Landscapes of Devils

GASTÓN R. GORDILLO

Landscapes of Devils

TENSIONS OF PLACE AND MEMORY

IN THE ARGENTINEAN CHACO

Duke University Press   Durham & London

2004

© 2004 Duke University Press

All rights Reserved
Printed in the United States of
America on acid-free paper ∞
Designed by C. H. Westmoreland
Typeset in Dante with Cather display
by Tseng Information Systems, Inc.
Library of Congress Cataloging-in-
Publication Data and republication
acknowledgments appear on the last
printed pages of this book.

A mis padres

The philosophy of praxis is absolute "historicism,"

the absolute secularization and earthliness of thought. . . . It is along

this line that one must trace the thread of the new conception

of the world. —Antonio Gramsci, *Prison Notebooks*

To proceed dialectically means to think in contradictions, for the sake

of the contradiction once experienced in the thing, and against that

contradiction. —Theodor Adorno, *Negative Dialectics*

Contents

List of Illustrations

Maps

Acknowledgments

I wrote this book about places and memories in a dazzling array of places, which in turn evoke their own memories. The recollection of the many debts accumulated on this journey cannot but begin in the Chaco. The people who are these pages' protagonists are an indissoluble part of who I am today, hence it is difficult to adequately convey the depth of my gratitude. Dionisio Díaz (deceased), Nicanor Jaime (*Nedói*), Secundino Lucas, Pedro Martínez, Marcelo Núñez, Emilio Rivero (*Locohé*), Toribio Sánchez, and Eusebio Solís (*Lagachidí*) have been crucial companions in my ethnographic forays, and in moments of confusion I always counted on their patient, illuminating comments. Their warmth and generosity have been directly proportional to the enjoyment I felt talking with them. Andrés Cardoso (*DaríloGo*), Miguel Jaime, Chicho Martín (*Cadácho*), Ramón Morales, and Esteban Moreno (*Táico*) have shared countless conversations and/or numerous hunting and fishing trips with me. It is especially from them that I learned what I know about the experience of Toba men in the bush and the Pilcomayo marshes.

It would be impossible to list here the rest of the Toba who in one way or another contributed with their voices and hospitality to the final outcome of this book. Nonetheless, I must mention Rodolfo Setacain and his wife Marta Moreno (deceased), Mateo Alto, Adolfo Caín, Martín Carlos, Pedro Cuchi, Emilio Cuellar, Celestino Cuellar, Alberto Díaz, José Ernesto, Manuel Estrada, Victor Filemón, Nélida Florentín, Antonio García, Ramón Jaime, Juan Larrea, Nicolás Larrea, Gil Lazarte, Fabreciana Luis, Tita Luis, Mariano Méndez, Luis Mendoza (deceased), Osvaldo Molina, Benigno Morales, Hugo Morales, Susana Morales, Pedro Nagadí, Andrés Pérez, Humberto Pérez, Norma Pérez, Quico Pérez, Santa Pérez, Julio Reginaldo, Orquera Reginaldo, Basilio Roque (deceased), Juan Rosendo (deceased), Evencio Sánchez, Teodoro Segovia, Luisa Segundo, Asuzena Tenaiquín (deceased), Valeria Urquiza, Dionisia Yanqui, José Manuel Yanqui, and Mario Zacarías. Throughout this book, I refer to people currently alive with pseudonyms.

In 1987, when I was an anthropology undergraduate at the Universidad de Buenos Aires anxious to learn what fieldwork was all about, Marcela Mendoza took me to the Toba villages for the first time, an experience that changed me forever. I cannot stop thanking her for that. Ever since then, Marcela has provided me with countless insights on Toba culture, memory, and history and shared with me invaluable information and documents. Our exchange of ideas became particularly intense and fruitful when I was completing my dissertation in 1998. Luis María de la Cruz has been my other crucial interlocutor on the Toba, and we had long conversations about some of the topics analyzed in this book. His work among the Toba on land claims and his commitment to indigenous rights have always been a source of inspiration. Additionally, Luis María enormously facilitated my fieldwork by allowing me to use his house in one of the Toba villages. María Lia Bargalló was my companion in four trips to the Toba villages between 1988 and 1991. Our fieldwork experience and her sensitivity shaped the contours of my future research in ways I could then not foresee.

In the city of Formosa, Ana Mosquera was a generous host with whom I shared concerns and projects. José Alsina (deceased) guided me into piles of documents at the Formosa Historical Archives, an institution he rescued from oblivion. Bishops Humberto Axt and David Leake, of the Argentinean Anglican Church, kindly shared memories of their experiences among the Toba. I am especially grateful to David Leake for allowing me to reproduce photos from his family archive.

Colleagues and friends in the Department of Anthropology at the Universidad de Buenos Aires contributed to this book in multiple, intricate ways. It was there—as an undergraduate student, teaching assistant, and graduate research fellow—that I learned what critical thinking is all about. Special thanks to Juan Martín Leguizamón, a brother in arms and a source of inspiration for his commitment to an anthropology grounded in people's concerns. For their intellectual stimulation I am also grateful to Ricardo Abduca, Fernando Balbi, Claudia Briones, Diego Escolar, Valeria Hernández, Leda Kantor, Axel Lazzari, Patricia Monsalve, Carlos Prego, Alejandra Siffredi, Héctor Hugo Trinchero, and Marcelo Urquía.

The Department of Anthropology at the University of Toronto provided the ferment to produce the dissertation that led to this book. I owe to Gavin Smith the motivation to ask the right questions. Richard B. Lee was a fundamental pillar of my subsequent work. It is hard to accurately express the strength of Gavin's and Richard's support as my dissertation coadvisors, how much I learned from them, and how much I admire them. The 1997–98 dissertation-writing group in Toronto created a weekly space of insightful comments and criticism. Thanks to Andrew Martindale, Robin Oakley, Warren Olivo, Dee Rose, Celia Rothenberg, Heike Schimkat, and Andrew Walsh.

John Comaroff made the most detailed, thorough, and challenging comments I could have ever expected from an external thesis examiner. The richness and scope of his suggestions were critical to redefine this book. The following people, some of them close friends, read parts of the manuscript in its various stages or enriched it with their observations: Arianne Dorval, Michael Lambek, Bill Levitt, Cynthia Milton, Juan Manuel Obarrio, Stuart Philpott, Natacha Pravaz, Valeria Procupez, Paula Pryce, Anke Schwittay, Gerald Sider, Renée Sylvain, Michael Taussig, Claudia Vicencio, and Pablo Wright. My dialogues with Elena Arengo on the intricate histories of the Chaco proved particularly influential. Kari Jones accompanied me through several stages of this manuscript's development and contributed much to it. Tomás Eloy Martínez helped me solve the mystery of Juan Domingo Perón's presence in San Martín del Tabacal, as the Toba currently remember it. In May 1998, my friend and colleague Hernán Julio Vidal passed away in a tragic accident while doing fieldwork in Patagonia. The final chapter owes much to my dialogues with Hernán on the cultural power of international borders.

I wrote and rewrote the revisions during an intense three-year North American tour that took me through New Haven, Cambridge, Ithaca, and Vancouver. As a visiting fellow in the Program in Agrarian Studies at Yale University (1999–2000), I had the privilege of enjoying a remarkably stimulating and collegial context in which to rethink, reread, and rewrite. Jim Scott was the legend who made this environment possible. Kay Mansfield's warmth and unconditional support had a lot to do with my fabulous year in Agrarian Studies. My cofellows at Yale critically read several chapters: special thanks to Henry Bernstein, Richard Grove, Cindy Hahamovitch, Jeanette Keith, Joan Martínez-Alier, Scott Nelson, Gabriele Rasuly-Paleczek, and Paula Worby. Rohan D'Souza deserves a special mention for asking the unsettling question, for his faith in the revolution, and for his sense of humor and friendship.

I turned around the manuscript, again and again, at Harvard University as a Visiting Scholar in the Rockefeller Center for Latin American Studies (2000–2001), at Cornell University as a Visiting Assistant Professor in the Department of Anthropology (2001–2002), and finally in Vancouver as an Assistant Professor in the Department of Anthropology and Sociology at the University of British Columbia. Colleagues and friends at these institutions further encouraged me to rethink some of the ideas presented in this book, especially Alexia Bloch, Rima Brusi, Felix Girón, Vince Brown, and Ajantha Subramanian.

Valerie Millholland, my editor at Duke University Press, supported this manuscript from the time I first contacted her. The two reviewers for the press provided me with a careful and thought-provoking reading that helped me tighten and improve the argument. Special thanks to Tania Li ("reader number two," as I learned later) for her challenging remarks on the conceptual, stylistic, and ethnographic knots I needed to untangle. Lynn Walterick's copy-editing skills saved me from those cryptic sentences and inconsistencies I thought I had left behind.

My parents Teresa Ana Schiaffino and Agustín Gordillo, their partners Ricardo López Alfonsino and Mónica Merlín, and my siblings Hernán, Camila, and Bárbara are all an important part of these pages. Mariano Cerdá and Javier Iñón know better than anybody the personal circumstances in which, over the years, I set out for the Chaco. Their friendship was a crucial part of my experience in the field. Florencia Esteverena was the immensely loving and patient light that helped me lead this manuscript through turbulent waters.

Fieldwork for this research was funded by the Wenner-Gren Foundation for Anthropological Research (Predoctoral grant no. 6503), the Universidad de Buenos Aires (Secretaría de Ciencia y Técnica), the University of Toronto (Connaught Foundation and School of Graduate Studies), and the Ministry of Education and Training of the Province of Ontario. My sincere gratitude to these institutions.

There is someone I never met but to whom I am also indebted: Alfred Métraux, who did fieldwork among the Toba in 1933 and 1939. Encapsulating the experience of many of us who love the Chaco intensively but often wish to find relief from its implacable geography, he wrote in 1939 in two parts of his diary: *Le Chaco est difficile à décrire, mais j'en aime tous les aspects. . . . J'en veux à cette radio qui m'arrache du Chaco.* — The Chaco is hard to describe, but I love everything about it. . . . I long for that radio that pulls me out of the Chaco.

Landscapes of Devils

Introduction

> The dialectic . . . is a logical absurdity as long as there is talk of
> the change of one "thing" into another "thing." . . . That is to say, its
> premise is that *things should be shown to be aspects of processes*. . . . Thus
> the knowledge that social facts are not objects but relations between men
> is intensified to the point where facts are wholly dissolved into processes.
> —Georg Lukács, *History and Class Consciousness*

The western Argentinean Chaco is dominated by a landscape that is flat, monotonous, and often overwhelming: *el monte*, the bush. The dirt roads that cut through the region are surrounded by forest and often look like frail marks of human presence trying to prevent nature from fully taking over. Wherever one looks, the thick succession of hardwoods, cacti, and shrubs, six to twelve meters high, extends like a mantle over a dry, dusty soil. In the northwest of the province of Formosa, one of the hinterland roads ends near the border with Paraguay, where a dozen Toba villages are scattered south of the marshlands formed by the Pilcomayo River. These hamlets momentarily break the dominance of the bush yet are also subordinated to its unyielding presence. From every household, while chatting next to a fire, making handicrafts, or preparing food, women and men can see the mass of vegetation surrounding them. Most of them enter the bush often to gather honey, wild fruits, or firewood, to hunt, visit their fields, or go fishing in the marshes. And many of their memories, anecdotes, and conversations hinge in one way or another on this place. Yet despite its sheer presence, people remember that the bush did not exist in the past. When they refer to their ancestors, who roamed those same lands in foraging bands prior to their defeat by the Argentinean army and the arrival of Criollo settlers in the 1910s, they emphasize that they inhabited a world of wide grasslands, free of forest.

These memories remind many Toba that the bush is not simply a

1. Bush trail in Toba lands. *Photo by author.*

natural component of the landscape but a historical product intrinsically linked to their incorporation within the Argentinean nation-state and their demise as a politically autonomous group. This history has constituted Toba subjectivity and produced the local geography, in a process in which the forces that made the Toba what they are today are the same that created the bush. This entanglement of space, history, and subjectivity involved not just the Chaco interior but also practices that connected the emerging bush with other geographies. In the early twentieth century, state violence, settler colonization, and the consolidation of a capitalist frontier 300 kilometers to the west drew the Toba and other indigenous groups into the orbit of sugar plantations as a seasonal labor force. This pattern of migration was a further and potent force in the making of the bush, as the place where people constructed a relative haven from labor exploitation yet also as the site deprived of commodities that fostered their annual return to the sugar cane fields.

In the mid and late 1990s, Toba men and women had stopped working at the plantations but their memories of "the mountains" — *kahogonaGá*, as they refer to the cane fields because of their location next to the first Andean ranges — were a forceful presence in their lands.[1] These memories remind most Toba that the spatial product of their immersion within a capitalist political economy, the bush, is also the place where they carved out relative shelter from it. The spatial sedimentation of this tension between exploitation and relative autonomy emerges in many aspects of Toba practice and subjectivity, among them the devil imageries that, in

Map 1. Relative location of the Toba

contrasting ways, impregnate the memory of the plantations and current experiences of the bush. As we shall see, the action of devils captures some of the major social contradictions constituting these geographies.

In this book I unravel the historical experiences, tensions, and places that have produced the bush as a contested social process. My premise is that places are produced in tension with other geographies and that these tensions are made tangible through the spatialization of memory. These spatial connections turn places, as Doreen Massey has argued, into processes that are necessarily "extroverted": that is, open to "a constellation of social relations meeting and weaving together at a particular locus" (1994:154, 142, 155). The constellation of social relations meeting to configure the bush links it not only to the sugar plantations but also to other places through a complex network of practices and memories. Some of these sites had by the 1990s disappeared; others had emerged only recently. Yet all of them were tied to the memory of the mountains and the grasslands in the making of the bush. In this study, I examine how these places have been constituted by state terror, Anglican missionization, disease and labor exploitation, healing and shamanism, sexuality, commodity fetishism, state hegemony, and practices of accommodation and resistance. Devil imageries, and the contradictory forms of estrangement and reciprocity they evoke, are one of the main threads weaving through the spatialization of these experiences.

The Absolute Spatialization of Practice

Influenced by the prioritization of time over space that has dominated Western philosophy since the Enlightenment, most anthropological studies of social memory have tended to focus on the temporal aspects of remembering: that is, on constructions of the past and their cultural, ideological, or political dimensions (e.g., Abercrombie 1998; Cole 2001; Lambek 1996; Rappaport 1990; Swedenburg 1991; Trouillot 1995).[2] And those who have conceptually tackled the spatial components of memory, for their part, have usually done so from a phenomenological perspective that overlooks the role of power relations and history in the making of senses of place (see Basso 1996; Casey 1987, 1996; Feld 1996).[3]

In this book I merge the experiential dimensions of place making with the political economy that makes it possible by examining the materiality of memory, its embodiment in practice, and its constitution as a social force in the production of places. In his *Prison Notebooks*, Antonio Gramsci advocated a theory of practice grounded in what he called, in opposition to idealism and objectivist materialism, the "absolute secularization and earthliness of thought" (1971:465). Here I expand this earthliness to include what I would call the absolute spatialization of practice. My analytical point of departure is the fact that every memory is, in a fundamental way, the memory of a place. Faces, casual encounters, or collective struggles are remembered not in a vacuum but in a locale that makes them meaningful. And this spatiality is crucial for an anthropological understanding of memory. This process does not involve memories unfolding on an arrested spatial matrix but a dynamic process of place production. Henri Lefebvre (1991) has forcefully argued that our gaze should move away from "things in space" (space as a rigid template) and toward *the production of space* (space as the *product* of action). This means, first, conceiving of memory as a component of practice involved in place making and, second, integrating Toba memories with the historical practices that have produced the bush physically, politically, and culturally.

My analysis draws on recent scholarship in anthropology and geography that has examined how places are historically made and unmade through practice, fields of power and struggle, and networks of social relations (see Gupta and Ferguson 1997; Ferguson and Gupta 2002; Harvey 1989, 1996, 2000, 2001; Massey 1994; Mitchell 1996; Moore 1998; Raffles 1999, 2002; Rodman 1992; N. Smith 1984; Stewart 1996). Yet in these pages

I examine an often-overlooked aspect of place making: that places are the result of the social contradictions embedded in them. The study of these contradictions is crucial to dismantle the appearance of places as well-bounded entities, for it reveals, first, the fractures and struggles that make them ongoing, unstable, and unfinished historical processes and, second, the relations that integrate them with other geographies.

In Toba historical experience, the most recurrent tension shaping local landscapes is the one opposing wage labor to hunting, fishing, and gathering. Henri Lefebvre (1991:365) argued that social contradictions create spatial contradictions. Likewise, the contradiction between what most Toba call *marisca* (foraging) and *trabajo* (work) expresses a tension between different social relations of production and experiences that have produced places of relative autonomy in the bush and places of exploitation in plantations and (more recently) farms.[4] Even though this tension is central to my argument, I do not analyze it in a bipolar fashion (or as the expression of a "dual economy"); rather, I examine it as the uneven spatial manifestation of a single social practice that involves further contradictions and multiple geographies and, for that reason, undermines a clear-cut distinction between neatly bounded places. As we shall see, the foundation of an Anglican station in Toba lands in 1930, where British missionaries banned dances and other practices regarded as immoral, turned the sugar plantations into places of sexual excess free of missionary discipline. Similarly, the nostalgia that in the mid-1990s many Toba expressed for the commodities earned at the plantations, as well as the availability of public-sector jobs in the nearby municipality, informed perceptions that the bush was a place of poverty, hardship, and unrewarding efforts. These dimensions illustrate that places are processes riddled with tensions and anticipate some of the multisited practices examined in chapters to come.

My approach to labor contradictions, rather than being based on an objectivist approach to production, fully immerses them in social subjectivity. This book draws on the work of a growing number of authors who, critical of reified and ahistorical notions of culture, have examined the dynamism of cultural production in particular historical and political settings (Comaroff 1985; Comaroff and Comaroff 1991, 1997, 1999; Gupta and Ferguson 1997; Roseberry 1989; Sider 1986; Smith 1991, 1999). In these pages, I analyze cultural meanings as they are produced by historical experiences. My use of this concept follows the legacy of Edward Thompson (1966; 1978a; 1978b), who has examined collective experiences that are as subjective as they are the product of fields of domination and confrontation. This historical notion of experience is critical to account for the cultural and spatial dimensions of practice, for it is *through* experience that history leaves a mark on memory and guides action in the production of places. Experience, in other words, is both a product and a creative force, in a process in which, as Raymond Williams put it, subjectivity is "under continual pressure from experience" (1961:101; see 1977:166).[5]

My reference to contradictions tearing through places and labor experiences requires a brief clarification of my understanding of the dialectic, which will nevertheless become clear only as my historical and ethnographic narrative progresses. One of the most widespread misconceptions about the dialectic is that it involves an "interaction" between *separate* entities in which they "shape each other."[6] Being a practice that undermines reified dichotomies, the dialectic in fact dismantles the very idea of interplay between separate "things." As Georg Lukács writes, the premise of the dialectic is that *"things should be shown to be aspects of processes"* and as a result "the knowledge that social facts are not objects but relations between men is intensified to the point where facts are wholly dissolved into processes" (1971:179–80, emphasis in original; see Adorno 1973:145). Similarly, I aim to show that places such as the bush, the plantations, or the mission station are eminently *relations* between social actors and that these relations dissolve these places' appearance of fixity. Yet my approach is not simply relational; it is dialectical in the sense that it takes these relations to unleash confrontations and oppositions. Among the Toba, such contradictions emerge in a spatialized habitus constituted by memory.

Of Places, Embodied Memories, and Devils

The people whose experiences, memories, and practices I examine in this book live in the west of the Gran Chaco region: a mostly semiarid plain that covers southeastern Bolivia, western Paraguay, and a good part of northern Argentina.[7] Also known as Toba-Pilagá (Métraux 1937) and western Toba (Mendoza 2002),[8] they form a group of 1,600 people historically and linguistically distinct from other Toba groups in Argentina, which live farther east and encompass a total population of about 30,000 (Arengo 1996; Cordeu and Siffredi 1971; Miller 1975, 1979, 1995, 1999; Wright 1992, 1997).[9] Eastern and western Toba use the term *Toba* to refer to themselves ("big forehead" in Guaraní, which refers to the now-abandoned practice of shaving their foreheads) and share the self-denomination *Qom* (people).

Yet these groupings have been constituted as social subjects through different historical experiences (examined in chapter 2). Unless stated otherwise, all future mention of "the Toba" indicates the western Toba.

During my fieldwork, the memories of the sugar plantations, the mission, or the grasslands were recurrent occurrences in my conversations with people and in the daily interactions I observed in households, public places, farming camps, or bush trails. On numerous occasions I would hear elder men and women remembering past experiences as part of long monologues. Some children would listen next to them and adults would often pay attention from the distance and make comments or ask questions while conducting other activities. These moments of memory production were particularly important in the early morning hours around the household fire, when family members gather to share a *mate* (a type of tea common in Argentina). At political meetings, it was also common to hear men insert memories within longer harangues about contemporary concerns. In addition to these everyday and relatively spontaneous sites of memory production, the Anglican services in local adobe churches provided more ritualized sites of commemoration. Sermons by Toba priests often hinged on the remembrance of the mission—destroyed by flooding in 1975—and the un-Christian, violent landscapes that dominated the region prior to its foundation.

While taping or making notes of memories in interviews or casual interactions, I repeatedly tried to locate the events being remembered in time. Yet dates were of little or no meaning to most people. It took me a while to realize that this responded not just to a cultural disregard for calendar time but to the weight of places in memory. As several chapters illustrate, what made these memories significant were, rather than their temporal coordinates, the geographies they evoked.[10] Places made these memories significant in another way: through the fact that they were produced at particular sites—the villages, the bush, and the marshes—and at a particular moment in the configuration of those sites: the mid and late 1990s.[11] This location profoundly shaped the memories I registered in the field and made them part of debates and concerns specific to that moment in their history, such as those triggered by the incipient social differentiation dividing the largest villages.[12] The spatialization of memory was also apparent in people's bodies. Memories were not only narrated or created ritually but also embodied in what Pierre Bourdieu (1977) has called "habitus": a set of dispositions for action. Differently constructed according to age, social status, and gender, the cultural sedimentation of

Toba historical experience has turned past memories into new values and patterns of behavior, in a process in which the marks memory leaves on the habitus remain when the remembrance of the experience that originated it may not (cf. Casey 1987; Connerton 1989). This embodiment is critical to place making, for as pointed out by Lefebvre (1991:162), "it is by means of the body that space is perceived, lived and produced."

The spirits the Toba call *payák* or *diablos*, devils, are probably the best illustration of the inscription of memory in their habitus and of the cultural and spatial significance of labor contradictions; for this reason, they are one of the main themes articulating different geographies throughout the book. For women and men, young and old, committed to the Anglican Church or critical of it, devils are a latent yet persistent presence in their lives. They are the dominant nonhuman presence in the places central to their practice and memories. Yet these spirits' behavior, features, and type of interaction with humans are deeply contingent on their location. The term *payák* represents for most Toba the condition of potentially dangerous creatures or phenomena that cannot be fully explained or understood and therefore people often use the term as an adjective (see Métraux 1937:174; 1946a:16). For instance, creatures such as *wosáq* ("rainbow" and the storms associated with it) or seemingly natural phenomena like *kadáachi* (whirlwinds) have or may have a payák nature. Yet this state is most graphically condensed in the beings—usually invisible but that can adopt changing physical shapes, like that of a hairy dwarf—which people also refer to by the term *payák*.[13] In fact, most people use this term in this sense: as synonymous with evil spirit.

Most Toba incorporated the term *diablo* as translation of payák through their experience of Anglican missionization. As part of a dualistic opposition between good and evil originally alien to local values, missionaries presented the Devil as the epitome of evil and emphasized that diabolical forces were behind practices at odds with the Gospels (as we shall see). Even though most Toba did not adopt the Christian idea of the Devil at face value, as a singular and distant entity, their interactions with the missionaries gradually enhanced the negative features associated with payák creatures, now seen as diablos. This merger between Christian imageries and figures prior to missionization was in turn reconfigured by the experience of labor migration and the contradictions it entailed.

During the decades Toba men and women worked at the cane fields, they saw the plantations as places haunted by scores of devils that were sources of terror, disease, and death, established no communication with humans, and made their alienation in those sites particularly apparent. The sedimentation of that memory of terror in their habitus, together with the articulation of different practices and social relations in their lands, enhanced the reciprocity that links foragers to bush devils, which are seen by contrast (despite their often whimsical behavior) as sources of bush food and healing power. As a result of this contradictory experience of place, in different sites the payák adopt heterogeneous features related to the labor practices, social relations, and tensions embedded in the landscape. The devils' behavior informs how people relate to places, and this bodily predisposition is, I will show, inseparable from social memory. The diablos, in short, capture some of the spatial contrasts created by decades of labor migration, and this introductory outline anticipates some of the conceptual and ethnographic knots I tackle in chapters to come.

On Epistemology and Method

When I set out to conduct the research that led to this study, my broadest aim was to overcome the dichotomy between objectivism and subjectivism by showing that the objectivity of places results from the historical and subjective forces that are behind it, a point inspired by Antonio Gramsci's insistence that "objective" should be understood as *humanly* objective and "subjective" as *historically* subjective (1971:446). If I accomplished this goal in any way, I believe it was mostly possible because I began my Chaco journeys with an "objectivist moment" that examined the fields of force in which social action is immersed.

I conducted fieldwork among the Toba on numerous occasions, involving different but closely interrelated research projects that span some fifteen years. Between 1987 and 1993—first as an anthropology undergraduate and then as a graduate research fellow at the Universidad de Buenos Aires—I spent a total of seven months in the Toba villages and worked on a perspective in political economy that examined the historical constraints imposed on people's everyday forms of livelihood (see Gordillo 1992, 1994, 1995a, 1995b, 1996). Concerned as I was with issues of labor, domination, and history overlooked in Chaco ethnography, "culture" was at the time tangential to my research. Yet as I gradually became interested in subjectivity, memory, and place, my previous work proved vital for understanding these issues and, further, for trying to dissolve the very distinction between "political economy" and "culture" as separate analytical fields.

In September 1993 I headed to the University of Toronto to pursue graduate work and process this epistemological transition. In August 1995 I returned for eighteen months to Argentina and the Toba villages to conduct the fieldwork and the archival and library research for my dissertation. In June 1996 I visited other places central in Toba experiences and memories: a farm near Embarcación (Salta)—where I met a group of Toba men and women working as harvesters—and San Martín del Tabacal, the sugar plantation that absorbed most of their labor migrations in the twentieth century. When I was writing and revising the manuscript first in Canada and then the United States, I returned to the Toba villages in August 1997, May 1999, and June–July 2000 (for a total of ten weeks) to wrap up final aspects of the research. Most of my conversations and everyday interactions involved men but the dozen interviews I conducted with women allowed me to explore experiences, memories, and areas of contention shaped along gender lines.

The three parts into which I divide the book can be considered moments in a movement that is simultaneously historical, spatial, and analytical. Because of the myriad relations I try to establish between different geographies, my narrative opens up various levels of analysis and works on their manifold interpenetrations as the chapters unfold. This book is eminently historical in the sense that I accompany people's memories on a journey that is as geographical as it is cultural and material. Believing that history is not just "the past" but the social forces that have produced *the present*, my narrative immerses the reader into the deep history that has created the memories I registered in the field. But I do so through an approach that, while committed to a rigorous historiography, tries to break down an objectivist distinction between memory (what "they" think happened) and history (what "really" happened).

Part I, "The Making of the Bush," integrates processes old enough to escape Toba social memory with the more recent events that led to the Anglican evangelization, the end of "the time of the ancient ones," and the emergence of the bush as a new geography. The making of Toba lands (as parts II and III show) is a process that continues in the present, yet these chapters examine how the bush was initially produced, physically and socially, by new experiences of confrontation. I begin by presenting the current layout of the places examined in the book and move on to ana-lyze the historical forces that, from the Spanish colonial era to the early twentieth century, configured the Chaco and in particular Toba territory as places fractured by violence, subjugation, and resistance. After analyz-ing current memories of the first migrations to the sugar plantations and the clashes with the Argentinean army, I examine how the foundation of the Anglican mission created a refuge from state terror but also a place subjected to a new type of discipline. Present-day memories, I argue, illus-trate that missionization triggered a politicized spatiality that configured the bush and the mission in tension with each other and also in contrast with the plantations.

Part II, "Bones in the Cane Fields," takes the reader to the foot of the Andes and in particular to San Martín del Tabacal. I first analyze the history of this plantation and the memories of the ethnic hierarchies and power relations that regulated Toba labor until mechanization put an end to their migrations in the late 1960s. Then I examine the death, disease, and terror many Toba project onto the cane fields, epitomized in devils and cannibals, and the simultaneous memories of money and commodities that turned San Martín del Tabacal into an alluring yet ulti-mately alienating place of wealth. The following two chapters focus on the fields of contention produced in the plantation, first, through the evening dances that defined this place in opposition to the mission, and second, through the forms of resistance that, even though challenging exploita-tion, ultimately reinforced people's estrangement at the cane fields.

In Part III, "Foraging until the End of the World," I analyze how the memories presented in the previous two parts coalesce in the cultural and political geography of the bush. First, I examine how the health, resilience, local knowledge, poverty, and noncommodified abundance most Toba associate with the bush are produced in tension with the memory of the disease, estrangement, and wealth projected onto the sugar plantations. I also examine these features in conjunction with the legacy of Anglican missionization and the action of the bush devils, as they are defined in contrast with the plantation devils. Second, I explore how recent labor migrations to farms and cattle ranches have affected the social configura-tion of the bush and how, in turn, work in these places is haunted by the memory of San Martín del Tabacal. I then analyze, intertwined with these practices and memories, the way in which people living in poverty have reproduced the collective use of the bush through struggles and negotiations with settlers, stage agencies, and their own leaders, a process that in the 1990s was creating new fractures in the local landscape. As part of my final articulation of disparate geographies, the last chapter examines how the bush is also made in relation to lands that, located across the Pilcomayo marshes, evoke the memory of landscapes of freedom.

I

The Making

of the Bush

I

Landmarks of Memory

No space ever vanishes utterly, leaving no trace.
—Henri Lefebvre, *The Production of Space*

When I lived among the Toba, people conjured in their narratives, first, the tangible places they experienced on a regular basis: their hamlets, the bush, the marshes, and the nearby village of Pozo de Maza. They also referred to places located farther away but regularly intertwined with their practices: the lands across the marshes, the town of Ingeniero Juárez (60 kilometers to the southwest), and the farms in Salta where many men and women migrate for work (over 300 kilometers away). Yet this mapping was permanently enmeshed in the memory of sites that have disappeared from their direct experience: to the west, the sugar plantations and in particular San Martín del Tabacal, and within their local geography the places that have been physically erased by history: the grasslands, the Pilcomayo River, and the Anglican mission. All these places, past and present, are tightly interwoven in local practices through memory. When Henri Lefebvre (1991:164) wrote that no space vanishes without leaving traces, he was thinking more about physical marks than about traces left in memory. In this chapter, I explore how both dimensions intersect: that is, first, how the current layout of places such as the bush, the marshlands, or the farms are marked by the spatial sediment left on them by past geographies and, second, how these marks foster memories of landscape transformations. I examine these processes with the aim of showing the deep historicity of these places, exposing the history behind their current configuration, and undermining their deceptive appearance of fixity, sharing Hugh Raffles's point: "It is the impression of stasis that beguiles. They may look secure, but landscapes are always in motion, always in process" (2002:34). I map these landscapes in motion by focusing on how their current layout has been transformed by labor and social relations, for, as Lefebvre argues, "social relations of production have a social existence to the extent that they have a spatial existence; they project themselves into a space, becoming inscribed there, and in the process producing that space itself" (1991:129).

This chapter is structured as a journey that begins in the Chaco interior and ends at the foot of the first Andean ranges in San Martín del Tabacal. Since I concentrate on the major changes that affected each place in the twentieth century, I temporarily leave aside the relations that produced these places in tension with each other. Those relationships are the object of the rest of the book, where I examine these locales in detail, dismember them, and then rearticulate them in their multiple interconnections. The villages are our starting point.

The Hamlets

When entering a Toba village, usually arriving by bicycle from another village, I often felt it was hard to tell where the bush ended and the village outskirts began. I would first see a *rancho* (adobe dwelling) partially hidden by vegetation, then another one equally obscured by trees and bushes, and the trail would gradually lead me to a clearing occupied by more visible and irregularly distributed clusters of adobes. In the late 1990s the Toba lived in twelve hamlets that congregated one, two, or more exogamous webs of extended families distributed in matrilocal households.[1] Most villages comprised less than 100 people but one held about 600. In the largest villages, households are scattered around an adobe church, a dispensary, a primary school, and a building (usually used for storage) of the *Instituto de Comunidades Aborígenes* (ICA), the provincial agency of indigenous affairs. Reflecting the incipient class differentiation recently created by public-sector employment, brick houses with corrugated iron roofs, where leaders and state employees live, usually occupy the village core and the straw and adobe ranchos of those who lack a stable income are scattered around them.

In casual conversations, many people point out that a few decades earlier those villages did not exist. Even though in the past people roamed those lands through hunting and gathering expeditions, they had their hamlets ten to twenty kilometers farther north, along the banks of the Pilcomayo River. Large floods produced this displacement early in 1975 by destroying those villages and forcing people to move to their current location. Many remember that the old villages by the river bore no marks

Map 2. Toba villages in the mid-1990s

of government agencies: state schools, dispensaries, or ICA buildings did not exist and people lived in relatively egalitarian places where everybody, even leaders, dwelled in ranchos. This configuration was tightly connected with other places washed away by the floods: the Anglican mission station and Sombrero Negro, a Criollo village two kilometers upstream.

Sombrero Negro was the main site of state presence in the area. Yet as part of the legacy of the violence I examine in chapter 3, the Anglican station immersed most Toba within a sphere of missionary influence that partially excluded state intervention. In 1996 Omar, a man in his late fifties, remembered the differences between Sombrero Negro and the old mission: "In Sombrero Negro there was a store, a *gendarmería* post [military border police], a police post. There was also a school, a government school. But Toba kids didn't go there. They didn't go. They always went to the mission school. They didn't know the state school. They didn't know it. But now it seems no kid knows the mission school." Omar shed light on the spatial differentiation marked in those days by missionary presence. Memories like this also define current villages, immersed within the

2. In a Toba village. *Photo by author.*

sphere of influence of state agencies, by their contrast with the patterns that shaped local practices until the mid-1970s.

The recent salience of *trabajo* (work) is another factor marking differences between current and past villages. Under the category "work," people include agriculture, herding, craftsmanship, seasonal wage labor, and most prominently public-sector employment. People define trabajo in opposition to *marisca*, which refers to hunting, fishing, and gathering of wild fruits and honey, to the point that most see "foraging" and "work" as mutually exclusive practices. Highly valued as a source of commodities, trabajo implies for most Toba a responsibility, regularity, and discipline relatively absent in marisca. This distinction is grounded in their experience of labor migration and has spatial dimensions equally informed by memory. People remember that in their old hamlets on the river everybody lived off marisca and that "work" — especially jobs in state agencies — emerged as a defining feature of their villages only in the late 1980s.

The consolidation of villages as places of trabajo involves, first, domestic practices conducted by women. Handicraft production — wool tapestry and handbags made of chagüar fiber (*Bromelia hieronymi*) — is the most visible female "work" within the household. Even though crafts have become meager and irregular sources of income, this practice is an important marker of female identity, to the point that women and men alike refer to it as "women's work." Women are also in charge of herding sheep and goats in the hamlets and their immediate surroundings. The soil ero-

3. "Women's work." *Photo by author.*

sion caused by goats, which leave a barren soil devoid of grass and shrubs, is one of the villages' distinctive spatial marks.

For men, jobs granted by state agencies are the most highly valued type of trabajo. These jobs have turned the largest villages into places increasingly fractured by social hierarchies, which are spearheaded by elected representatives in the Pozo de Maza municipality and delegates to the ICA and (less prominently) skilled public-sector employees such as teaching assistants, nurses, and midwives. These jobs are turning these households into an indigenous petite-bourgeoisie with distinctive interests and, in a few cases, entrepreneurial spirit. Some leaders have invested in hundreds of goats and sheep and, most important, cattle, a particularly controversial commodity because it is the symbol of settler identity. As a recent expression of this differentiation, some leaders have begun hiring relatives or settlers to look after their animals. This means that these leaders are creating a class cleavage not only through their jobs but also through the investment of their salaries in petty commodity production.

Most Toba read the strains created by this differentiation through the language of reciprocity, for they see wealth accumulation as an infringement of the sharing values that define them as Aborígenes, a marker of identity that merges (as we shall see) ethnicity with conditions of poverty. Criticism of well-off leaders for their "stinginess" is often accompanied by memories of an egalitarian past near the river, when it was unthinkable that a leader owned cattle. Ordinary people often challenge this differentiation by putting pressure on their leaders to redistribute part of their resources through patterns of generalized reciprocity (Gordillo 1994; see also Lee 1979, 1988, 2003). Thus, many submit their leaders' behavior to permanent scrutiny and pay regular "visits" to their households to demand foodstuffs. This social pressure affects the spatial configuration of villages, turning better-off households into public places in which ordinary people partially contain the tendency to produce a more individualized and self-enclosed space. These forms of contention have spatial implications of a different sort. Even though they are contested places, villages are the site of the leaders' and public-sector employees' power and resources. People living in poverty base their livelihood elsewhere, at a place they actively defend as a collectively owned space.

The Bush

I left the village on a borrowed bicycle early in the morning, heading to a hamlet located ten kilometers away, where several men were waiting for me to begin a several-day hunting expedition. The bicycle first took me to the narrow trail that starts winding down through the relatively open bush of the village surroundings. The ground was relatively free of vegetation, except for the cacti and algarrobo trees that were all around me. After a few minutes, the bush became thicker and the trail carved a path through a mass of vegetation. A cow, roaming freely in the bush as cattle do in the region, saw me coming and moved languidly to one side of the path. The trail was now full of bumps, many of them the product of footprints left by cattle on hardened mud. After navigating for twenty minutes through that extension of thick bush, I reached *la picada*, a perfectly straight trail opened for oil exploration in the 1980s by the then state-owned, now privatized, oil company YPF (*Yacimientos Petrolíferos Fiscales*). Five to six meters wide and able to accommodate a pickup truck, la picada looks like a giant cut made in the heart of the bush, extending with exasperating precision toward its dissolution on the horizon. As I entered la picada and headed north toward the marshes, I felt immersed in a world primarily defined by three colors: the whitish dust of the trail, the blue of the morning sky, and that presence in dark tones of green that engulfed everything on the sides: the bush.

The trails that cut through the region and the encounters with cattle are permanent reminders that the Toba are not the only actors making use of the bush and that this place is deeply marked by the presence of Criollo settlers and state agencies. Toba memories often contrast this spatial configuration with the times when those lands were grasslands, *nónaGa* or *campo*, where only Aborígenes lived. Those were the open landscapes roamed by the *yagaikipi*, the ancient ones (*los antiguos*), as most Toba call their non-Christian ancestors in contrast to themselves, the new ones (*dalaGaikpi*).[2] In 1996, Enrique, a man in his fifties, was remembering the times of the ancient ones and told me, pointing to the vegetation that began a few meters from his household: "This isn't like it was before. All this is dense bush now. But they say that before, there was no bush. . . . Before, there were no cows, there were no Criollos, there were no roads. And all this was open country. There was thick bush only at the edge of the grasslands. If you wanted to eat ostrich [*Rhea americana*], you chased them galloping on horseback with *boleadoras* [throwing balls]." Like many other Toba, Enrique was defining the savannas of yesteryear by the absence of some of the markers that characterize the bush today: cattle, Criollos, and roads. And he remembered the nónaGa by evoking a practice defined by movement and velocity, ostrich hunting on horseback, which is currently impossible to re-create in the bush.

In the early twentieth century, grasslands covered both banks of the Pilcomayo River and stretched, intertwined with patches of bush, fifteen to twenty kilometers into the hinterland. The bush dominated the landscape only in the Chaco interior.[3] According to old people, those grasslands had been created by a *dóle aló* (big fire), a mythical fire forced the first ancient ones to hide underground. At the turn of the century, the grasslands were indeed the product of fires set by the Toba and other indigenous groups to send messages, hunt, and as a weapon in warfare. Those fires reproduced wide areas of open country, halted the growth of trees, and pushed forests into the hinterland (Morello and Saravia Toledo 1959:18; Morello 1970:37).

The first Bolivian and Argentinean explorers in the area marveled at the sight of those grasslands, which they saw as full of potential for cattle herding. Looking for pastures for their cattle, the first Criollo settlers arrived on the Pilcomayo in 1902 and founded Colonia Buenaventura, 150 kilometers upstream from Toba territory. The Criollo colonization brought decisive landscape transformations. Suffering land encroachment and military reprisals, indigenous groups stopped making fires. Cattle depleted the grass and began eating wild fruits and spreading tree seeds (through their feces) over wide territories. As a result, in a few years trees

4. Grasslands near the Pilcomayo in the late 1920s.
Photo by Enrique Palavecino. Archives of the Museo
Etnográfico Juan Ambrosetti, Facultad de Filosofía y
Letras, Universidad de Buenos Aires.

were growing in areas formerly covered with prairies (Morello and Saravia Toledo 1959:20, 76–77; Morello 1970:34, 39). By the 1920s, the social changes brought by the settlers and by the military defeat of indigenous groups were having profound spatial implications; they were creating a radically different landscape of monte and overgrazed strips of sandy soil.[4] As the Criollos moved with their cattle downstream, this landscape transformation reached Toba territory. By 1939, grasslands had mostly disappeared from their lands and had become part of a collective memory. That year the wife of an Anglican missionary living among the Toba wrote: "The old Indians remember when all this area was subtropical grassland without trees—they could see for miles across the flat land" (D. Tebboth 1989:68).

In the 1990s, memories of the grasslands regularly informed Toba experiences of the bush, yet in contradictory ways. During my first fieldwork in 1987, I was surprised to hear many people refer to the landscape that surrounded us as nónaGa, "open country," when all I could see around us was a pretty convincing bush.[5] I soon learned why people used that term. The bush surrounding that particular village was not as thick as in other areas and this relative openness (hard to decipher for urban eyes) indicated that decades earlier those areas had indeed been open country. I also noticed that people often reserved the term "bush" (*viáq, monte*) to refer to the thickest and oldest sections of forest, which form a dense ensemble of trees and weeds and are also called "large bush," *viáq ádaik* (see figures 5 and 6). It took me a while to train my gaze and be able to distinguish the viáq ádaik from the more open sections of bush and to understand how the distinction between the two is soaked in memory. Because of the burden of old geographies in their memory, many Toba use the term "bush" and "open country" as echoes that, reverberating from the past, project themselves onto the present as if unaware that the present is a different place. And this particular fusion of language, space, and memory stresses the continuity of past landscapes into the present.

Yet the memory of grasslands shapes perceptions of the bush in altogether different ways, confirming how dependent meanings are on the context in which they are produced. When people want to emphasize the profound transformations that have affected their lands, they emphasize the contrast between the open spaces of the past and the forested landscape of the present. With this historical contrast in mind, people talk about "the bush" in a way that includes the relatively open areas of forest within it. This time, the bush represents for them the current configuration of their lands *as a whole* and "open country" symbolizes a historically specific geography that has now disappeared. Segundo, a man in his late seventies, had referred several times to the landscape surrounding his village as nónaGa, open country. Yet he was once remembering the ancient ones and told me, while looking around us: "Before, all this used to be open country. Now, it's dense bush." Segundo's memory of the spatial fracture that separates the past from the present turned those open sections of forest into "bush." He reminded me, and himself, that as the yagaikipí's was a world of grasslands, the world of the new ones is one dominated by the bush.

These spatialized memories are anchored in the practices and social relations of production through which most Toba regularly re-create the bush as a collective place, a re-creation that in the 1990s had legal recognition through the granting of a collective land title to all villages. These

(*top*) 5. In the bush sections many Toba call "open country."
(*above*) 6. Hunting in the "big bush." *Photos by author.*

relations of production are based on the unrestrained access to land and its resources and the immersion of foodstuffs within circuits of generalized reciprocity. In this regard, marisca is associated with values of sharing and autonomy from the cash economy that stand in tension with those of trabajo, the practice that symbolizes the villages. Marisca is also a crucial symbol of aboriginality for, unlike trabajo, it is what most readily distinguishes Aborígenes and settlers.[6] This aboriginality is also a class marker and many people consider marisca as the practice that sets poor and well-off Toba apart.

Unlike trabajo, secluded within the villages and the fields and subjected to control by merchants and state institutions, marisca is defined by widespread mobility in the bush and the marshes, flexibility in the treks' direction and length, and relative autonomy from direct relations of domination.[7] Men conduct brief trips near the village surroundings to capture small animals—rabbit (*Sylvilagus brasiliensis paraguarensis*), viscacha (a rodent, *Lagostomus maximus*), and charata birds (*Ortalis carnicollis*)—and roam farther into the thickest sections of bush if they want to hunt large mammals like corzuela (*Mazama*, deer) or peccary (*Tayassu tajacu* and *Catagonus wagneri*). Some men set out with an axe with the explicit aim of searching for honey, but many hunters simply gather it any time they come across a beehive. Women, for their part, enter the relatively open sections of bush to gather algarroba pods and also enter the viáq ádaik to gather chagüar plants for their handicrafts.

Marisca depends heavily on the changing availability of natural resources throughout the year, and this spatialized temporality is another feature that sets it apart from trabajo. Wild fruits, honey, and animals are particularly plentiful in the wet season, between November and May, when they cover between 50 and 70 percent of household consumption (Gordillo 1995b:119). In May, resources in the bush are scarce and large shoals migrate upstream the Pilcomayo, marking the peak of the fishing season, when the marshes become the primary source of food. The decline of fish abundance by late July signals the beginning of the months of scarcity, August and September, when marisca's productivity decreases substantially. Even though this seasonality constrains the frequency, direction, and duration of foraging trips, marisca is not simply an "ecological adaptation" to the Chaco environment; rather, it is a practice primarily guided by conditions of poverty, market constraints, and spatiopolitical strategies (as several chapters will show). Men living in poverty set out to the bush to hunt and gather honey on a regular basis, even during *nakaviagá* (winter), but women's forays into the bush have a more markedly seasonal character. The ripening of chañar (*Gourliea decorticans*) in October and especially algarroba (*Prosopis alba* and, to a lesser degree, *nigra*) in November signal the beginning of "the fruit season," when women enter the bush in groups and cover large areas. They also gather mistol (of the smaller variety, *Zizyphus mistol*), bola verde (*Capparis speciosa*), sachasandia (*Capparis salicifolia*), and poroto de monte (*Capparis retusa*), some of which are available until the end of summer.[8] Through these gathering trips women produce most of the foodstuffs people consume at this time of the year.[9]

Marisca makes many people move between the bush and the villages and this oscillation contributes to defining both places in contrast with each other. Yet these connections also make the bush a potent presence in the hamlets. The memory of San Martín del Tabacal and the more recent perception of the contrast between their lands and towns such as Ingeniero Juárez and Formosa accentuate this semantic expansion of the bush into the villages. These memories and experiences make many people define "the bush" as home: a place of their own that includes not only thick and open forests but also their hamlets. When people in the villages say, as they often do, "here in the bush" they produce this meaning that implicitly delimits their lands as a whole in relation to other geographies. This is why for many Toba "the bush" often overshadows the Pilcomayo marshlands, another place that evokes memories of vanished landscapes.

The Marshlands

When I arrived at the hamlet I was heading to, my companions were sitting around a fire ready to leave. A boy diligently put my bicycle inside a rancho and I sat down for a few minutes to drink from a warm mate gourd somebody put in my hands. My break did not last long. A few minutes later, as I was still soaked in sweat from the ride, we all set out on foot to the marshes. We marched on a narrow bush trail and each of my six companions carried a rolled blanket, a small bag, and a shotgun or rifle. As we got closer to the marshes, the vegetation gradually opened and we soon left the dry, hardened hinterland soil behind and began walking on grass. Bright shades of green, which contrasted with the darker, dustier colors of the hinterland bush, surrounded us. As the space gradually opened in front of us, we were immersed in a landscape I always found startling, beautiful, and uncanny. Standing twenty to thirty meters apart and towering over an intensely green veneer of grass and shrubs, countless dead trees extended in all directions. Many of them were partially covered in lush shrouds of weeds and stood over shallow water. As we proceeded toward our boats, dozens of birds flew here and there, filling the air with lively sounds. That ghostly landscape of shallow water and dead trees was testimony of the bush that had once covered the area, drowned by the floods that, in this region, brought an end to the Pilcomayo River.

In the early 1970s the Pilcomayo flowed further north and those marshlands did not exist. According to old people, the river was originally dug up

7. The Pilcomayo marshes. *Photo by author.*

by a huge water snake called *lék.*[10] Ever since that moment, the Pilcomayo was for generations deeply embedded in Toba livelihood and identity and, for that reason, its disappearance had a profound impact on them. In the mid-1990s people over thirty remembered the river with deep nostalgia and gave me detailed accounts of those days and the landmarks that defined them. The river, I learned, was at points over 100 meters wide and was delimited, as figure 8 shows, by steep banks and sandy beaches. More important, the river was within their immediate reach: men, women, and children took baths several times a day and men set out to fish day and night. Like the other groups of the Pilcomayo, men usually fished in teams using two types of nets, *uanaganaGát* (a depth net) and *heélaGae* (a surface net), either in groups or individually.[11] Figure 8, a photo taken in the Pilcomayo in the 1930s, shows a fisherman with a *uanaganaGát* net, used in this case on the margins of the river. People remember that the high productivity of fishing allowed them to store large quantities of fat and roasted and sundried fish to be consumed in August and September. References to fish abundance permanently permeate memories of the river. In 1996 Pablo, a man in his early seventies, told me about the days prior to the flooding: "It was nicer, much nicer. People didn't suffer. We always ate fish. . . . When there was a river, all sorts of fish came out."

Because of the enormous amount of sediment carried from the Andes and the low gradient of the Chaco plains, the Pilcomayo River has always

8. The Pilcomayo River in the 1930s: Man fishing with net.
Archives of the Museo Etnográfico Juan Ambrosetti, Facultad de
Filosofía y Letras, Universidad de Buenos Aires

been prone to changing its course and forming marshes. Yet in the 1970s
this process was probably accentuated by the deforestation of the Andean
slopes and the increase in the pace of sedimentation. Early in 1975, the
first wave of annual floods saturated the riverbed with sediment and, in
this area, the river literally turned into a mud bloc. When the last wave
of floods arrived in March, the water overflowed the riverbanks and in-
undated a wide area. The flood destroyed the villages, Misión El Toba,
and Sombrero Negro and brought dramatic changes in the landscape.
With the riverbed filled up with sediment, water formed new and wide
networks of streams and swamps five to ten kilometers south of the old
course. After losing everything, over a thousand people had to relocate in
new hamlets built on the southern margins of the marshes.

Twenty years later, the old villages, the mission, and the Pilcomayo
riverbed were covered with thick layers of sediment, several meters deep,
and located in areas where no Toba lived. Only some hunters who trek
across the marshes are able to recognize the places once so central in their
everyday life. Segundo once went on a marisca trip to what used to be
the mission and remembered how *enlame* (sediment) and thick bush had
covered it all: "It seems that it all changed. The house of the missionary
was totally covered. . . . Right after the floods, you could only see the corrugated iron above the enlame. Now, all that's thick bush. I once went
there and got out with my pants torn to pieces. It's really thick. It's not like
before." Segundo's account sheds light on the profound spatial changes

9. Fishing in the marshes. A settler's cow observes
from the distance. *Photo by author.*

brought on by the floods. After a few years, the bush took over the places
that had once been carved out as socializing spaces by Toba, settlers, and
missionaries. As a further and compelling sign of this landscape transformation, the bush imposed its presence over what remained of the river.

In the years following the floods, most Toba had to adapt their livelihood to the new geography created by the marshes, over five kilometers
wide in the summer and early fall. Men had to alter their fishing techniques, for fish spread over a wide network of shallow streams and swamps
that do not allow for the use of nets and the organization of fishing teams.
Fishing became an individual practice, less productive than in the past
and conducted primarily with an iron-headed cane (*chiquena*) and hooks
and nylon lines.[12] Changes in the landscape also reformulated senses of
place, for the river's disappearance increased the semantic, spatial, and
practical importance of the bush. The marshland is not as close to Toba
everyday experience as the river was. Because of the expansion of the
marshes during the annual flooding, most people live at least a few kilometers away from them and drink fresh water from drilled wells. Owing
to this distance, their fishing expeditions require long walks or a bicycle
ride.

Yet the marshlands, like the river, are a central reference point and
the most important source of food. Even though men fish all year, many
households establish temporary camps in the marshes to take advantage
of the relative abundance of fish between May and July.[13] Many men also

10. Flood horticulture on the marshes' edges. *Photo by author.*

fish while preparing small fields usually no bigger than one or two hectares, for flood horticulture.[14] Given the low rainfall (less than 600 milli-
meters a year), this farming technique, which many Toba have practiced
for generations, is the most productive in the area.[15] These fields have
turned the marshes' shores into places characterized by marks of trabajo,
where men and women plant watermelon (*Citrullus vulgaris*), pumpkin
(*Cucurbita maxima*), anco (*Cucurbita moschata*), melon (*Cucumis melo*), and
corn (*Zea mays*). Most households cultivate for self-consumption, but a
few households are developing a commercial agriculture and reinvesting
in tools, seeds, and small amounts of pesticides. This capitalization is con-
solidating their status as petty commodity producers and remaking local
spaces, for the most active farmers have formed separate hamlets near the
marshes to take advantage of floods and also be farther away from the
intense demand by people from other villages. Yet despite these marks of
trabajo scattered along their shores, the marshes are primarily defined by
marisca and the patterns of mobility and seasonality examined above. In
addition to fish, this place provides most Toba with an abundant source
of beehives, wildlife, and wild fruits. As a result, marisca expeditions permanently cover both the bush and the marshes, and the annual expansion
and retreat of water creates a wide transition zone between the two that
is an important source of foodstuffs.[16]

When I accompanied Toba men into the marshes, *laheGó* ("the other
side") was a frequent topic of conversation. For years I was intrigued by

the myriad stories and memories people told about that invisible place hidden behind that large mass of water and vegetation. In June 2000, with the six hunters with whom I had reached the marshes' edge, I was finally about to set foot on laheGó.

The Other Side

It took us about two hours to cross the marshes, slowly navigating the intricate network of streams, vegetation, and swamps. We left the two boats on one of the last strips of shallow water, loaded our gear, and began walking toward the hinterland. After a few hundred meters, the grass gave way to dry, hardened soil. We passed by the rancho of a Criollo and for a couple of hours followed a trail surrounded by thick bush yet wide enough to expose us to the intense Chaco sun. After walking through a dusty area eroded by cattle we reached the dry creek that was to be our camp for the next four days. While we were putting plastic sheeting and blankets on the ground, Roberto told me that the old Pilcomayo riverbed, and hence the border with Paraguay, was only a few kilometers to the northeast. Someone turned on a radio. When the time was announced, one of the men joked about the spatial liminality of those lands, caught in between the marshes and the international border: "It's three o'clock in Argentina. I wonder what time is it in laheGó."

For most Toba, the other side (*la banda* in Spanish) is a contradictory place located in a no-man's-land of sorts. The lands extending between the marshes and the old river are Argentinean territory but are relatively isolated from Argentinean villages, and the Criollos who live there maintain regular links with Paraguayan *estancias* (cattle ranches).[17] More important, those lands were the Toba's home and therefore memories of a past prior to the flooding are memories of those same places. Yet the floods' impact and the fact that no Toba inhabit those lands anymore turned laheGó into an unfamiliar landscape, where it is often hard to recognize old sites. Some women go to the other side in October and November, when the marshlands are shallow, to gather fruits from the chañar trees that abound in the area. Some men, for their part, trek through those lands to work in the estancias in Paraguay. Yet the abundance of wildlife, fostered by the fact that very few people live there, is the primary force that attracts hunters to laheGó.

After resting at the camp for a couple of hours, we went to see the place

11. Grasslands on "the other side." *Photo by author.*

my companions had told me so much about: the grasslands. In the villages, people referred to them often and evoked images of wide campos that were "like before," full of animals hard to see on their lands. As we walked there I did not know what to expect. I almost anticipated being disappointed, for I found it hard to believe that grasslands of any significant size could still exist in that part of the Chaco. As we left the last sections of bush behind, my curiosity became awe. There they were: grasslands as far as the eye could see, stretching for kilometers toward a minute line on the horizon that marked a distant bush strip. After a few minutes, my companions spotted the first ostriches in the distance. They were invisible to me. As I relished that impossible landscape, I tried to imagine how those lands might have looked a hundred years earlier, with bands of ancient ones trekking a world free of trees, Criollos, cattle, and anthropologists.

The first times I accompanied foragers into the marshes, many years earlier, I often noticed large columns of smoke emerging from the other side. My companions would comment that Criollos were setting fires to clear the ground for cattle. Only much later I made a connection between those fires, which prior to the early twentieth century produced the grasslands, and the reemergence of extensions of open country on the other side. Paradoxically, the descendants of the settlers responsible for the grasslands' demise were recreating in laheGó, the ancient ones' home, a landscape reminiscent of the Toba's past.

Yet whereas laheGó, north of their villages, evokes a past of autonomy defined by foraging, the south connects them to the places that led to the ancient ones' demise. Those are also the places where the Toba learned the meaning of "work."

Paths to Distant Places

Pozo de Maza, a village of about 500 Wichí and Criollos located about twenty-five kilometers away from the marshes, is the southern limit of the area most Toba recognize as their familiar locality. Traversed by the dirt road that connects the area with Ingeniero Juárez, the village comprises a handful of brick houses, a couple of *boliches* (general stores), a school, the quarters of gendarmería, and the site of the municipality with jurisdiction over the Toba villages. A few hundred meters away, out of sight from the main road, is the Wichí hamlet. *La comuna*, as the municipality is locally known, is the main source of public-sector jobs in the Toba villages and the center of local relations of patronage, party factionalism, and political conflicts. When talking about the upheavals in Pozo de Maza, some men like to point out that at the time of the ancient ones this site was a hunting ground of the *mañiGodipí*, "the ostriches," the Toba band that reached farther into the hinterland. This memory asserts that the place was originally Toba territory, implicitly contesting the current Wichí and Criollo presence in the area. Adults also remember that for decades Pozo de Maza was simply a Criollo post lost in the hinterland, where hundreds of Toba men, women, and children stopped for one night in their long walk to the railway line, on their way to the sugar plantations. In those days the current road, built in 1984, did not exist. Angélica, a woman in her late fifties, told me while pointing to the road fifty meters away from us: "In the past, this was just a trail. There was no road, just a trail for horses. When they came from the San Martín plantation to take the people out, people went on foot to Maza. If there was no truck there, we went on foot to Juárez." Like many others, many Toba remember the past configuration of the hinterland as the by-product of their experience of labor migration, which turned those vast extensions of bush into a place of passage to the *ingenio* (sugar plantation).

Founded in 1931, Ingeniero Juárez is the political, administrative, and economic hub of western Formosa and the Toba's most important regional point of reference. The town expanded in the mid-1980s following the discovery of oil in the region, and in a few years its population reached about 11,000, comprising mostly Criollos but also a large Wichí contingent. A group of Toba displaced by the 1975 floods set up a *Barrio Toba* (a neighborhood of about 250 people) in the outskirts and this presence increased the connections between the hamlets and Ingeniero Juárez. In the 1990s some people went to town relatively often: to visit relatives, do paperwork at state agencies, take relatives to the hospital, or sell handicrafts or produce. This experience accentuated the contrast between "the bush" and "Juárez," not only for the Toba. Every time I arrived in town after a long stay in the Toba villages I experienced culture shock, and the Criollos who would see me stepping out of a pickup truck, usually covered in dust, would marvel at my boldness for living "in the bush." Yet many Toba remember that decades ago Ingeniero Juárez was a small train station equally lost, as it were, "in the bush." Mariano described what the town looked like in those years: "Juárez was very small. There were no people, very few people. Only three merchants lived there. The merchants had little houses made of wood planks. No bricks. Nothing. Just wood planks." I asked him whether the town had streets. "Just one street. But it was very short. Everything was bush." Memories like this underscore the geographical transformations created by the town's growth and how these changes reversed the predominance of the bush still apparent in most northwest Formosa.

The railway connecting Formosa to Embarcación, inaugurated shortly after Ingeniero Juárez was founded, took several generations of Toba to the sugar plantations of Salta and Jujuy. Once a symbol of the forces of civilization and progress cutting through the wilderness, in the late twentieth century the railroad was almost in ruins, the result of widespread budget cuts.[18] In 1965 a dirt road was built parallel to the railway. After Tabacal mechanized the harvest, farms located in eastern Formosa and Salta began recruiting Toba men and women directly from their villages by truck by way of this road. In the 1990s this road was the main means by which many Toba left "the bush" to work for wages in distant places. One of their most important destinations was *tadéwo*, the west.

The Bean Farms

The contractor in charge of the farm agreed to take me to see the Toba working for him. He seemed flattered by my interest in his work but also intrigued by the fact that I knew his harvesters. We were in Embarcación, a town located on the easternmost foothills of the Andes, at the end of

12. Toba camp at a bean farm north of Embarcación.
Photo by author.

the old railway line coming from Ingeniero Juárez. The contractor was working for one of the farms that since the 1970s had transformed the landscape of the region, turning thousands of hectares of forests into bean fields.[19] The following morning, before dawn, I met him again and we both got on his pickup truck to head to the *finca* (farm). While driving he explained the details of the harvest and repeatedly praised the Toba for being "hardworking" and "clean," as opposed to the Wichí, whom he defined as "useless for work."

It was daylight when we got off the main road and, a few minutes later, entered the finca. We parked near a rudimentary store where workers buy food and other staples. When I stepped out of the truck, some Toba men who were coming to talk with the contractor recognized me and smiled in surprise. In a few seconds, I was shaking dozens of hands. Some were people I had seen only a few times but others were friends. I was as excited as I was shocked to see them in a place so different from the Chaco interior. I was finally in tadéwo, at one of the fincas I had heard so much about. We were chatting near a forest strip, where they had erected their camps with poles, corrugated iron, and pieces of nylon sheeting. A few hundred meters to the west, across the road that connects Embarcación to the Bolivian border, I could see the foggy, densely forested hills that mark the end of the Chaco plains.

About eighty Toba were working in that farm, looking for the trabajo unavailable in their villages and the Chaco interior. They came from three different hamlets and had formed several work teams, usually families or groups of friends. Most were single men and women or young couples with children. Yet a few were in their forties and fifties and remembered that, when they were teenagers, thick forests covered that area. In those days Embarcación was not unfamiliar to them. Hundreds of Toba used to get off the train there on their way to San Martín del Tabacal, which is located only twenty kilometers to the west next to the town of Orán, at the gates of the San Francisco River Valley. In the 1990s, for many men and women working in that farm, the memory of Tabacal was, as we shall see, a spectral presence.

San Martín del Tabacal

I arrived in Orán at night and the following morning the air was damp and foggy. A compact mass of mist and clouds crawled down the slopes of the hills west of the cane fields, which extended in all directions and surrounded Orán like a green sea. It was June of 1996, almost three decades after the Toba had worked in San Martín del Tabacal for the last time. The plantation had undergone major changes since those days. Once a thriving symbol of the power of the Salta sugar barons, San Martín del Tabacal had been for years in serious debt to public and private banks. When I was there, an American company was about to purchase 60 percent of the shares. The Patrón Costas family, the original owner of the ingenio, retained 4 percent of the shares.[20] Thirty years earlier, the plantation had begun a mechanization scheme that ended the labor migrations which, every year for over seven decades, had taken several generations of Toba from the Pilcomayo to the San Francisco River Valley and back. Years after the mechanization, while working near Embarcación, some Toba went to the ingenio to visit the place where they had spent such a significant portion of their lives. Some were struck by the changes that had erased the marks of their presence. Horacio, a man in his late fifties, remembered: "I don't know what year it was. I went to the San Martín plantation to see. I was watching. It's not like before. It changed. Now, machinery does the work. The places where we used to live aren't there anymore. Only cane fields. The *lote* [lot] where we lived is an orange grove now. . . . In the past, you could never see the dam at Vado Hondo. But now you can see it from the distance. That used to be bush." Horacio was contrasting the ingenio's new layout with his memories of their first trips to Tabacal, when jungle covered most of the land, the plantation was small, and some fields were planted with tobacco. The ingenio, after all, was named after the *tabacales* (tobacco fields) of the area.

I took the local bus to the town of Tabacal, the plantation headquarters and site of the sugar refinery, a few kilometers from Orán. While I looked out the windows, I kept wondering about the mountains so many Toba had told me about. People depicted them as an imposing presence overlooking the cane fields from the west. To my frustration, all I was able to see that hazy morning were hills, obscured by clouds, that did not look particularly impressive. I got off near a large portico formed by four arches, where one could read engraved in stone *"Patrón Costas"* and, on another arch, *"año 1920."* The architecture struck me as the remnant of another epoch resisting the flow of time, the symbol of the vanity of an earlier era of bourgeois power. The town of Tabacal, built in a re-created Spanish colonial style, was behind. A few hundred meters away, the factory chimneys pumped huge columns of white smoke. As I walked below the arches and headed toward the factory, passing near trucks loaded with sugar cane, I felt I was going back in time to those days when hundreds of Toba men, women and children got off the train, stood near those arches, and waited to be distributed in their lotes (the plantation's units of residence). A few weeks later, back in the Toba villages, I told several men about my visit to Tabacal and all of them compared my impressions with their memories of that same place. Tomás told me, remembering the arches: "They left the people there. People got off the train there, in front of the factory. . . . When we got off, we rested for one night. The following morning, they distributed the people. . . . The factory boss arrived. He ordered the *capitán* [indigenous leader] to take people to a lote, and other people to another lote, and other people to another lote. I remember, when I was young." Yet that day of June 1996, with the harvest in full swing, there were few workers in sight: just trucks waiting to unload tons of sugar cane.

The refinery was more impressive than I had imagined: a dark, enormous building with several thick, tall chimneys saturating the air with smoke and industrial noise. Many Toba had told me they feared and avoided that place, especially because of the dangers that lurked in its basement. I stayed for a couple hours, observing the imposing, almost living machinery and taking notes. Later that morning, the clouds began dispersing. I had been in Tabacal for about three hours and decided to head

(*top*) 13. Sugar refinery, San Martín del Tabacal.
(*above*) 14. The mountains, San Martín del Tabacal.
Photos by author.

back to the road and explore the cane fields. As I walked away from the refinery, I noticed that the sky was sunnier and I looked once again to the west. I remember shivering at the towering mountains that dominated a now-clear valley. Images cascaded into my mind: the scores of devils that came down from those ridges to spread disease among the Toba, the fabulous treasures hidden somewhere in those heights, the cannibal men who descended in search of human flesh. I always believed, and still do, that the old notion of *Verstehen* (understanding) is based on the naïve assumption that a supposed intersubjective communion can overcome different cultural and class experiences. But that morning, as I looked at the mountains and at the factory pouring its breath into the sky, I could not help feeling that somehow I was closer to understanding what many Toba had been telling me for a long time.

2

Heaven and Hell

This is the face of the province called Chaco! which the Spanish soldiers
look upon as a theatre of misery, and the savages as their Palestine and
Elysium. — Martin Dobrizhoffer, *An Account of the Abipones*

In the 1670s the site where San Martín del Tabacal now stands was indigenous territory covered with jungle. The ruins of Santiago del Guadalcázar,
founded in 1624 and abandoned eight years later, were the only remains
of a brief attempt by the Spanish to control the region. Yet this was still a
disputed territory. The juncture of the San Francisco and Bermejo rivers
was an entry point into the Chaco for Spanish military expeditions coming
from the highlands. In 1673, as they descended from the same mountains
that centuries later would evoke terror among the Toba, Spanish troops
from Jujuy could see the Chaco in front of them like a vast, dark ocean
rolling toward the east. Those men formed one of the parties sent simultaneously from different fronts by the governor of the Tucumán province,
Angel de Peredo, against the *indios infieles* (infidel Indians) of the Chaco.
The column led by Governor Peredo had departed from Esteco, on the
Salado River, and approached the Bermejo from the south. On reaching
this river, Peredo dispatched groups of soldiers "in order to take the infidels out of the dens of thick forests, where they hide with their families
under the protection of wild animals" (Lozano 1989:217).[1] When the Jujuy
troops arrived in the same area, various indigenous groups had managed
to flee across the river. The synchronized movement of military parties,
however, cut off several escape routes. When the campaign was over, the
Spanish had been able to capture 1,800 men, women, and children. The
captives were taken to Esteco, where Governor Peredo distributed them
as serfs among his troops. Father Pedro Lozano wrote about this event:
"And all the soldiers and corporals were so anxious to have Indians serving
them, that they judged that all the prisoners were not enough to award
their merits" (1989:229).

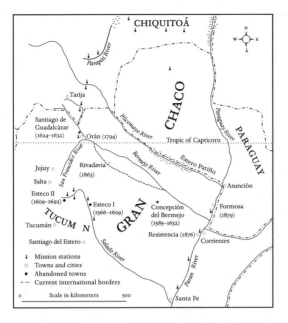

Map 3. The Gran Chaco: Sixteenth to
nineteenth centuries

The campaign led by Angel de Peredo was one of the many *entradas*
(forays) made by the Spanish in order to obtain serfs and slaves from the
Chaco interior. These entradas shed light on the tense spatial configuration of this region during the colonial period, as a territory torn between
efforts by the Spanish to obtain their labor through enslaving expeditions
and attempts by indigenous groups to rely on the intricate local geography to resist those raids and, in turn, attack frontier settlements. In this
chapter I analyze the spatial dimensions of these fields of force by examining the historical emergence of the Chaco as an indigenous haven, the
origin of the western Toba as a distinct sociopolitical entity, and the final
military assault on the region conducted by the Argentinean state.

The Making of the Chaco Frontier

The social landscape that the Spanish encountered in the Chaco was the
result of the mingling of populations and cultural influences that for mil-
lennia had converged into the region from the Pampas, the Amazon basin,

and the Andes (Métraux 1946b:210). Prior to the arrival of the Europeans, the configuration of the region had been shaped by the Guaraní migrations to the western edge of the Chaco in the fifteenth century (from what is today southern Brazil) and the powerful influence of the Inca Empire along the eastern slopes of the Andes. Portuguese and Spanish explorers first entered the Chaco in the 1520s and 1530s, trying to reach the Inca riches from the Atlantic coast. They encountered hunter-gatherer groups organized in small bands and, in the western edge of the Chaco, slash-and-burn agriculturists (Chané, Guaná, and Guaraní-Chiriguano).[2] These expeditions also met fierce resistance. Since the Gran Chaco was a mostly semiarid region with no silver or gold, its direct control did not become a priority for the crown. From the mid-sixteenth century onward, however, the Chaco interior became for the Spanish an important source of serfs and slaves (Gott 1993:155; Susnik 1971:9-11).

Attempts to control indigenous labor were especially important on the western frontier of the Chaco, the province of Tucumán, where the Spanish founded towns such as Santiago del Estero (1553), San Miguel del Tucumán (1565), Esteco (1567), Salta (1582), and Jujuy (1593). Esteco and Concepción del Bermejo (the latter founded farther east in 1585) were among the first Chaco settlements where the native population was subjected to *encomienda* (see Lozano 1989:98, 111; Gullón Abao 1993:36). Imposed by the Spanish during the early colonial period, encomienda was a type of servitude through which the crown granted an *encomendero* rights over the labor of a specific indigenous population. The latter was obliged to provide him with unpaid personal services and an annual quota of goods or cash. The encomendero did not have rights over their land and, at least formally, had to guarantee their evangelization and "education." Yet in Tucumán encomienda became a highly exploitative system combining feudal and slave elements (Rutledge 1987:84-91; Rosenzvaig 1986:50-57).

Various groups were subject to encomienda relations along the Salado River, yet attempts to impose these relations in the Chaco interior failed. In the 1630s the Spanish had to abandon Concepción del Bermejo and Santiago del Guadalcázar (another encomienda center) following widespread indigenous rebellions (Zapata Gollán 1966:27-29; Gullón Abao 1993:37). The fields of accommodation and resistance created by labor exploitation had deep spatial implications, for they contributed to producing the Chaco interior as a region located beyond Spanish reach. By the mid-seventeenth century, Guaycurú groups, most notably the Mbayá (on the Paraguayan frontier) and the Abipón (in the southern Chaco), adopted the horse and developed highly mobile units of mounted warriors. Their attacks on towns and settlements, as well as the looting and rustling of cattle and horses, put a steady pressure on the Spanish frontier. For over two centuries, these and other groups made the Chaco a region from where they launched raids and a haven that enabled them to resist enslaving raids, military expeditions, and missionization attempts. In 1784, summarizing some of the tensions tearing through the Chaco geography, the Jesuit missionary Martin Dobrizhoffer (1970:124) wrote: "This is the face of the province called Chaco! which the Spanish soldiers look upon as a theatre of misery, and the savages as their Palestine and Elysium." Evoking Roman and Judeo-Christian imageries, Dobrizhoffer illustrated that the Chaco became an indigenous bastion through its transformation into a place hostile to European troops.

Trackless Woods for Fortifications

The consolidation of the Chaco as a "theatre of misery" for the Spanish severely undermined labor control in Tucumán and on the frontiers of Santa Fe and Corrientes, where the presence of vast tracts of forests encouraged people to escape labor servitude. Throughout the seventeenth century, the number of *indios encomendados* in Tucumán plummeted as a result of high mortality rates and recurrent flights (Rutledge 1987:92, 96–99; Gullón Abao 1993:53).[3] Facing serious labor shortage, the Tucumán authorities organized several expeditions to "chase Indians" in the Chaco interior, among them those led by Peredo in 1673 and Andino in 1679 (Zapata Gollán 1966:40–41; Gullón Abao 1993:51). Yet the region's geography posed serious obstacles to these attempts at reproducing a declining labor force. The indios, Father Lozano complained, "flee to the thickest forests, which we know well are impenetrable to armed Spanish" (1989:226). These fields of contention transformed the Chaco into a place of indigenous autonomy perceived by the Spanish as a treacherous green fortress, where nature was an ally of savagery and provided "trackless woods for fortifications, rivers and marshes for ditches, and plantations of fruit trees for storehouses" (Dobrizhoffer 1970:124).

During the colonial era, numerous accounts reveal the meanings of freedom and well-being that indigenous groups projected onto the Chaco interior. In the late eighteenth century, Martin Dobrizhoffer wrote that the Abipón "were strongly attached to their native soil, a soil abounding in delightful fruits and wild animals, and fortified with so many lurking-holes; and [they] . . . dreaded the vicinity of the Spaniards with as much anxiety as servitude, having learned that the one was often the occasion of the other" (1970:263). Accounts such as this indicate that features associated with indigenous lands were perceived in their contrast with experiences of domination in places under Spanish control.

These spatialized meanings of autonomy were also fostered by missionization attempts. The Jesuit order was active on the Chaco frontiers for over two centuries — until the crown expelled it from Spanish territories in 1767 — yet flights to the bush permanently drained the missions' population.[4] Father José Cardiel wrote that missionized Indians always longed for the Chaco, to the point that when they talked about their lands they used "the most magnificent expressions, like when we talk to them about Paradise" (1920:375). Disease and social control at the missions directly informed these idealized memories of the bush. In the early eighteenth century, at the Jesuit *reducción* (mission) of San Esteban de Valbuena, on the Salado River, a Lule chief urged his followers "to abandon the reducción and what they called captivity and to return to their woods where they would enjoy their old freedom and live healthy and strong, not like in Valbuena, where due to a certain epidemic they were dying and coming to an end" (Lozano 1989:411). This view of the bush as a place of health and freedom defined in opposition to the disease haunting the missions was part of processes also affecting areas deeper into the Chaco.

Located at the heart of the region, forming large marshlands, and inhabited by militarily autonomous groups, the Pilcomayo posed formidable obstacles to the Spanish. Dozens of expeditions to this river failed because of the swampy territory and indigenous attacks, which contributed to the perception that this territory was the most remote and most mysterious in the Chaco (Lozano 1989:59; see Gordillo 2001). Yet this perception was not the result of this area's geographical isolation but of its configuration as an indigenous bastion, produced through warfare and wide trade circuits (cf. Palermo 1986). In 1721, for instance, Father Gabriel Patiño reached the mid-Pilcomayo and noted that indigenous groups had acquired horses, sheep, and cow leather through warfare, barter, and direct trips to the Salta frontier (Arenales 1833:26, 23–25, 27).

The conflicts and displacements mentioned above did not involve an interaction between rigid social entities spinning off each other, to use Eric Wolf's (1982:6) metaphor, as "billiard balls." Rather, these processes profoundly reconfigured the ethnic landscape of the Pilcomayo and eventually the origin of the western Toba as a distinct sociopolitical entity. In the seventeenth and eighteenth centuries, Spanish chronicles are full of references to Toba groups located between the foot of the Andes and the mid-Pilcomayo (Lozano 1989:218–19, 263; Arenales 1833:25–28). Most of these references allude to the so-called Bolivian Toba, who had an early and conflictive relationship with the Spanish.[5] From the existing sources, it is not possible to determine whether the Toba examined in this book, living 200 kilometers downstream, were then part of a distinct grouping. Yet genealogical analysis conducted by Marcela Mendoza (2002) shows past links between some western Toba bands and the Bolivian Toba. This may indicate that in the past both groups were in close contact or formed a single sociopolitical unit and, later on, a cluster of bands moved down the river and formed a new grouping, probably around the mid-nineteenth century. A few decades after their ancestors arrived at the lands occupied by present-day Toba, social relations brewing farther west would have a deep impact on them.

Sugar Cane and the Making of New Frontiers

By the end of the eighteenth century, relations of production in the province of Tucumán were undergoing important changes and haciendas based on cattle raising and sugar cane cultivation had gradually replaced the encomiendas, in decline since the seventeenth century (Rosenzvaig 1986:77). These haciendas hired indigenous people relying on new social relations increasingly based on wage labor, and their gradual expansion became particularly apparent in the San Francisco River Valley. By the late eighteenth century, the Spanish defeated the last outbreaks of indigenous resistance in the valley, and haciendas such as San Isidro and San Lorenzo were producing sugar cane (Gullón Abao 1993:120–21; Rutledge 1987:108–9). In 1794 the Spanish founded San Ramón de la Nueva Orán, not far from the ruins of Santiago de Guadalcázar. This town further transformed the valley into a new type of geography, based on sugar cane cultivation and the exploitation of *indios reducidos* (missionized Indians) and indios infieles from the Chaco, who entered the valley in search of commodities (Gullón Abao 1993; Teruel 1994). Yet this was a political economy still constrained by the vast territories to the east, where indigenous groups retreated when labor conditions become too severe (Gullón Abao 1993:284).

In the decades following independence from Spain (1816), new haciendas such as Ledesma and San Pedro consolidated sugar cane production. By the 1830s, this region was extending its influence into the Chaco interior by attracting more indigenous workers and through direct attempts at colonization. With Orán as a stepping stone, Criollo settlers began occupying the banks of the Bermejo River. This expansion was the first systematic attempt since Concepción del Bermejo, abandoned three centuries earlier, to occupy and transform the interior of the Chaco geography. Deprived of lands and exploited by settlers, some Wichí retreated to other lands "where they could live better, in complete freedom and far from our contact" (Uriburu 1873:105–6). Others found temporary shelter in short-lived missions founded on the Bermejo, between 1857 and 1868, by Italian Franciscans (Gobelli 1916; Teruel 1995). But in 1863, shortly after settlers founded Colonia Rivadavia on the Bermejo, the Wichí launched a widespread rebellion, triggered by land encroachment and labor exploitation. The repression unleashed by the national guard and local militias was swift and brutal, and hundreds of men, women, and children were slaughtered (Uriburu 1873:106–7). For many Wichí, the bush in the Chaco interior became the only place where they could avoid extermination. In 1872 the Argentinean explorer and businessman Emilio Castro Boedo met a group of Wichí who had fled Rivadavia. They told him: "The Christians deceive us a lot; they kill us, chase us, and make us flee to the bush where we live like poor things, . . . naked and starved to death if we don't hunt" (1873:228). The bush was still a refuge from terror; yet it was a refuge in which living conditions were deteriorating because of the growing dependence on market goods. The 1863 massacres anticipated the way the Argentinean elites were to deal with one of the last indigenous territories within the nation.

A *True Hellhole: The Military Assault on the Chaco*

When after decades of civil warfare Argentina emerged in the 1870s as a unified nation-state with growing links with the world market, the expansion of internal frontiers and the control of border areas became state priorities. This involved the final assault on the last indigenous strongholds in the country: Pampa-Patagonia and the Chaco. The Buenos Aires elites regarded these regions as *desiertos*, deserts: empty geographies with enormous yet dormant economic potential defined by their absence of civili-

(*above*) 15. Army troops attacking
indios "protected by the density of
the forests," 1884. From Angel
Justiniano Carranza, *Expedición al
Gran Chaco Austral, bajo el comando
del gobernador de estos territorios,
coronel Francisco B. Bosch* (Buenos
Aires: Imprenta Europa, 1884).
(*left*) 16. A true hellhole. From
Arthur Thouar, *A travers le Gran
Chaco: Chez les indiennes coupers de
tétes.* Paris: Phebus, 1891.

zation, market relations, and state presence (Arengo 1996; Wright 1998). Yet these were "deserts" inhabited by armed indigenous groups that had yet to be defeated. This is why the Argentinean national project forged in the late nineteenth century hinged on the violent erasure of what was seen as its negative counterpart.

The final assault on the Chaco gained momentum in the 1880s, shortly after the army finalized "the conquest of the desert" in the Pampas and Patagonia. The bulk of military pressure focused on the southern and eastern Chaco. In October 1884, the minister of war, Benjamín Victorica, led a large campaign involving 1,500 men from five regiments who converged from the south, east, and west on the middle course of the Bermejo. Like the Spanish before them, the Argentinean troops advanced over a geography that most of them saw as the embodiment of the savagery they were fighting against. El monte encapsulated a wild nature and a savage humanity that seemed to conspire against the spatial expansion of the nation's civilizing mission. The naturalization of indigenous resistance and the fetishization of nature turned the bush, in the words of an army officer, into the Indians' natural "ally" and the soldiers' most feared "torment" (Molinari 1949:11–12). Michael Taussig (1987:75) wrote that during the rubber boom the Amazon jungle came forth "as the colonially intensified metaphor for the great space of terror and cruelty." In the Chaco, indigenous resistance in the bush evoked similar anxieties. That place, an army officer wrote, was "a true hellhole" where soldiers felt asphyxiated (Molinari 1949:11, also 77–78). The bush was the overwhelming presence of the Indians' absence; it fostered the suspicion that indios constantly watched the troops' movements "protected by the density of the forests" (Departamento de Guerra 1889:229; see Taussig 1987:78).

Indeed, for the groups resisting this large-scale military assault, the bush enabled them to partially compensate for their lesser firepower. Men avoided clashes in open spaces and preferred to engage in hit-and-run tactics conducted in forested areas. When attacked by the army, women and children usually fled to the thickest bush sections while fighters confronted the troops (Ministerio de Guerra y Marina 1889:176). These strategies were not enough to stop the army, and the machinery of violence of the Argentinean state prevailed. Yet the massacres triggered by troops were not unrelated to their fear of "the green desert" of the Chaco. Referring to the rubber barons who terrorized the Colombian and Peruvian Amazon, Taussig (1987:133) wrote: "The terror and torture they devised mirrored the horror of the savagery they both feared and fictionalized." In the Chaco, soldiers were immersed in a similar spiral of violence in which their fear of the bush and their horror of savagery fostered the terror they unleashed on the indigenous population.

Early in 1885, Victorica's campaign was over. After numerous battles and skirmishes with Toba and Mocoví groups of the southern Chaco, the army killed hundreds of warriors, took thousands of prisoners, and captured an enormous bounty of horses, cattle, and sheep. The region had been for the first time penetrated from several fronts, many groups had been defeated or disbanded, and important *caciques* (indigenous leaders) had been killed or captured. Mimicking the savagery they were claiming to suppress, several officers displayed in public the heads of caciques killed in battle (Fotheringham 1910:450; cf. Taussig 1993).

The 1884–85 campaign, however, did not result in the definite conquest of the Chaco. Troops did not raid the hinterland between the Bermejo and the Pilcomayo and many indigenous groups fled north to the Pilcomayo (Scunio 1972:296). Yet the pressure was mounting and the campaign's shock waves reached most corners of the Argentinean Chaco. In 1883 and 1885, Argentinean cavalry detachments clashed with various groups on the Pilcomayo, not far from western Toba territory (Ibazeta 1883–1884; Scunio 1972). And in 1884 a Bolivian military expedition traveled through that area on its way to Asunción, becoming the first ever to connect the Bolivian Andes with the Paraguay River along the Pilcomayo (Thouar 1991). These forays, and the fact that other indigenous groups arrived in the region escaping the army, most likely created among the western Toba the perception that new, powerful forces threatened their autonomy.

Wedges of Capitalism

At the time of Victorica's campaign, capitalist investment in the Argentinean Chaco was scarce and restricted to timber production on the Paraná and Paraguay rivers (Iñigo Carrera 1983; Arengo 1996). State violence changed this. In a few years, the looting of the southern and eastern Chaco had begun. The legal parameters for the expropriation of indigenous lands had been set up in 1876, by a federal law through which huge tracts of lands in the (more humid) eastern Chaco and on the Bermejo were distributed to investors and speculators. By 1889, 5,600,000 hectares of land had been distributed to just 112 estates (M. González 1890:xii–xv). Since most concessions became unproductive *latifundios* (large estates) held by

17. "The Indian . . . will have no other choice than to surrender
entirely to labor, without any monetary cost to the state."
Archivo General de la Nación, Buenos Aires.

speculators, the government passed new laws aimed at encouraging small
and mid-size productive units (Iñigo Carrera 1983:10, 49–51, 58). Through
this massive land expropriation, the government also aimed at forcing the
recently defeated indigenous groups into becoming a cheap labor force.
In 1905 the Formosa governor outlined the direct connection that existed
between the tightening of "the desert" and the creation of an indigenous
proletariat: "[The most] efficient and secure means of civilizing the Indian
and incorporating him into production and labor [is]: the advance of colonization and the gradual narrowing, by the settlers, of the desert. Once the
civilized man has entered, he will expel [the Indian] from his present pos-
sessions, where he finds easy means of subsistence and then he will have
no other choice than to surrender entirely to labor, without any monetary
cost to the state" (Luna Olmos 1905:59).

The expansion of capitalist relations into the eastern Chaco turned
land into a new type of space, what Henri Lefebvre (1991) would call
"abstract space": a quantifiable, measurable commodity sliced into lots
to be made available on the market. This commodification required the
physical destruction of the retreats indigenous groups had held for centuries. As Luna Olmos's words reflect, this obliteration of "the desert"
created a new social subject: people deprived of means of production and
forced to engage in wage labor as their only means of survival. As a result

of this massive geographical and social reconfiguration, in the southern and eastern Chaco several Toba and Mocoví groups, now part of a land-less proletariat, settled in the outskirts of towns. Franciscan missionaries and state agencies produced places where some of them were to be con-gregated for their re-education and civilization. The most important of such places were the missions of Laishí and Tacaaglé (1901) and the *reduc-ciones indígenas* of Napalpí (1911) and Bartolomé de Las Casas (1914). As Elena Arengo has pointed out (1996), these reducciones became the site of an intense civilizing project, where government officials intended to reshape these groups' subjectivity and turn them into agriculturists and disciplined laborers. Other groups in the eastern Chaco were cornered in parcels of federal land left out in the interstices of a growing landscape of estates that were fencing off lands and clearing forests for cattle and, from the 1920s on, cotton. For these Toba and Mocoví groups, marisca became a secondary, part-time activity, an occasional reminder of what their life had been like in the past.

The production of new geographies through capitalist relations had a very different expression in the western Chaco and the regions surround-ing the Pilcomayo River. In the early twentieth century, state presence in this area was still thin. The semiarid lands of the region were less at-tractive to investors, and in Formosa — a national territory that became a province only in 1955 — most lands in the west of the territory remained in the hands of the federal government. The expansion of capitalism re-configured this region not through land expropriations but through its transformation into a huge source of labor for the plantations of the San Francisco River Valley.

The sugar industry had been expanding rapidly since the 1880s. Le-desma, San Pedro, and San Isidro imported steam machines from Europe and in 1882 a British engineer named Roger Leach formed a society that turned hacienda San Pedro into a modern company called Ingenio La Esperanza, which he later ran with his brothers (Rutledge 1987:134–35, 160). This leap into capitalist modernity turned the old haciendas into ingenios: units administered by a centralized company that owned the sugar cane fields and the refinery and hired large numbers of wagework-ers.[6] Federal credits, tariffs, and the arrival of the railway in Salta and Jujuy greatly encouraged this transformation. By the 1890s there were four large ingenios in full expansion in the San Francisco River Valley: Ledesma, La Esperanza, La Mendieta, and San Isidro, which were rapidly turning the valley into one of the most dynamic capitalist frontiers in Argentina.

Continuing with a trend initiated in the eighteenth century, the growing demand for labor targeted the Chaco. Since some indigenous groups still relied on foraging, in areas near the frontier this recruitment also involved the army's coercion (Uriburu 1873:107; Schleh 1945:332; see Iñigo Carrera 1984). Ledesma and La Esperanza, the largest plantations, also began sending contractors to the Pilcomayo, by then the last part of Argentinean territory where the army had not secured a direct presence.

The siege to the Gran Chaco, which for centuries had shaped the region in a violent process of struggle, accommodation, and displacement, was coming to an end. The Chaco interior ceased being the impenetrable "hell" that had haunted generations of Spanish and Criollos and the "paradise" that had sheltered militarily autonomous indigenous groups. Yet the tension between oppression and autonomy tearing through the region did not disappear; it was reconfigured in new ways. In the Pilcomayo region, the Toba's initial incorporation into the orbit of the plantations was tied to the transformation of their lands into a new type of place.

3

Places of Violence

[State] sovereignty implies "space," and what is more it implies a
space against which violence, whether latent or overt, is directed
— a space established and constituted by violence.
— Henri Lefebvre, *The Production of Space*

Poor Toba people, they were most scared of the military.
If it weren't for the San Martín plantation, there would be
no Toba left. — Patricio, 1997

The early twentieth century stands as a particularly meaningful moment
in Toba memories. It was "the time of the ancient ones": a time when the
Toba were proud, fiercely independent hunters, fishers, and gatherers. In
current memories, those times stretch back to a blurred past that includes
events probably taking place in the 1890s and dissolves, without reference
to genealogies, into a distant temporal horizon. When asked about their
deeper history, old people recite stories about the cultural hero *uaiacalá-
chigi* (fox) or mythical events that shaped the world, such as the arrival of
women from the sky or the fire that forced people to hide underground.
In these accounts, people remember their past as a landscape of savannas
and wide vistas, defined negatively by the absence of settlers, cattle, and
trees. The end of those times is therefore the history of the demise of that
geographical and social configuration. And this was a history of violence.
Allen Feldman (1991:20) has argued that violence is not the "expression"
of deeper historical processes external to it but, rather, a transformative
practice that produces historical subjects. Inscribing the productive character of state violence in space, Henri Lefebvre (1991:280) wrote that state
sovereignty presupposes not just any space but one "established and constituted by violence." Likewise, the incorporation of Toba territory within
the sovereignty of the Argentinean state required the production of a new

space *through* the violent dismemberment of the yagaikipí's political and military autonomy. Seen from the eyes of the state, the end product of this civilizing violence was a geography that gained meaning through its immersion within "the national order of things" (Malkki 1995). In Toba memories, this violence is in contrast a force that constituted their lands as a place of their own, which their ancestors *defended* arms-in-hand against state agents. In this chapter, I explore this spatialized history and the way most Toba remember it by analyzing how state violence was related to the first trips to the sugar plantations. This requires an examination of the way the ancient ones recreated their lands prior to their journeys to the mountains.

That's the History of the Ancient Ones

At the turn of the century, the Toba occupied both banks of the Pilcomayo River and roamed wide areas of the Chaco hinterland, organized in exogamic bands under the lax leadership of a *haliaganék*, a shaman and warrior. During the fishing season most bands settled near the Pilcomayo, and at the peak of the gathering season, in the summer, they converged into larger villages (Mendoza 1999, 2002).[1] Most Toba remember that warfare was a central aspect of their ancestors' lives. They often portray the grasslands of the past as places torn by clashes between the ancient ones and the *TegaGaikpí*, the Nivaclé from across the Pilcomayo, and the *KaGaikpí*, the Wichí groups from upstream. Toba warriors raided enemy villages to capture sheep, weapons, and captives (women and children) or because the TegaGaikpí had obstructed the flow of fish with fishing fences. Clashes were often associated with rituals like the one illustrated by figure 18, in which men returning from a successful raid celebrated the seizure of booty and scalps. Alfred Métraux took this photo in 1933, when these rituals were about to be abandoned owing to the recent Anglican missionization. Yet this staged image illustrates the type of decoration (feathers, jaguar furs, chagüar fiber masks) and body painting associated with warfare "at the time of the ancient ones."

Internalizing decades of Anglican socialization, in the 1990s many people remembered the yagaikipí's violence as a sign of their brutality, ignorance, and heathenism (see Gordillo 2002d). Yet they also emphasized that this was violence generated *by* the ancient ones; it was a marker of their agency, independence, and pride. It was also their burden, for many

18. Toba men performing a warfare ritual for Alfred Métraux, 1933. *Photo by Alfred Métraux. Archives of the Museo Etnográfico Juan Ambrosetti, Facultad de Filosofía y Letras, Universidad de Buenos Aires.*

Toba remember their ancestors as trapped by an almost innate drive to fight. As Pablo, a man in his early seventies, put it: "Poor people, the old people. They couldn't sleep in peace. They were fighting all the time." This violence had further, spatial implications, for it produced their territory as *Toba* land. It was through their clashes with the Nivaclé and Wichí, and later on with the settlers, that the ancient ones asserted control over a wide territory. Memories of warfare are spatialized by constructing the times of the ancient ones as a place of fierce autonomy they had to fight for. Gervacio, a man in his forties, remembered that this is what defined "the history of the ancient ones" when he told me, "The ancient ones only thought about war. They defended the land. They defended it, defended it. That's the history of the ancient ones."

This armed defense of their lands by Toba, Nivaclé, Wichí, and Pilagá had hindered several expeditions to the area and reinforced the Pilcomayo River's reputation as an untamed territory. Yet the expansion of the capitalist frontier farther west was disseminating commodities that were gradually changing local consumption patterns and undermining this autonomy. These changes, as well as the threat of military reprisals, were also making many Toba more willing to interact with civilian and scientific expeditions. Explorers Domingo Astrada (in 1903) and Gunardo Lange (in 1905) reached their territory and noticed that some Toba possessed firearms, iron tools, and pieces of industrially designed clothing. They were also struck by their insistent demand for clothing and tobacco (Astrada 1906:122–25; Lange 1906:63–65). Lange (1906:64) wrote that many Toba were particularly fond of cloths "of lively colors." These demands expressed the ancient ones' contact with what John and Jean Comaroff (1997:220) have called "the banality of imperialism, the mundanities that made it so ineffably real." The acquisition of commodities also became a political strategy aimed at incorporating firearms that could empower the Toba's capacity to confront their older enemies and eventually resist the army. Circulating through looting and trade, most of these goods arrived in their territory from the west. At some point, probably in the late 1890s, Toba men decided to travel to that place by themselves.

The Country of Wonders

The ancient ones were probably lured to the sugar plantations by "Indian hunters" who offered gifts in exchange for their migration to the cane fields (see von Rosen 1904:13–14).[2] The journey on foot took up to two months and, given the dangers and uncertainties posed by a trip to an unknown region, it is likely that initially only young men participated (Mendoza 2002; see Niklison 1989:120). Shortly after 1910, Ledesma and La Esperanza had systematized labor recruitment and replaced the "Indian hunters" with large and well-organized expeditions of *mayordomos*, which herded cattle to feed hundreds of people during the journey (Niklison 1989:63, 117; Vidal 1914:23–24).

In 1909 the Swedish ethnographer Erland Nordenskiöld (1912:6) lived among a group of Nivaclé near the Pilcomayo; he wrote that they saw the ingenios as a "country of wonders." Ninety years later, many Toba transmitted a similar sense of wonder when remembering their ancestors' first impressions of the plantations. The mountains were a major source of awe. The visual impact of those ridges was so compelling that even today many Toba refer to the plantations as "the mountains."[3] In 1997 Mariano told me about the impression those ridges made on the yagaikipí: "Everybody was looking at the mountains. They were thinking that they were very high. That's what people were afraid of." This estrangement was accentuated by the contact with commodities they had never seen before: new types of clothing, such as pants, and new types of food, such as sugar, *yerba mate* (the herb used for the mate tea), or flour. In the 1990s, many Toba enjoyed telling stories that highlighted the misinterpretations this situation created. For instance, many remembered that the yagaikipí tried to cook sugar by pouring it into boiling water. Others described how they threw away the yerba mate because they thought it was "an animal's dung." Recalling these stories, people usually could not avoid laughing, with tender compassion, at the "ignorance" of their ancestors.

Many Toba also remember that the ancient ones learned that working at the ingenio required a new political economy of time, organized in concepts such as "weeks," "months," and "Sundays." But rather than seeing this new time division as an imposition by capitalist discipline, as analyzed by Edward Thompson (1993:352), many remember that at kahogonaGá the ancient ones discovered the "real" flow of time. In 1994 Patricio, a man in his early seventies, told Marcela Mendoza: "They didn't know what a day was, what a week was, that on Sundays people don't work. Little by little, people were learning. The *patrón* [boss] gave them advice. And people began getting an idea of what the end of the month was. . . . The patrón of La Esperanza said: 'We're going to work until the month of November and then we'll let you go.' They didn't know what a month meant. But they worked." Patricio was also pointing out that, despite the yagaikipí's learning process, there was a sharp cultural gap between them and their patrones. This ethnic and class divide accentuated their estrangement at the ingenio. In those years, European visitors were struck by the contrast between modernity and savagery that characterized the plantations (B. Grubb 1911:86–91; Muir 1947:224, 228; Nordenskiöld 1912:4). At La Esperanza, for instance, thousands of "half naked savages" lived in huts not far from "tennis courts, a swimming bath, a squash court, ice, bacon, white-skinned Englishwomen and children" (Muir 1947:224). Some of these visitors noticed that indigenous workers were equally amazed by these contrasts. On Sundays the Leach brothers organized polo matches at La Esperanza, and Barbrooke Grubb (1911:91), a British missionary, wrote, "I thought it remarkably strange one day, while watching a polo match, to see little bands of Chaco savages passing along and gazing wonderingly at this strange game of the English."

Yet the ancient ones' alienation from the places, commodities, time schemes, and habits of their bosses was anchored in exploitative conditions that estranged them, first and foremost, from their labor. In the

19. Toba men at La Esperanza, wearing chiripas. From
W. Payne and T. Wilson, *Missionary Pioneering in Bolivia,
with some Account of Work in Argentina*. London: H. A.
Raymond, 1904.

early twentieth century, La Esperanza and Ledesma employed together
more than 5,000 indigenous people from the Chaco: Wichí, Toba, Chorote, Pilagá, and Nivaclé. This labor force was complemented with Guaraní (then called *Chiriguanos*) from the Bolivian Chaco and Kolla peasants
from the highlands of Argentina and Bolivia. Criollos coming from various parts of northern Argentina formed the permanent workforce. In 1913
a total of 12,100 people worked at the Jujuy plantations (Vidal 1914:19).
Early in the century, the Chaco groups were employed as cane cutters;
they cut off leaves and top ends and transported the cane to the small trains
that took it to the factory. Women worked together with men, usually
carrying the cane cut by their husbands (Niklison 1989:72).[4] When in the
mid-1990s the Toba remembered the work of the ancient ones at kahogonaGá, many emphasized how strong and hardworking they were. "In
the past, the Toba were the ones who endured the work the most, more
than the Wichí," Ernesto, a teaching assistant in his mid-thirties, told me
in 1995. "The owner of the ingenio liked them a lot. They worked all day
long. At five in the morning they were already up, until noon, and then
from one to six in the afternoon. But they were tough. No way around it.
They were strong for work."

In contrast with memories like this, which highlight that the ancient

ones were highly regarded by their bosses, administrators saw their indigenous labor force as unproductive and undisciplined. A La Esperanza
administrator complained that the Toba "are horribly lazy and will only
work at all if paid by results" (Muir 1947:229). Indeed, far from being docile
workers or full-time proletarians dependent only on wage labor, the Toba
and the other Chaco groups still held considerable political and military
autonomy in their lands. This situation turned the plantations, first, into
contested places often shaken by violent forms of resistance. In the 1990s
many people remembered that since the ancient ones were proud people
with a defiant spirit they did not take exploitation easily and assaulted
abusive foremen often. These incidents, similar to those analyzed by Ann
Stoler (1985:52–53) in the Sumatra rubber plantations, were the product
of an early engagement with wage labor by people not accustomed to its
class hierarchies and unfamiliar with collective forms of struggle such as
strikes. Second, those fields of force were also created by the fact that these
groups had not given up places of relative autonomy in the Chaco. When
the *zafra* (harvest) came to an end in November (or early December), indigenous workers were paid in kind in the so-called *arreglo grande* (big
agreement) and, loaded with goods, returned to their homes. Noticing
the spatial tension between the bush and the ingenios unraveled by that
moment, an inspector of the Argentinean Labor Department wrote in
1917: "The Indians are in a hurry to return to their lands of origin. . . . You
can note their haste to leave the ingenios and reach for the trees loaded
with fruits" (Niklison 1989:91).

The Protective Shade of the Bush

In 1909 Erland Nordenskiöld witnessed the return of a Nivaclé group from
the ingenios and noticed the excitement caused by the commodities they
had earned there: "They displayed everything that they had brought: old
rifles, uniforms, sugar, matches, powder, mirrors, adorned military caps,
aniline colors, etc., things that looked extraordinary to the other Indians,
who were also no less in wonder at the stories they were telling about the
trip. It was not less amazing, for these Indians, than what the story of an
earthling coming back from a trip to the Moon would have been for us"
(1912:6).

Most Toba were going through similar experiences and facing similar
challenges, for they were incorporating these foreign goods while try-

20. Explorers near the Pilcomayo with unidentified indigenous
companions and a hunting trophy (a jaguar), 1918. *Archivo
General de la Nación, Buenos Aires.*

ing to reassert control over their territories and bodies. First, men and
women used cloth brought from kahogonaGá to create a new type of
clothing that was to become a symbol of their aboriginality. They replaced
their previous garments (made of chagüar fibers and animal skins) with
long cloth "skirts" wrapped around the waist, known in Spanish as *chiripa*,
combined with hats and handkerchiefs. In the 1990s, people remembered
this clothing style created by the experience of wage labor as a crucial
bodily marker of ethnicity, shedding light on how their aboriginality became intertwined with a class experience.[5] More important in terms of
the reproduction of indigenous places in the Chaco, in addition to cloth,
horses, and riding gear, the ancient ones brought back home Winches-
ter and Remington rifles, bought from itinerant merchants outside the
ingenios (Niklison 1989:95–96). People currently remember that these
rifles increased their capacity to fight the Wichí and Nivaclé and, later on,
the Criollos and the army. Paradoxically, these firearms helped the Toba
maintain their lands as a territory free of state control while making them
increasingly dependent on the plantations.

The fact that the western Chaco was still located beyond the direct
control of the army posed labor-recruitment problems. First, on several
occasions indigenous groups attacked and even killed mayordomos sent
by Ledesma and La Esperanza, especially when they felt they had been

cheated in the previous seasons (Niklison 1990:47–48). Second, as part of their attempt to maintain margins of autonomy, many people traveled to the sugar cane fields only on an irregular basis. As a result, the mayordomos had to organize long journeys over extensive areas in search of new groups, which because of their mobility were hard to locate (Niklison 1989:110; Zavalía 1915:37). As a labor inspector put it: "The Indian does not go spontaneously to the plantation. It is necessary to go and look for him in the very heart of the jungle, where he has built his unstable camps" (Vidal 1914:21). Recruitment problems became so serious that between 1910 and 1914 the number of indigenous workers recruited by Ledesma and La Esperanza declined by half (Vidal 1914:28).

In the western Chaco, the early twentieth century was then characterized by a recurrent tension between, on the one hand, the indigenous groups' attempt to maintain a margin of maneuverability in the bush while obtaining valuable goods in the plantations and, on the other, the administrations' effort to pull them out of the Chaco and turn them into a reliable labor force. This contradiction was producing a new type of geography: a region that for capitalist sectors reproduced a cheap mass of laborers and that for indigenous groups granted them partial autonomy from labor exploitation. In 1916 labor inspector José Niklison (1990:47) wrote that the plantations had a debilitating effect on indigenous bodies but that the return to the Chaco enabled them to recover under "the protective shade of the bush." This protection made many groups project onto the bush some of the healing and sheltering qualities I analyze in part III. Yet these dimensions were partially shattered by the gradual advance of the Criollo settlers and the army.

It Was the Soldiers Who Died!

The level of violence in the Pilcomayo region increased significantly with the beginning of colonization. In November 1902, soldiers rounded up and executed over 130 Wichí men, women, and children returning from Ledesma (Astrada 1906:38). A few weeks later, settlers founded Colonia Buenaventura on the Pilcomayo. Facing land encroachment and violence, some Wichí groups temporarily crossed to Bolivian territory or moved downstream. Others stayed in their lands trying to adjust to the Criollos' presence. Colonia Buenaventura grew rapidly, colonization moved downstream, and the first settlers arrived in Toba territory shortly after 1910. In

September 1911 the army launched a large campaign in the region with the aim of neutralizing the indigenous armed resistance, securing the control of the border with Bolivia and Paraguay, and founding forts near the river. According to the report by Colonel Enrique Rostagno, the officer in charge of the campaign, "not a single shot was fired." Rostagno noted in passing, however, that the groups he came across were "very afraid" of the military (1969:21, 33). These groups, including the Toba, were by then aware of the army's firepower and often tried to avoid open confrontations with regular troops; yet they challenged the presence of settlers in myriad ways, and these growing tensions eventually led to clashes.

In the mid-1990s many Toba argued that prior to their first encounter with the Criollos, their ancestors stumbled on cattle roaming the area ahead of their owners. Since the yagaikipí thought they were wild animals of a rare kind, so the story goes, they killed them. In these narratives, people tend to portray the ancient ones as naïve victims of their own uncivilized ways. "Those poor people didn't know the Christians," Patricio told me. "They didn't know the cows. . . . People saw a cow and killed it. [They said] 'It seems it has no owner.' Poor people. They were ignorant. They knew nothing. They didn't know there are believers. They didn't know there are cows." This trope of ignorance defines cattle, Christianity, and private property as natural, taken-for-granted dimensions that only primitive people could ignore. Yet this trope does something else: it partially justifies killing cattle and exonerates the ancient ones for doing it. This explanation is particularly significant because most Toba argue that the army attacked the yagaikipí because of this innocent, unintended violation of private property rules. This collective memory overlooks the fact that for a few years their ancestors imposed their own regulations on the settlers and, far from ignoring their codes of ownership, charged them head of cattle for pasture use (Mendoza 2002). In December 1916, on their return from the sugar plantations, Toba men killed a settler, burned down his house, and stole his cattle for failing to comply with this payment (Mendoza 2002; Rodas 1991:58). This signaled that the ancient ones were willing to defend their lands the same way they had fought their Wichí and Nivaclé enemies.

Responding to reports about a "Toba uprising," in March 1917 two regiments of cavalry converged on the area, 150 men strong. Joined by two dozen settlers, the troops attacked the yagaikipí near their largest villages in Laguna Martín and Sombrero Negro, near the banks of the Pilcomayo. In the mid-1990s, most Toba had only a vague recollection,

21. Cavalry regiment near the Pilcomayo, 1911.
Archivo General de la Nación, Buenos Aires.

if any, of the events immediately prior to the clashes. Yet their collective memory of the actual battle was particularly graphic. Most adults had heard accounts from their parents or grandparents and would give me meticulous, vivid descriptions of the fighting. Many people emphasized their ancestors' skills in warfare, their ability to hide undetected, and the soldiers' clumsiness in a place that was not their own. More important, they would give me a version of the battle's outcome at odds with the one portrayed in the regional historiography. Federico Rodas (1991:59), a regional historian, interviewed a Criollo who joined the troops and argued that, after putting up a fierce resistance, many Toba fled to the bush and crossed the river to avoid extermination. He added that those killed by the army were more than those who escaped. Most Toba, on the contrary, claim with conviction that their grandparents suffered almost no casualties and killed an enormous number of soldiers. Take, for instance, these three men in their sixties and seventies, to whom I spoke, independently of one another, about the clashes. I asked Segundo whether any ancient one died. He said, emphatically: "Nothing, nothing! Sixty soldiers died. No Aborigen died. One was injured, shot here." Segundo pointed to his leg and added: "But it healed." Mariano, for his part, told me that over "two hundred" soldiers died. When I asked him about Toba casualties, he replied with a subtle smile, as if measuring my reaction: "Not even one Toba died. The soldiers almost caught a little old man. But they didn't see him because he was beside a large tree." Agustín was remembering the battle along with his friend Nicacio, and the two were interrupting each other in their haste to add details. Agustín said, "Many soldiers died. Like one thousand, or fifteen hundred." I asked him whether many Toba died. He raised his finger and said emphatically: "Nobody died! Only a very old woman died. She couldn't escape from the hut. The Criollos say that two thousand Aborígenes died. But they're wrong. Nobody died. It was the soldiers who died!" Most Toba acknowledge that the ancient ones had to cross the Pilcomayo River to Bolivian territory. But they did so, most agree, only because they ran out of ammunition. Moreover, the retreat did not change the status of their victory. After Mariano told me that the Toba crossed the river, I asked him who won the battle. He looked a bit surprised at my question and said, "The Toba won."

As James Fentress and Chris Wickham note (1992:6), it is tempting to emphasize the subjective components of memory when people's accounts include what seem to be improbable events. But memory is always informed by meanings important for those who remember. The memory of "true" facts is as culturally constructed as the memory of what seem to be unlikely events. The point is to unravel the meanings and fields of force behind the production of *any* memory. What is significant about the memories examined above is, first, that they evoke clear meanings of resistance to the state. The emphasis on the ancient ones' victory and the denial of their status as victims ("it's them who died!") illustrate that these memories have been shaped by current concerns over ethnic pride and, as we shall see below, locality. Explorers who met the Toba at the turn of the century were struck by their "insolence" and "arrogance" (Campos 1888:153; Astrada 1906:122). This arrogance — in addition to being an ideological construction by white observers — revealed that at the time, warfare was central in the socialization of Toba men and in the re-creation of their control over their territory. When in the 1990s Toba men remembered their grandparents fighting the army to defend their lands, they were evoking this pride and projecting new meanings onto it. And this projection is colored by a historical experience of oppression. When remembering these clashes, people put the negative features they often attach to the yagaikipí momentarily aside. The latter are no longer ignorant people who inspire compassion; rather, they are brave, skillful, unbeatable warriors who awake admiration, for they did something no Toba man would dare do today: take up arms to fight the state.

The memory of the victory over the army has important spatial dimensions. Despite the violence the military unleashed on them, the Toba are still *there*. Current memories, in other words, are informed by the experience of having overcome attempts by the army to wipe them out of their lands. What matters for current generations is that the ancient ones were not exterminated; that despite their temporary retreat they were able to reproduce relative control over their territory, even if under new, more adverse conditions. That capacity to resist state violence was, indeed, a victory of sorts: the symbol of a resilience that gains force as people remembered it eighty years later. Yet these memories have further spatial components that stand in tension with this recollection; they are torn, first, by the realities of the present, in which people are immersed within the sovereignty of the Argentinean state, and second, by the recollection of the events that followed the attack by the military, which illustrate that the ancient ones did not feel secure in their lands any longer. When people remember what happened after the clashes, they reveal—usually unaware of contradicting their previous accounts—the terror that their grandparents may have experienced at the army's hands. These memories also uncover that the military altered the geographical reconfiguration of the region and forced the Toba to look for protection elsewhere.

They're Working People!

After running out of ammunition and retreating across the river, the ancient ones moved downstream to the wide marshlands then known as Estero Patiño, could not return to their territory, and temporarily stopped migrating to the ingenios. For several years, the yagaikipí lived off foraging in contact with Pilagá groups, occasionally selling skins and furs to itinerant merchants, and eluding army patrols. As the military was imposing its power over the central Chaco, the bush was no longer an indigenous stronghold; at most, it became the last refuge where small groups on the run could avoid extermination. Expressing this spatial configuration,

Juan Mac Lean wrote in 1908, "Our Chaco Indian feels horror at the military uniform; when he sees it, he escapes to the bush right away" (Beck 1994:62).

Yet by 1920 this was a severely dislocated bush. Living in hiding was not enough to guarantee protection from the army, which by then had forts all over the region, and the ancient ones needed commodities that had become important for their social reproduction. The social and spatial disarticulation created by state violence strengthened the perception that, in those circumstances, only those who had a vested interest in their survival could protect them. In the mid-1990s, several people told me that their ancestors were able to return to their lands and reassume the migrations to kahogonaGá because of the mediation of Robustiano Patrón Costas, the owner of San Martín del Tabacal, the newest plantation in the San Francisco River Valley.

As if not talking directly about the battle made them more willing to acknowledge the power of the army, people agree that the contractors sent by Patrón Costas asked the military "not to kill the Toba." In 1996 Ernesto imitated what those contractors had told the soldiers: "No! How come you're going to kill them! . . . They're working people! With them we work in the factory and we have sugar!" The emphasis on their new role as "working people" outlines the integration in a new class formation that blurred their previous status as proud warriors; it also illustrates that what saved them from the army's attempt "to kill them all" was that they had become useful workers producing "sugar." In contrast to memories of the clashes, this time some people acknowledged openly that the yagaikipí were terrified of soldiers. Patricio told me about the 1917 battle in detail and emphasized that "not even one Toba" had died. Yet a few minutes later he said, to my amazement at his capacity to shift gracefully between contradictory statements, "If it weren't for the San Martín plantation, there would be no Toba left. The San Martín plantation defended the people. . . . In 1919, Patrón Costas remembered the Toba: 'Very hardworking,' he said. He sent a mayordomo to look for the Toba. And he chatted with the people so that they came to work. They were most scared. Poor Toba people. They were most scared of the military." I asked him why they were scared. "Because maybe the military didn't forget and wanted to fight. But since people already had a mayordomo, [the latter] told the commander they had to stop messing around. He told them they had to stop killing people, that people had to work so that Argentina keeps growing. It's true. Argentina was already rich. And Tabacal defended the

22. Toba family on the move in a landscape still marked by
grasslands, 1918. *Archivo General de la Nación, Buenos Aires.*

Toba well." These memories reveal the ways in which class and nation-
hood are amalgamated in Toba memories of their violent incorporation
into a new political economy. They are also suggestive of the way in which
people in the 1990s traced back their inclusion within the imagined com-
munity of Argentina, as "very hardworking" laborers contributing to the
wealth and growth of the nation, despite the fact that for decades they
lacked citizenship rights (as we shall see). Patricio's account also illustrates
that in the years that followed the clashes the ancient ones were seeking protection from new actors and that their very survival depended on
this protection. Filtered through the sedimentation of decades of labor
in Tabacal, this memory has strong paternalist overtones and is personalized in the figure of Robustiano Patrón Costas, a point to which I return
in chapter 7.

In 1921 the German-Argentinean ethnographer Robert Lehmann-
Nitsche (1925:187) met a group of Toba working at Ledesma and they told
him about their "bloody" fighting with the army and their recent return
to their lands. But returning to the sugar cane fields as "valuable" workers
did not guarantee protection from violence. In those years, the ingenios
deployed troops to curb unrest by "wild Indians" and were places subject
to their own forms of repression (Muir 1947:231–34; Niklison 1989:48).
This contradictory experience haunts current memories and stands in
clear tension with the memories of Patrón Costas as a protective figure.

Old men remember that prior to the foundation of the Anglican mission in 1930, on various occasions the San Martín del Tabacal administration threatened "to kill them all," often because of men who assaulted abusive foremen. This time, people make it clear that the ancient ones were terrified of soldiers. Mariano recalled that after one of these incidents they all returned home: "People quit work, because they were afraid, because the soldiers wanted to kill them all."

Yet home had become a different place. Their lands were no longer an exclusively indigenous territory and the army was an overreaching presence that had secured the region as part of the Argentinean nation. The spatial mark left by state violence was nowhere more apparent than in the consolidation of the Criollo presence in Sombrero Negro and in a dozen *puestos* (dwellings and their corrals) scattered around a wide area, which signaled the introduction of new spatial fractures and social relations. Most Criollos owned only a few head of cattle and some sheep and goats and looked after the cattle of better-off settlers. Yet some began hiring Toba men to build corrals or chop wood, creating relations of patronage that represented a new, local balance of power. In a landscape increasingly marked by diminishing grasslands, the bush became a contested place that Toba men and women had to reproduce through tense interactions with settlers. In the 1920s Toba men organized a few raids against their old enemies, the Nivaclé and the Wichí, in what became their last attempt at reproducing violent forms of control over their territory. That old style of warfare was becoming part of the past, engulfed by a present marked by the need for commodities, the rise of massive forms of wage labor, and the monopoly by the state over legitimate means of violence.

The construction of the railway Formosa-Embarcación further altered the geographical layout of the hinterland, for it produced a deep wedge through the Chaco that connected the Paraguay River to the foot of the Andes and facilitated Criollo colonization. The final stage of railway construction also involved Toba labor. In 1929 a group of men worked for a few months clearing forest for the railway line. Seventy years later, Marcelino, a political leader in his late fifties, remembered that when labor contractors arrived looking for them, the ancient ones were initially distrustful: "They thought that they wanted to kill them. But they didn't." This account indicates that at the time memories of terror were fresh; it also shows that some yagaikipí were carefully calibrating their strategies in their relationship with the *do'okohé* (the whites).

In this conjuncture, a group of white-skinned men arrived on the banks of the Pilcomayo, eighty kilometers upstream. These men had plenty of resources and were different from settlers, soldiers, and contractors. Many Toba soon saw them as potential allies. They had already seen them on their way to the cane fields at a place called Algarrobal; what they did not know was that those men had been thinking about them for a long time.

4

Searching for Our Fathers

The ancient ones were suffering a lot. They were fighting a lot.
So, they said: "What are we going to do now? We have to go and
look for a father, because we don't have a father."

— Mariano, 1999

Every Sunday morning the bell would ring at around 8:30. I would usually
finish my cup of coffee and head to the small adobe church, 200 meters
away. Men, women, and children would be converging on the same site
from all corners of the village, some wearing their best clothes. As we
entered the church, men sitting on the left and women and children on the
right, the air was always impregnated with a silent solemnity, broken here
and there by forced coughs and children's whispers. Javier, the local pastor,
would begin the service and we would all stand up for the opening psalm.
Throughout the service, directly or indirectly, we would all be reminded
of the British missionaries who arrived in 1930 to change the Toba's lives
forever. The Anglican *cultos*, in this regard, are crucial sites in the production of memories about the experience of missionization. In fact, they
are the Toba's primary ritual of commemoration. As Paul Connerton has
argued (1989:53), commemorative rituals are not simply "symbolic representations" that "express" values and memories. They are bodily performances that *produce* memories; in the words of Edward Casey (1987:217),
they are moments of "intensified remembering." Toba cultos are such
moments. Through sermons, singing, and prayers people are reminded
of the state of ignorance in which the yagaikipí lived prior to the arrival
of the missionaries and of the positive changes brought by the latter. As
Javier said on one of those Sunday mornings: "We're civilized already. We
have electric light. We have houses. We know how to read. In the past
we knew nothing. We didn't know how to read. We didn't use tables. We
didn't use spoons. . . . Now we're like men, we're not like animals."

23. Prayer next to Toba church, 1997. *Photo by author.*

The portrayal of the ancient ones as ignorant of current markers of civility is particularly strong among committed Anglicans yet is also shared by ordinary Toba. These memories are intertwined with accounts that, on the contrary, portray the ancient ones as strong, brave, and worthy of admiration. Even orthodox Anglicans produce these contradictory memories. Javier is not only a priest but also a nurse. A few months prior to the service mentioned above, I was talking with him about a flu epidemic affecting several children. This reference to current health problems made him remember the ancient ones in a way strikingly different from the remembrance he invokes during service. "People are very flabby now," he told me. "The ancient ones ate a lot of proteins and honey. . . . Now, people eat carbohydrates only. . . . Now, we have no idea how to fight. The ancient ones cut the head of the Chulupí [Nivaclé] and drank *aloja* [fermented drink made of algarroba or honey] with it, like a plate. I'm not brave enough to do that." We both laughed and Javier added: "The ancient ones were very good at running. They didn't get tired." This image of the yagaikipí as healthy and bold and the new ones as weak and flabby is recurrent among most Toba and reveals that missionization created ambiguous memories of their pre-Christian past. The fascination with the ancient ones' fighting skills, particularly apparent in the memory of the battle with the army, also indicates that there is a persistent ambiguity in the way many people remember the missionaries' interactions with the yagaikipí. In this chapter, and the two that follow, I analyze the contradictory memories of the Anglican mission and how they relate to tensions and experiences of violence that, in the 1930s and 1940s, contributed to reconfiguring the local geography. But first I examine the circumstances of the arrival of British missionaries in the Argentinean Chaco, their close connections with La Esperanza, and the intense expectations many Toba had of them. This story begins in the southernmost tip of South America.

A *Letter from Spaniard Harbor*

In August 1851, seven Englishmen led by Captain Allan Gardiner of the British Royal Navy were dying of starvation, scurvy, and exposure on the beach of Spaniard Harbor, Tierra del Fuego. For months, they had been unsuccessfully trying to attract the local indigenous groups, Selk'nam and Yámana, to pursue missionary work among them. Out of provisions and facing harsh weather, Gardiner seemed to have longed for warmer lands and less elusive objects of conversion. Before he died, early in September, he wrote a letter addressed "to the Toba chiefs of the Pilcomayo River":

> This letter comes to you with greetings. Our country which is called Great Britain, lies far, very far from yours. . . . Our God . . . has given us a Book in which we are taught all that He would have us do. . . . We have sent this Book to many other nations. . . . Why should the Toba nations be the last to receive this Book? It grieves us to think that you are still ignorant of it. . . . Let two of our people visit you, let them dwell with you securely until they have learned to speak to you in your own language. . . . We are your friends, though you know us not. . . . Farewell, captains, and all the Toba nations. May you be ever happy (quoted in Young 1905:207–8)

In 1844, seven years prior to his death in Tierra del Fuego, Allan Gardiner had founded in England a small missionary society called the Patagonian Mission (Makower 1989:20). Even though most of his work focused on Patagonia and Tierra del Fuego, in 1846 Gardiner made a trip to the Bolivian Chaco and paid a short visit to the Toba of the upper Pilcomayo. This brief experience left a profound mark on him and would have a lasting influence among his followers. Renamed in 1864 the South American Missionary Society (SAMS), the society founded by Gardiner gradually turned its attention toward the Gran Chaco. In 1889 Barbrooke Grubb, a member of the society, started missionary work among the Lengua of the

Paraguayan Chaco; a few years later, he began to consider expanding Anglican evangelization to the western Argentinean Chaco. In 1898, aware that thousands of "heathen Indians" worked at the sugar plantations of the San Francisco River Valley, Grubb contacted the Leach brothers, the owners of La Esperanza, "as to the possibilities and advisability of starting mission work on or near their estate" (Hunt 1912a:22–23). The project had to be postponed for several years, but in 1911 the first group of British missionaries, among them Grubb, began working in La Esperanza.[1]

The SAMS arrived in the San Francisco River Valley at a time when British influence in Argentina was particularly prominent. Additionally, the presence of the Catholic Church among indigenous groups of the western Chaco had been undermined by the failure of the Franciscan missions established on the Bermejo between the 1850s and 1860s (see Teruel 1995).[2] This national and regional context allowed Grubb and his followers to consolidate and eventually expand their agenda of Protestant evangelization. Since the Leach brothers were concerned about the difficulty of recruiting mobile groups, they strongly supported Grubb's missionization plan, which included following these groups back to the Chaco and settling them in stations. As one of the missionaries wrote: "The Government, as well as private firms, now realize that the Indians are a valuable asset to the labour supply . . . and endeavours are even now being made to settle them upon reservations, where they can be more easily governed, and where the missionary could have a permanent station and brilliant prospects of evangelization" (Hunt 1913:62). This convergence between the interests of missionaries and plantation owners implied an attempt to create a new spatial configuration in the Chaco interior, which, by undermining indigenous mobility, would favor labor recruitment and missionary work.

In 1914, after interacting with indigenous workers in the cane fields for three years, the British missionaries founded their first station, Algarrobal, erected in lands donated by the Leach brothers on the Bermejo (B. Grubb 1915:42). This mission was strategically located forty kilometers east of Embarcación at a place where indigenous groups converged on their way to the plantations. In the mid-1990s, some Toba remembered that, intrigued by the news about white men who provided assistance and protection, the ancient ones began stopping at Algarrobal on their way to kahogonaGá. Their first interactions with the missionaries were brief, but the yagaikipí soon began referring to them as *kade'tá*, "our fathers." This term, probably influenced by the Criollos' use of the Spanish word *padre*

24. Left to right: Julián Rumalda, Colin Smith,
and Alfred Leake at Algarrobal, 1927.
Courtesy of David Leake.

(father) to refer to priests, expressed the expectations of protection created
by the conflicts with the settlers and the army. In 1999 Patricio recalled
what his father witnessed about those first interactions with "the gringos"
(as they were also to be called): "People were thinking: 'There's a father.
There's a father.' They already knew that there were gringos from somewhere else. They stopped to rest at Algarrobal. The missionary asked:
'Who are these people?' A Wichí answered: 'These people are Toba; they
come from far away.' The missionary felt sorry for them [and said]: 'Poor
people. Poor things.' " I asked Patricio why he felt sorry for them. "Because he saw they had nothing," he told me. Remembered through the
lens of Patricio's current Anglican identity, the yagaikipí could not but be
deprived of everything the missionaries were soon to give them.

In April 1927 a young missionary named Alfred Leake arrived at Algarrobal from Britain. In contradistinction to the image of "poor things"
conveyed by Patricio, Leake was deeply impressed by the "tall and proud"

Toba who passed through the mission as if they "owned the place" (Makower 1989:73), a sign that the ancient ones maintained the body language of a recent independent past. These interactions became more regular and intense once the SAMS accomplished its old dream of establishing a mission on the Pilcomayo. In November 1927 Alfred Leake and Colin Smith founded Misión Selva San Andrés among the Wichí, upstream from Toba territory (Makower 1989:62–65). In the 1990s many Toba remembered that the news of the foundation of San Andrés created high expectations among their ancestors as to the possibility of countering the power balance imposed by the army and the settlers.

Happy the People!

People currently remember that the haliaganék (headmen) had a meeting and decided to send a delegation to San Andrés to request the foundation of a station in their lands. The main reason was that they "wanted to have peace." This strategy had important spatial dimensions, for rather than considering moving to San Andrés, the Toba leaders wanted the missionaries to come and live among them, in the hope that attracting a new actor into their lands would aid them in reasserting control over their own territory. In 1999 I asked Mariano why the ancient ones asked for a mission, and he replied:

> Because the ancient ones suffered too much. They were suffering a lot. They were fighting a lot and had no peace. When they went to the ingenio, the Wichí always attacked them. Then, the army came and chased them away. They didn't want to take it anymore. So, they said: "What are we going to do now? Who has power to live among us?" They said there was a father [and said]: "We have to go and look for a father, because we don't have a father. Because over there [in San Andrés], those people are living in peace."

The search for "a father," remembered as an explicit strategy to put an end to suffering, was a search oriented toward those places, "over there," where violence had ended. Further, it was a strategy remembered as the result of an absence: that of a protective and powerful "father" that, they realized, they "didn't have." The first Toba deputation arrived in San Andrés in early June 1928 and several weeks later a larger delegation of 200 people formally made the request for a mission (Hunt 1933:328). Cur-

25. "The missionaries arrived. Happy the people!"
Photo by author.

rent memories, confirmed by missionary reports, outline that the Toba chiefs wanted a mission in order to obtain "protection" and "education" (see South American Missionary Society 1928:100). The labor migrations had already made the yagaikipí feel estranged from goods and forms of power alien to them, and the clashes with the army had confirmed that they were unable to confront these new forces effectively. The demand for protection and education reflected the ancient ones' awareness that their survival depended on being safeguarded from and learning about the forces unleashed by the do'okohé.

The missionaries were extremely enthused by this petition by, as one put it, one of the "noblest" and "fiercest" groups in the Chaco (Hunt 1928:119–20). When Barbrooke Grubb learned in Britain about the request, he wrote shortly before his death, having in mind the letter written by Gardiner in Tierra del Fuego: "We have long been drawn to them, and they seem to have been in a wonderful way drawn to us. The fierce, hated Toba . . . truly, it is remarkable . . . it is of God" (Hunt 1933:328–29).

Missionization plans gradually gained force and in May 1929 Alfred Leake and Henry Grubb explored Toba territory to choose the station's location. Large crowds welcomed them. Nicacio, then a young boy, was there. In 1995 he remembered the arrival of "Alfredo" and "Enrique" as a moment of great excitement. While telling me about it, he raised his right arm and made quick exclamations: "The missionaries arrived. Happy the people! Some sang. Some had little flags. Happy the people! Enrique spoke Mataco [Wichí] very well and Alfredo also spoke Mataco. My dad also understood Mataco, so they talked. They said: 'Let's have a service with everybody.' But a lot of people were there! A lot! . . . People were happy, for they had a God now. They didn't fight anymore. They were all brothers with the Chulupí and the Mataquitos." Nicacio remembered the arrival of the missionaries as an exhilarating event that separated a time of warfare from a time marked by their discovery of a "God" that they *had* to have in order to cope with new geographies of power. This new era was also marked by the transformation of their old enemies into "brothers," a process parallel to the rise of class-based notions of aboriginality in the sugar cane fields (as we shall see).

Following the advice of Toba chiefs, the missionaries chose a site two kilometers upstream from the Criollo hamlet of Sombrero Negro. This location was politically significant because it challenged the Criollo presence in that village, the hub of settler activity in the area. Grubb and Leake, however, seemed to have mixed feelings about the role they were about to play. In the report about their trip to Sombrero Negro, they expressed discomfort about the Toba's purely utilitarian enthusiasm toward the mission: "But let there be no misunderstanding regarding the Toba's desire for and enthusiasm after a mission. What is it they want? . . . [I]t appears that their idea of a mission is first and foremost a protector. Harassed off the land their ancestors roamed over, pressed into service on the distant cane-fields, threatened by their white neighbours, they seek a champion to plead their cause and to fight their battles, and they look to a 'mission' to do it" (Grubb and Leake 1929:95).

Alfred Leake and a fellow missionary founded Misión El Toba on October 30, 1930, seventy-nine years after Allan Gardiner, on that desolate Tierra del Fuego beach, had envisioned Anglican missionary work among the Toba of the Pilcomayo. Following Gardiner's original directives, Leake was to live among them and teach them about "the only true God." The Toba, for their part, succeeded in bringing to their lands "a champion to plead their cause and fight their battles." The station would have a lasting impact on the local geography. Yet as state terror had eroded some of the sheltering qualities of the bush, the mission would produce new types of places and new types of contradictions.

5

A Kind of Sanctuary

I dreamed I was taken to the mission. The missionary said:
"What's wrong?" [I said:] "Those people over there want to hurt me."
[The missionary said:] "If they want to hurt you we'll chase them, we'll
burn their houses down. Nobody will hurt you." — Kedók, 1933

The foundation of the mission is for most Toba *the* turning point in their
history. In their memory, the end of the times of the ancient ones was
caused not by their first migrations to kahogonaGá, the arrival of the Criollos, or the clashes with army, but by the construction of Misión El Toba
by Alfredo. The emergence of this new place is remembered as the beginning of an era of peace. Some emphasize that with the mission the
ancient ones stopped being violent, brutal, and heathen; yet many argue
that peace was the outcome of the missionaries' capacity to halt army violence. Tomás captured this view of the times prior to the mission when
he told me, "It was very bad when there was no missionary. Everybody
wanted to kill the Aborígenes." In the pages that follow, I analyze how
current memories of the Anglican mission hinge on the perception that
this place created a drastic reconfiguration of the local geography, especially vis-à-vis the military. This process transformed the mission into a
sanctuary of sorts that counteracted the previously unrestrained exercise
of violence by the state yet also awakened partially unfulfilled, and hence
fraught, expectations of education and material wealth.

Strange and Wonderful Powers

The construction of the mission created spatial patterns originally alien to
the Toba. The missionaries' house, the school, and a building divided into
store and dispensary formed the core of the station. This was from the out-

set a place delineated by the missionaries' social and moral directives and by the protection and knowledge projected onto them. Because of these expectations, people from different bands converged in the mission and established their camps next to it. In those early years, most Toba referred to the missionaries as *pa'agén taganaGáik*, teachers, and more commonly kade'tá, our fathers. Kade'tá, however, was also the term Alfred Leake encouraged as translation of God, following the Christian metaphor of God as Father. Uneasy with such an association, the missionaries ended up discouraging the use of kade'tá to refer to them (Makower 1989:85–86).[1] The initial use of this term by the Toba did not mean that they saw the missionaries as godlike; yet they did see them as men with shamanic powers. Leake was aware of this. He wrote that people often asked him to cast spells on shamans, cause rain, or expel the settlers from their lands. These requests made him realize that "in the eyes of the Indians, we were endowed with many strange and wonderful powers" (1933:67).

These references indicate that many Toba were projecting onto the missionaries their own conceptions of leadership, based on the figure of haliaganék as a powerful shaman. Yet the missionaries were also strangers in a place the ancient ones saw as their own; thus, their emergence as new leaders implied that their coexistence with Toba chiefs was often tense. The missionaries held regular meetings with the haliaganék and chan-neled important decisions through them (cf. O. Leake 1934:10). Yet some leaders demanded a more active participation in local affairs. In the early years of the mission, for instance, they often disrupted the passive role assigned to the congregation during service. Bishop E. Every (1936:111) noted that when "a chief thought he grasped a point in the discourse, he thought it his duty to turn round and drive it home to those round him, a practice which was disturbing to say the least of it" (cf. Grubb 1931:88).

Despite these forms of competition, Alfred Leake and his colleagues gradually consolidated their role as prominent political figures, protec-tors, and teachers. Initially, the school played an important role. By 1933 it had ninety students, mostly young men, and the same year Alfred Métraux wrote that "the eagerness of the Indians to read is extraordinary" (1933b: 206). But schooling also included contradictions that anticipated further tensions. Many Toba were interested in the missionaries' teachings not so much to convert to Christianity but to empower their capacity to under-stand a changing world (Métraux 1933c:79). The missionaries, on the contrary, regarded schooling mainly as a tool for religious conversion

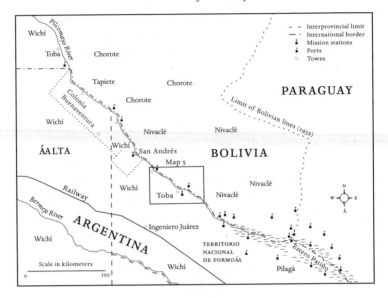

Map 4. The Pilcomayo in the early 1930s.

(O. Leake 1932: 93; cf. Comaroff and Comaroff 1991:63–64). These diverging expectations, together with the regimenting aspects of formal education, seem to have undermined many Toba's initial enthusiasm. In 1934 the men's school was "rather up and down" and the women's school was still closed (O. Leake 1934:9). Schooling had an erratic progress thereafter, hindered by the prolonged absence of many children involved in foraging expeditions and labor migrations (O. Leake 1937; Leake 1940). Because of these factors, the illiteracy rate among the Toba continued being very high.

In the 1990s people remembered that their grandparents relied on other means to learn from the missionaries. The Sunday service attracted people living in smaller hamlets spread along the river. As Tomás put it: "Since Alfredo had teachings and we lived in Jesús María, we went to the mission to listen." Every Saturday large numbers of people converged in the mission on foot and horseback to attend the service the following day. This event socialized men and women in new values and immersed them in new forms of commemoration of their pre-Christian past. Men also visited the store in Sombrero Negro to barter skins (iguanas, alligators), furs (wildcats, jaguars), and feathers (especially rhea) in exchange for salt, flour, cloth, and ammunition. The proximity to the Criollo hamlet, in this

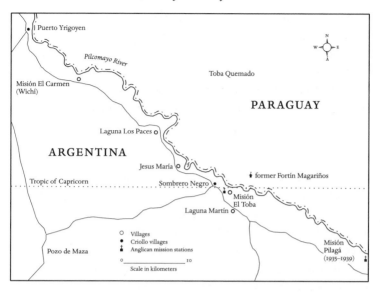

Map 5. Misión El Toba, Sombrero Negro, and main Toba villages: 1930s–1975.

regard, further consolidated Misión El Toba as a regional point of reference. Yet this attraction, also fostered by the threat posed by the army,
was countered by tensions that made people regularly oscillate between
the station and the bush.

Only the Word of the Lord

In contrast to other areas in the world in which missionization entailed an
early attempt to turn herders or hunter-gatherers into farmers (Comaroff
and Comaroff 1991, 1997), the first generation of missionaries did not en-
courage a shift to agriculture. Because of the adverse regional conditions
for farming, they regarded foraging as the only viable (although not ideal)
form of indigenous livelihood. Yet the mission was a place of *trabajo*,
even if based on limited resources. People remember that the missionaries promoted carpentry, by training men in the craft, and craftsmanship,
by buying "women's work." Women highly valued this purchase. In 1996
Fabiana, a woman in her fifties, remembered those days with nostalgia:
"Alfredo bought handicrafts. He had a store. Women were working with
handicrafts all the time. In those days, men didn't have work and we had

work. Men had to go to the bush. It was only with the missionary that we got some money to drink mate." Fabiana remembered the mission as a place separate from the bush and dominated by female labor: a place that excluded men's work and enabled women to make their own money. Men, however, were not altogether excluded from the mission's goods. Some were hired on an irregular basis to erect buildings, participate in the carpentry workshop, and fetch wood or water. And when hundreds of men and women departed for the sugar plantations, the missionaries distributed foodstuffs among the elderly and the children who stayed home (D. Tebboth 1989:93, 117, 164).

Despite these forms of assistance, in the mid-1990s some men made clear that their grandfathers were disappointed on discovering that trabajo and commodities at Misión El Toba were not as abundant as expected. In 1999 Enrique remembered the spatial implications of this disillusionment: "At first, the mission was a large village. When people first arrived it was a big place, for people thought the mission would give them work. But it gave them nothing. The missionaries only taught the word of the Lord. That was it. There was nothing. So people left. . . . Since people saw there was nothing at the mission, and since they were far from the places where they had something to live with, they got back where they lived." This account sheds light on the contrast between the bush and the station as different types of places. And Enrique highlighted this tension by pointing to the immateriality of what the gringos had to offer to most Toba men ("only . . . the word of the Lord").[2]

This factor seems to have contributed to decreasing the initially high population at the mission and many people spread along the river in hamlets such as Laguna Los Paces, Jesús María, and Laguna Martín. Yet movement between these sites and Misión El Toba continued. In 1933 Henry Grubb (1933:41) reckoned—when the total Toba population was 700 or 800—that the station population fluctuated between 200 and 400, "the numbers varying from time to time." This fluctuation reveals that many Toba were attempting to take advantage of the benefits of missionization without giving up the resources and relative autonomy provided by the bush. In those years, foraging became particularly important because, owing to serious conflicts with foremen in San Martín del Tabacal, no labor contractor arrived in the area between 1932 and 1936 (O. Leake 1936:126), which forced people to rely on marisca expeditions on a more regular basis. Mobility in the bush was also part of an attempt to challenge the presence of Criollo settlers and maneuver vis-à-vis the threat posed

26. A light in the bush. From *South American Missionary Society Magazine*, vol. 79, no. 862, May and June 1945.

by army patrols. But unlike the times prior to the arrival of Alfred Leake, this mobility had now a crucial point of reference: the mission.

A Kind of Sanctuary

In Great Britain, as figure 26 illustrates, the SAMS often portrayed its work in the Chaco as a source of light countering the darkness of indigenous heathenism. In this image, the dazzling beams of missionization illuminate a native from an "untouched tribe" grateful to receive the word of Christ. Yet missionaries in the Chaco knew that the relative success of their stations had little to do with spiritual enlightenment. By the 1930s, the Argentinean army had curbed the most important expressions of indigenous unrest in the Chaco. Yet the Pilcomayo was the last region where small, highly mobile Pilagá and Nivaclé groups occasionally clashed with the military. Troops attacked Nivaclé who crossed the border into Argen-

tinean territory and unleashed massacres in Pilagá hamlets to the southeast of Toba lands. The atrocities committed by the military created widespread terror in the region. A missionary noticed that among the Pilagá
"consternation was general and great at the sight of a military uniform"
(Makower 1989:110).³ This pattern of violence was having profound implications in the consolidation of the Anglican missions as protected places
that attracted previously dispersed populations. At San Andrés, a missionary wrote: "Several entire villages have moved down to join our people
here . . . all prompted by the desire to shelter under the wing of the Mission, on account of alarm due to various military movements" (South
American Missionary Society 1933:35; see also Métraux 1967:171–72). The
convergence of diverse groupings into the missions made clear that the
latter were effective havens *because* they were unmistakably differentiated
from the bush.

Likewise, Toba living in smaller villages converged in Misión El Toba
in moments of danger. Early in 1932, for instance, a group engaged in serious conflicts with Criollos and moved en masse to the mission, fearing an
attack by the army. One of the members of the staff wrote, "They seem
to look on the mission as a kind of sanctuary!" (O. Leake 1932:93–94). In
the geographies of violence produced by the military, the station became
indeed a sanctuary: a place under missionary control that because of its
civilizing values put limits to the previously unrestricted deployment of
state violence.

The news of this protection travelled fast and soon attracted indigenous groups from other areas. By 1932, Pilagá, Toba from the lower Pilcomayo, and Toba from the Bermejo had visited Misión El Toba asking the
missionaries to found stations for them (Grubb 1933:42; Arnott 1933:6).⁴
In 1935 hundreds of Pilagá that had temporarily roamed Paraguayan territory as a result of repeated clashes with the Argentinean army arrived
at El Toba (Arnott 1936:68–70). Unlike other groups, they did not plan to
leave. Since the population of the mission grew from 500 to 1,000, the de
facto appropriation of the compound by the Pilagá forced the missionaries to establish a separate station downstream. In October 1935, the SAMS
founded Misión Pilagá, thirty-five kilometers to the southeast (Grubb
1936:8).

This tense geography punctuated with protected places, however, was
regularly tested and challenged by the army. The Anglican stations were
not beyond the reach of state sovereignty and the missionaries had to
keep a delicate balance between their advocacy of indigenous rights and

their compliance with Argentinean law. Some incidents reveal this predicament and also the dissuasive power of the missionaries' presence. Currently, several Toba remember that the army was once very close to attacking the station, an event that according to mission diaries took place in October 1938.[5] Because of conflicts with settlers, troops arrived on several trucks, set up machine guns within the mission's perimeter, and "wanted to kill everybody." When remembering this episode, some men project onto the missionaries the warlike features of their old leaders. In 1933 Alfred Métraux (1937:190) noticed a similar attitude. His main informant, Kedók, told him about a dream in which he arrived at the mission fleeing his enemies. He dreamed that the missionary told him, "If they want to hurt you, we'll chase them, we'll burn their houses down. Nobody will hurt you." Similarly, some people told me that when the soldiers approached the mission, Alfred Leake instructed men on how to fight. According to Ernesto, Alfredo said to them: "You will have to fight with whatever means, either with a stick, with a machete, with an axe, with anything." These accounts are noteworthy because they portray the missionaries as bold, confrontational figures, willing to protect the Toba at whatever cost, even if that involved resisting the army through violent means.

Yet when the clash looked imminent, people agree, the missionaries were able to convince the officer in charge that the Toba were civilized and faithful to the Argentinean nation. Contradicting the accounts noted above, Mariano recalled that one of the missionaries "stopped the war" by pleasing the officer's inquisitive eye:

> Soldiers came from far away, maybe from Buenos Aires. They wanted to kill everybody. . . . Right there, the missionary talked to the Lieutenant. [He said]: "What is this? How is it possible that you want to kill these people? You have to kill the one who's guilty! That's the one you should kill. But just one." That's what he said. . . . The missionary was already there. He stopped the war. . . . The Lieutenant asked: "What do you teach?" [The missionary answered]: "I teach them that they don't have to fight. I make a little school." Right there [the Lieutenant said]: "Let's see. What do the children sing?" They sang the anthem right there. And the man was happy. He was clapping his hands. The man wasn't angry anymore and left. The missionary had many permits from Buenos Aires.

This account has several significant dimensions. First, it begins and ends with references to the national center of power, Buenos Aires: the

imaginary origin of the troops and the source of the missionaries' legiti-
macy. This spatial convergence made soldiers and missionaries the only
valid interlocutors of the dialogue remembered by Marcelo, turning the
Toba into a latent, invisible presence in the background. Second, rather
than being remembered as confrontational, the missionary was willing
to sacrifice the life of "one Toba," the one "guilty" of an unmentioned
crime, to save the rest. Yet, this incident also underscores the tensions that
existed between missionaries and institutions of the state. The Toba were
being immersed within the values of the Argentinean nation by a non-
Argentinean institution, which took over tasks carried out elsewhere in
the Chaco by government agencies (cf. Arengo 1996). Further, the missionaries were Protestant foreign nationals in a mostly Roman Catholic
country and were working in a sensitive border area, shaken in the 1930s by
the Chaco War between Bolivia and Paraguay. When in the 1940s the previously favorable national context for British institutions and businesses
was gradually replaced by a growing anti-British nationalism, the tensions
between the Anglican missions and state-run institutions increased.[6]

Facing the distrust of state officials, Alfred Leake and his colleagues
had to legitimize their presence by demonstrating the success of their
civilizing project and, more important, their commitment to national
symbols. As illustrated by Mariano, and as confirmed by other accounts
(Saint 1936:176; Tebboth 1989:37), when military officers or important
visitors arrived at Misión El Toba, the missionaries usually made school-
children perform the same ritual: sing the Argentinean anthem. In order
to disperse rumors that they taught foreign cultural elements, they also
took pains to show visitors that their schools followed "official programs"
(Saint 1936:176). These attempts to comply with state law became particularly tense when the missionaries handed offenders over to the police
or began legal actions against persons denounced by their peers (South
American Missionary Society 1933:39; Makower 1989:87).[7] These interventions became for many Toba a source of ambiguity about the missionaries' allegiances. Yet the latter still provided them with an institutional
protection that was vital in helping them cope with the challenges posed
by their immersion within new fields of power.

This dimension was so important that when the missionaries at Misión
Pilagá were not able to halt abuses by the army, the station collapsed soon
thereafter. In 1937, soldiers executed seven men from the mission on a
hunting expedition. Even though the missionaries repeatedly demanded
an official inquiry, the massacre severely undermined the Pilagá's confi-

dence in them (Arnott 1937:112–13; Makower 1989:111–13). In 1939, after a gradual decline, the station was abandoned and the Pilagá returned to their old territories to the southeast.[8]

In Misión El Toba, only a few kilometers upstream, the missionaries were successful in creating a protected place. Yet this success engendered contradictions that were to reconfigure the geography formed by the mission and the bush. The protective quality of the mission was defined in its contrast with the bush, for the local cleavage that separated wilderness from civilization was fundamental to put limits to military intervention. Yet this cleavage also produced places of contention, for Misión El Toba became not just a sanctuary but also a locale subject to new forms of discipline.

6

"In the Bush, You Can Do Anything"

> The gambling which often took place between the opposing teams
> in a hockey match . . . and the immorality associated with some of
> their dancing were banned on the mission station.
> — Henry Grubb, *The Land between Rivers*

In the mid-1990s most adult Toba remembered Alfred Leake as a man with
a strong zeal to make their ancestors abandon their old ways. Many argued
that initially he was not like that: he just "watched" the "customs" of the
ancient ones and took pictures and notes without interfering with them.
Yet once Alfredo gained a cluster of followers, many agree, he changed
this attitude and began a firm campaign against these practices. When I listened to men and women remember Alfred Leake's eager attempts to suppress shamanism, drinking, dancing, or singing, I usually noticed a subtle
but persistent ambiguity in their accounts. On the one hand, for most
Toba Alfredo was certainly doing the right thing. He was *the* missionary,
their protector and guide, and most would probably agree that Alfredo
wanted to suppress those practices "for their own good." As Tomás put it:
"Alfredo defended us from all the vices." On the other hand, people usually
maintained a cautious distance from the depiction of his actions. That is,
they remember the people censured by Alfredo as passive, resigned victims of his rebukes, as if expressing sympathy for those not allowed to
perform what, after all, were just their "old customs." The tensions per-
vading these memories shed light on the forms of accommodation and
resistance triggered by missionization. In this chapter, I explore the spatial
inscription of this experience and the way it produced the mission compound and the bush as politically charged places. Through these forms of
contention, as we shall see, the Toba were immersed in discourses about
"Satan" originally alien to them.

Alfredo Didn't Like It: The Spatial Politics of Conversion

In April 1939, on his second ethnographic expedition to the region, Alfred Métraux arrived at Misión El Toba coming on foot from Misión Pilagá. The missionaries gave him a cold welcome. At dinner, Leake told him that he regarded ethnographers as "supporters of paganism" who "bounce upon people" and "ransack past old things." In his diary, Métraux wrote: "I'm astonished at Leake's fanaticism, who says that the social work accomplished by the mission doesn't count at all and only sees the Indians' conversion to Christ" (1978:77, 78). In other Anglican stations, Métraux was equally struck by the missionaries' "fanaticism." In San Andrés, one of them talked to him about "the Devil" and the "perseverance of darkness" as if he were "a monk from the Middle Ages" (1978:78, 79, 80).[1]

In his uneasiness as an ethnographer interested in practices condemned by the missionaries as diabolical, Métraux was expressing that the Anglican stations had become places submitted to a tightly enforced moral economy. As the Jesuits before them, the first generation of British missionaries in the Argentinean Chaco considered that many indigenous practices were inspired by "the Devil" (Grubb 1948:15; 1965:7; South American Missionary Society 1933:36). Shamanism in particular was regarded as the most serious obstacle to evangelization, as "Satan's chief weapon" (South American Missionary Society 1935:121; 1949:25–26). In Toba memories, the primary targets of Alfred Leake's campaign were clearly the pioGonáq. Figure 27 shows a famous Toba pioGonáq, Carancho. He is holding one of the symbols of the shamans' power, a large *poketá* (gourd) that they used in their healing chants and whose monotonous sound marked these men's presence and power in every village. The missionaries' campaign against the pioGonáq played a central role in the introduction of devil imageries among the Toba. This campaign was as religious as it was political, for most missionaries knew that their prestige depended on undermining the shamans' social and symbolic power.[2] This was also a struggle over local spaces, through which the missionaries tried to turn the station into a place free of diabolical influences. Their crusade targeted not just shamanism but a wide array of practices. In fact, when I asked people about a particular "custom" of their ancestors, it was not rare to hear them add: "Alfredo didn't like it."

Current memories reveal that the missionaries created at Misión El

27. Carancho, one of the most powerful Toba
shamans, in the early 1930s. From John Arnott,
"Los Toba-Pilagá del Chaco y sus guerras."
Revista Geográfica Americana 1(7): 491–501.

Toba a spatialized micropolitics through which some of them repeatedly
invaded domestic spaces suspected of harboring shamans or practices
they disapproved of. People remember that every time Alfredo saw, heard,
or learned through others that the pioGonáq were practicing their craft,
he went directly to their homes to stop them. Eduardo is a man in his early
forties and a lay member of the Anglican Church. Yet when he told me
about Alfredo's attitude toward the pioGonáq, he put more emphasis on
his controlling and spatially invasive personality than on the evil nature of
shamanism: "That man controlled the people a lot. At night, a pioGonáq
was singing. And then the missionary went to look for him. He talked to
him so that he left that custom." These intrusions also included attempts
to suppress the *dónagan*, a singing of seduction and grief performed by
men at night with a poketá. Mariano remembered that Alfredo used to tell
them at the service: "That singing is the Devil's singing. I don't want you
to sing. You must sing with the word of God." As with shamans, people

agree that if late at night Alfredo heard somebody singing, he would get up, grab a lamp, and head toward his home to halt him.

The spatialization of missionary surveillance included a conscious attempt to produce new types of domestic spaces, in which households were expected to follow new patterns of order and hygiene. After the Sunday service, Alfred Leake personally inspected each household near the mission compound and instructed people on how to manage it. Leake's son, David, remembered: "It was a visit, but it also had something of the nature of an inspection—if things weren't clean enough, the family would be told to sweep up!" (Makower 1989:123). Similarly, some Toba recall that Alfredo's incursions in search of shamans or nonbelievers were often followed by demands for cleanliness. Mariano told me that he once saw Alfredo arrive at the house of a pioGonáq who was drinking aloja. He heard Alfredo tell the man: "It's stinking here! You don't have to live here. You have to live over there." Mariano added: "The missionary always went to see those who did bad things, those who didn't obey." These situations reveal the command Alfredo exerted over the mission space, in which he was able to dictate even the location of individual households.

As part of this spatialized politics, people remember that missionary surveillance also targeted public places and practices performed collectively. First, the missionaries censured "vices" such as smoking and chewing coca leaves, acquired through the Criollos and plantation workers. Second, they disapproved of practices central in the socialization of previous generations: the *nomí*, a collective dancing; the *polké*, a game similar to field hockey that involved gambling; and the *nimatáq*, the aloja-drinking feast conducted by men. Missionaries regarded these collective events as "satanic practices" and "Satan's victories" (Métraux 1978:81; Grubb 1965:57); thus, they banned these practices at Misión El Toba. Henry Grubb (1965:18) explained the reasons for the ban: "As we got to know the Toba better, we found that some of their customs were quite inconsistent with the Gospel and the way of life we preached. We had not the least desire to turn them into imitation foreigners, but the gambling which often took place between the opposing teams in a hockey match and brought great hardship upon the losers, and the immorality associated with some of their dancing, were banned on the mission station."

This account shows that some missionaries were caught up in the contradiction of wanting to convert the Toba to their "way of life" yet denying that such conversion could imply mimicking British values. Yet many Toba do remember that Alfredo worked hard to stop their ancestors from imitating and reproducing their old practices. Some people are fond of recalling one particular incident that exemplifies the missionaries' abrupt appropriation of public places. Mariano told me that Alfredo once learned that several men were drinking aloja from a hollowed yuchán trunk. He then grabbed an axe, took another missionary and several Toba followers with him, and walked to the feast site. Mariano imitated what Alfredo said to those men: "What you're doing, you won't do it anymore! You can't do it because I'm with you. Now, I'm going to pour all this away and cut the yuchán to pieces." The men remained silent and the two missionaries axed the yuchán to pieces. Mariano added: "Then, there was nothing left of what the old men were doing."

A similar zeal to produce the mission as an orderly place involved the condemnation by the missionaries of "fist fights" among women. These brawls began when a wife, along with her female relatives, picked a fight with a woman involved with her husband, a fight that often included the female kin of the accused woman (see Mendoza 1999:100–102). Men did not participate, and Tomás commented about it: "The old women were tough." Mariana, one of those "tough" women in her youth, remembered that Alfredo always attempted to stop those fights invoking their alleged connection with the Devil. She imitated what he used to tell women: "Fighting is something of Satan. You don't have to hit other women. We're all brothers and sisters." Alfred Leake (1933:114) once described how he had to intervene "with gentle pushes" to halt the "wild disorder" caused by women hitting each other and disturbing a "peaceful Sabbath atmosphere." These interventions were informed by the tension between, on the one hand, savagery, disorder, and chaos as markers of an untamed indigenous space, and on the other, peace, order, and gentleness as signs of the new spatial configuration brought by missionization.

Accentuated by Alfredo's commanding presence, these experiences turned Misión El Toba into a place delimited by the reach of the missionaries' disciplinary gaze. The fear of missionaries created a "public transcript," to use James Scott's (1990) phrase, through which many Toba avoided contesting them in public places. Aware of this, Leake (1933:67) wrote: "One of the things that struck us before we had been long with the Toba . . . was their apparent fear of incurring our wrath. . . . A Toba will rarely if ever disagree with a missionary to his face." Such spatialization of a public transcript of consensus surfaces repeatedly in current memories. In 1996 Pablo remembered that when Alfredo interrupted a drinking party, people simply kept quiet: "People didn't want to be contrary to Alfredo.

They didn't want to be against the missionary. People simply went away. They didn't want to say anything in front of the missionary. They didn't want to get in trouble."

The persistent action of the missionaries as kade'tá, charismatic leaders, shamanlike protectors, and teachers gradually undermined the Toba's initial resistance to "religion." In November 1934, the first Toba converted. Four weeks later, sixteen men followed him, "confessing their sins, claiming salvation through Christ and asking for the indwelling presence and help of the Holy Spirit." By mid-1935, there were about 250 Toba converts (Makower 1989:80). Jean and John Comaroff (1991:250–51) have rightly argued that conversion to Christianity on colonial frontiers is part of a broader historical transformation that goes beyond the forging of a new religious identity. Among the Toba, this conversion was profoundly intertwined with experiences of state terror, conflicts with settlers, and labor migrations. Additionally, their adoption of Anglicanism did not involve a smooth and unambiguous embrace of new values; in fact, this process was far from fitting the canons the missionaries regarded as ideal. In 1937 Alfred Leake lamented that many Toba did not appear to "have entered really deeply into the things of God" and that women were "particularly unresponsive" (Makower 1989:81).

The daily interaction with the missionaries was nevertheless having a deep, cumulative effect on Toba subjectivity. This was an interaction that rather than involving a circulation of messages—or a "conversation," to use Jean and John Comaroff's metaphor (1991, 1997)—implied a cultural production reconfiguring practices, bodies, and places. By the mid-1930s, some people had constructed at their own initiative "prayer huts," *tamnaGaikí*, to gather and pray in Misión El Toba and other villages (South American Missionary Society 1937:59). This was a sign that some Toba were internalizing new spatial patterns and that their hamlets were becoming new types of places. In a few years, Toba "evangelists" were preaching in other hamlets on a regular basis and spreading Anglican codes of morality and discourses on "the Devil" beyond the station. Devil imageries, in this regard, gradually entered local practices, blending with the payák spirits previously inscribed in Toba subjectivity. These new forms of cultural production involving payák as diablos contributed to the remaking of perceptions of place in the mission, the bush, and the plantations, as we shall see.

Evangelization also reshaped Toba bodies. People abandoned emblems of the ancient ones' identity, such as earlobe piercing, face tattooing, and long hair among men and short hair among women. In conjunction with their experience in the sugar cane fields, in the 1940s and 1950s people acquired pieces of clothing rarely worn until then: pants among men and dresses among women, which gradually replaced the chiripa (cloth wrapped around the waist). The discipline imposed within the station also succeeded in taming some of the bold gestures that had initially struck some missionaries. In 1936 Bishop E. Every (1936:111) wrote about the transformations he noticed at Misión El Toba from one year to the next: "I was astonished at the change in these people during the last year, I mean in refinement and manners. They are just as hearty in their welcome of a visitor whom they know, but they no longer shout and make interminable speeches all together. . . . And they are quite reverent at the services. Now they hardly ever interrupt, and even the small children are kept quiet."

Another visitor was equally struck by the changes. In 1939, when Alfred Métraux visited Misión El Toba for the second time, he hardly recognized the place he had been six years earlier. He noticed that the mission and the indigenous dwellings had been reorganized to create a more orderly place: "I'm going to the Mission, which I hardly recognize: two new buildings have been built. . . . The Toba live now in huts with walls plastered with mud, grouped inside an enclosure" (1978:64). Like Every, Métraux noticed an altogether new bodily attitude. In 1933 he had seen many Toba attending service with painted faces and feathered heads (1933b:207). This time, to his dismay, he found "dressed Indians" singing "boring" psalms "without beauty" (Métraux 1978:64).

These cultural, bodily, and spatial transformations, however, did not involve people passively yielding to evangelization. The ambiguity that overflows current memories of Alfred Leake leads us not only to the ambiguity of the early experience of missionization but also to the spatially inscribed forms of contestation it created.

Ambivalence and Shamanic Resistance

After his 1934 visit to Misión El Toba, Bishop Every (1934:101) wrote that "like children incapable of sustained attention, the first flush of their enthusiasm had died down." What Every read as innately childish (qua primitive) behavior marked the consolidation of a more ambiguous attitude toward evangelization. Condensing this ambivalence, in 1935 a visitor in

Misión El Toba noted: "In general, adult Indians profess a respectful submission not exempted of a certain distrust towards the reverend missionaries" (Saint 1936:178). It is also noteworthy that most Toba gradually referred to the missionaries as *dingolé'ee*, "gringos," a term that rather than
kinship, proximity, and reverence ("our fathers") emphasizes social and
cultural distance.

In the 1990s people remembered that back in those days attitudes vis-à-
vis the gringos were far from homogeneous. Two broadly defined groups
stood in tension with each other: the core of "believers" who closely followed the missionaries' directives and those who, on the contrary, re-
jected their presence. Shamans were clearly positioned among the latter,
for their power was regularly undermined by the missionaries' actions.
Yet most people seem to have adopted a middle ground, engaging with
Alfredo and his colleagues while maintaining a distance from them, trying to harness their goods and services while being critical of their order
and discipline (cf. Comaroff and Comaroff 1991:247).

This accommodation and the resistances resulting from it were profoundly spatialized. As noted, at the station open signs of noncompli-
ance were rare and people tried to deflect the gringos' directives with an
indifference that the latter often read as signs of irreverence and pride
(see D. Tebboth 1989:192, 197). Likewise, shamans expressed their dissent
through indirect means: refusing to attend religious services, spreading
negative rumors about the missionaries, or being hostile to those Toba
who had become devoted Christians. Yet some pioGonáq also used their
powers to challenge the missionaries more directly. People remember that
some shamans repeatedly tried to kill Alfred Leake through sorcery but
that they failed because his spirit was too powerful. Mariano, for instance,
told me how in one of these attempts several shamans died, struck by a
lightning bolt: "A pioGonáq wanted to kill Alfredo that night. There was a
light, coming out of the door of Alfredo's house. The other pioGonáq were
close to Alfredo's house. And some of them were touched by a lightning
bolt and died." I asked Mariano whether Alfredo himself sent the lightning
bolt. "Well, he was begging. He was praying. He begged that they didn't
get him. So, God gave it to him. . . . All the devils went away. They couldn't
do anything. All of them died." This action reveals that some shamans
tried to take over the mission's spatial core, the missionaries' home, relying on the bush devils that had given them shamanic power. Their defeat
and the perception that God himself protected Alfredo underscored that
the mission station had become a place impervious to the influence of

payák spirits. This event also reveals that the missionaries' struggle against shamans was necessarily a struggle against the payák, now seen as devils defined in opposition to the Christian God. And the failed attempts to challenge Alfredo at the mission also reflected that more effective resistances, shamanic or not, had to be conducted elsewhere.

Indeed, in other hamlets people disobeyed the missionaries' norms more openly. In Laguna Martín, three kilometers downstream from El Toba, people continued singing and dancing for a longer period of time than at the mission. In this regard, overt signs of contestation were in direct relationship with the distance from the missionaries. As Mariano put it, remembering a pioGonáq from Laguna Martín: "He sang because the missionary was far away." Yet even those critical of evangelization were not free of ambivalence. After all, they also benefited from the protection granted by the mission and from its material resources. This ambiguity informed the making of local places. Dora Tebboth (1989:106), the wife of missionary Alfred Tebboth, captured the spatial dimensions of Toba ambivalence when she wrote that people at Laguna Martín "have moved just far away from the mission not to come regularly to church, and yet near enough to hear local gossip and to sell any handiwork they make." The tensions weaving together the station and the hamlets included yet another place, which played a crucial role in the production of forms of dissent.

In the Bush, You Can Do Anything

Men and women continually moved from the mission to the bush and back seeking food or firewood, and this mobility accentuated the contrast between both places. Unlike the smaller hamlets, regularly visited by Alfredo and the evangelists, the bush was a place alien to the missionaries and well beyond their reach. As a result, many Toba turned the bush into a haven from the sanctuary founded by Alfred Leake. The making of a place free of missionary control was associated, first, with attempts to escape rebukes. Mariano remembered that he once saw Alfredo heading straight into the hut of an old man who was drinking aloja. He described this man's desperate escape to the bush as follows: "His wife was looking at the road [and told him]: 'Look! Here comes Alfredo!' The old man got up and fled as if he were an animal. . . . He was afraid. He went to the bush. . . . He ran into the bush."

The bush was a shelter for people on the run and also the place to carry out practices banned at the station. Leake (1933:67) wrote in one of his quarterly reports: "In the first hot season drinking-feasts were held very quietly or in hiding in the forests away from the villages. On one occasion we came across a small drinking party behind a rough bush fence." Drinking and dancing in faraway places became common practice when entire households set off to conduct foraging expeditions, especially during the fishing and gathering seasons, when few people stayed in the hamlets and the mission. These foraging camps, *nemacháqa*, provided an ideal opportunity to carry out censured practices without restraint; they also turned the bush into a place with a gravitational force of its own, which countered the forces and social relations converging on Misión El Toba. This process also contributed to grounding devil imageries, central to the missionaries' discourse and now increasingly so to Toba views of the payák, in the bush.

This spatialization of dissent became so important that in the 1940s several missionaries considered that the "returns to the bush" were undermining the evangelization project through the reproduction of practices at odds with strict Anglican codes. In 1942 Dora Tebboth (1989:134) lamented that these foraging expeditions were encouraging "a return to witchcraft, dancing, immorality, coca-chewing, stealing, [and] cow-killing." Yet what for her was a source of dismay, for many Toba was an assertion of autonomy and of bodily and spatial control. In 1996 Segundo remembered that those who were "into vices" often participated in these foraging expeditions. Emphasizing that the bush was a place that allows people to avoid moralistic forms of surveillance, he added: "In the bush, you can do anything: chew coca, drink aloja, sing. . . . You can look for a yuchán tree to make aloja." The consolidation of foraging camps as places where people could do "anything" eroded Anglican evangelization from another angle, by threatening missionary control over the station. Massive retreats and foraging trips affected school attendance and religious services, thus temporarily weakening the most important venues for Anglican socialization (O. Leake 1937:38; Leake 1940:9).[3]

Yet in the long run, despite these setbacks, the cultural and social influence of the mission continued being profound. Currently, new generations more fully socialized into Anglican values agree that those types of bush camps were at odds with "religion" and remember them as something of the past. In August 1997 I was talking with Regino outside a church packed with people listening to Anglican bishops who were touring the region. The atmosphere reverberated with prayers and religious songs, and Regino remembered that when he was a "nonbeliever" he always lived in the bush. As he was speaking, his memory was molded by the contrast between the church next to us, the bush in the background, and his past experiences. "Before I became a believer," he said, "I was always in the bush, foraging. I liked it that way, wandering, hunting in the bush. Ever since then, up to now, I've been with this religion for thirty-three years."

"After you converted, did you continue setting up those camps?" I asked him.

"Not anymore, because all that's gone. When I wasn't a believer, the vices always kept me going there: drinking wine, chewing coca."

"You mean, the vices made you continue returning to the bush?"

"Maybe that's why. Maybe that's why I liked to go out, because of the vices."

"What did you do in the camp?" I asked.

Regino shrugged: "We always stayed, like that, in the bush. We had to look for a place where it was possible to hunt animals. That's the way it was. . . . We stayed maybe for one or two months, because there was nothing. There were no jobs like there're now." He looked around us. "These new ones already have a *carguito* [little job]. In those days, there was nothing. You had to go out and set up a camp. You had to stay there."

"Did you go with your family?"

"I did. But we were always fine. Nothing happened. I didn't mention the spirit of God at all. . . . I didn't think about praying. . . . I never said thanks to God."

The massive Anglican service next to us reminded us that those days were gone. Yet Regino's account exposed some of the contrasts shaping the bush back then, as a place deprived of markers of religiosity such as "praying" and "thanking God." Regino also stressed that the lack of *trabajo* in state agencies ("carguitos") had clear spatial implications and forced people to leave the hamlets and set up bush camps. As we continued talking, he added that those camps produced bodies at odds with civility and cleanness. He first thought about "converting," he told me, when he saw his face in a small mirror. His long, thick hair, dense beard, and face covered with dirt struck him. He had become the true picture of a bush-man, a *viágahik*. Impressed by his description and trying to go along with him, I said: "It seems that your beard was just like mine." He gave me a serious look and as he raised his finger told me, "But you're not chewing coca!" By saying so, Regino was returning to his initial point: that bodies shaped by life in the bush were deeply connected to "vices." His spatial journey to "religion" reveals that for many Toba the bush was fractured by the conflicting allegiances generated by missionization. For those who wanted a respite from the gringos, the bush became a geography under the control of devils fostering the forces of witchcraft, a place of freedom where they could reproduce the good things of the past ("we were always fine"). For the "believers," the bush became a place of vices that created untamed bodies at odds with the habitus encouraged at the station. This contrast was so important that converting to Christianity was, for people like Regino, tantamount to "dropping the bush." This conversion was not a rejection of all the bush stood for as a source of livelihood and a place of autonomy and aboriginality; but it implied renouncing the bush as a site removed from, and defined in opposition to, the moral values and body language inculcated by the missionaries.

These memories, and Regino's present attitude, illustrate the transformations most Toba have gone through since the early days of the mission. On the one hand, the resistances articulated in the station, the smaller hamlets, and the bush reproduced some of the practices condemned by Alfredo, most notably shamanism. Currently, the consumption of coca leaves, wine, and tobacco persists, especially among young men, even though many people see them as vices with negative connotations. Yet the missionaries' perseverance and decades of Anglican socialization made the Toba gradually give up most of the ancient ones' "customs." The first practices that were abandoned were the rituals and attire associated with warfare. In 1933 Alfred Métraux (1937:180, 396) noticed that men had destroyed all the scalps taken from Nivaclé warriors. Even though in the 1940s missionaries complained about a widespread increase in aloja drinking (Tebboth 1989:170, 134), eventually men stopped consuming aloja altogether. In the 1990s people remembered this beverage as a symbol of the past. Group fights among women evolved into occasional, individual hand-fights. Some Toba danced in smaller villages for a few years but the nomí was abandoned there as well. Men and women, however, continued dancing at a distant place, well beyond the missionaries' reach: the sugar plantations. In this regard, the mission, the hamlets, and the bush were culturally and spatially defined not only by their mutual contrast and the practices examined above but also by the migrations that every year took hundreds of men, women, and children to the foot of the Andes.

II

Bones in
the Cane
Fields

7

The Promised Land

San Martín del Tabacal is . . . the Biblical miracle of the promised land.

— Ernesto Aráoz, *Vida y obra del Doctor Patrón Costas*

The memories of Misión El Toba are narratives about a place that is currently covered with sediment and vegetation across the marshes but was once located in Toba lands and affected the local configuration of the bush in direct ways. The memories of the sugar plantations, by contrast, evoke a place that was part of a spatially distant and altogether different geography. This distance accentuates perceptions of the difference between Toba lands and the ingenios; yet it also turns the latter into an invisible presence in the bush. People's practices in their lands are regularly informed by the memories of terror, devils, death, wealth, sexual freedom, and estrangement that made the ingenio such a potent and contradictory place in their experience. Because of this dense polysemy, "the mountains" haunt generations of Toba in ways that often surpass their capacity to make sense of them. In the chapters that follow, I try to capture these enthralling dimensions by examining the power relations, experiences, and imageries that emerge from current memories of the cane fields, with the ultimate aim of showing (in part III) how these memories — together with those of the mission, the grasslands, and the river — coalesce to constitute the bush.

When men and women talk about the plantations, sometimes they make reference to Ledesma and La Esperanza, where they worked earlier in the twentieth century; but more often than not their accounts focus on San Martín del Tabacal, which absorbed most of their labor migrations between the 1930s and 1960s. In this chapter I analyze the consolidation of this ingenio as one of the most powerful in northern Argentina and the ways in which many Toba remember its expansion as an eminently spatial transformation.

The All-Out Struggle against Nature and Men

In 1918 a society led by Robustiano Patrón Costas, a prominent member of the Salta aristocracy, bought lands near the town of Orán. Shortly after, the new company hired 1,000 men to clear tracts of jungle and open cane fields. In July 1920 the factory milled sugar cane from the first harvest. Years later, Patrón Costas remembered that "the all-out struggle against nature and men had begun" (Aráoz 1966:57). Since its very conception, the regional and national elites saw San Martín del Tabacal as the symbol of a civilizing struggle against the untamed savagery of nature and the undisciplined primitivism of workers. A biographer of Patrón Costas wrote that the plantation was "the first trail of progress opened in the thick jungle of the Chaco salteño" and added that this place was destined to become "the Biblical miracle of the promised land" (Aráoz 1966:27). Guided by this utopia with religious overtones, Tabacal radically altered the spatial configuration of the area; it created "pleasant" cane fields that contrasted with the "dark and untamed mass" of the jungle (Sweeney and Domínguez Benavides 1998:117). Figure 28 sums up this portrayal by naturally blending the cane fields with their owner. We see Patrón Costas emerging from a mass of canes as if that symbol of progress was his sole creation. Those are cane fields without workers, absorbed by a man whose spotless uniform reveals his class status and distance from manual labor. When remembering the ingenio, many Toba also make reference to the contrast between the jungle and the cane fields. In fact, their memories of the plantation's growth focus on the spatial dimensions of this expansion and stress that as the fields spread, the jungle gave up terrain. This process also reduced the tobacco fields that had made many Toba call this plantation *kol'eá* (tobacco fields). But contradicting bourgeois representations of this landscape transformation, many Toba emphasize that it was their labor that made the cane fields expand.

Toba memories of the power structure of San Martín del Tabacal are nevertheless strongly personalized in the figure of Patrón Costas. As member of a patrician family, Patrón Costas led the plantation on a personalized basis, maintained high visibility among his workers, and promoted the image of being an accessible and sensitive boss. Many Toba internalized this image. The protective aura that many project onto Patrón Costas is also an aura of power fostered by the resonance between the first part of his composite last name, Patrón, and his status as patrón, boss

28. Robustiano Patrón Costas. From Ernest
Sweeney and Alejandro Domínguez Benavides,
Robustiano Patrón Costas: Una leyenda argentina.
Buenos Aires: Emecé, 1998.

of the plantation. In fact, his class status was symbolically stronger than his actual name, and most Toba understood patrón in this latter context, usually referring to him in Spanish as *el patrón Costas*, "the boss" Costas. This paternalism is akin to the one associated with Alfred Leake, for many people remember both men as commanding figures who protected the Toba, first and foremost, from the military. Yet memories of Patrón Costas, as we shall see, are firmly intertwined with class hierarchies and forms of terror absent at the mission station.

Some people, in this regard, remember that their main patrón was connected with powerful figures in Buenos Aires. When in 1930 a military coup overthrew the democratically elected government of Hipólito Yrigoyen, Patrón Costas emerged as a staunch supporter of the new conservative regime and projected his influence, already prominent in Salta, onto the national arena.[1] Elected senator for Salta in 1931, the following year Patrón Costas became provisional president of the senate; in 1940, at the peak of his political career, he became vice president of Argentina (Luque Colombres 1991).[2] Patrón Costas's rising influence paralleled San Martín del Tabacal's expansion, fostered by tariffs and other policies implemented to favor the sugar barons. Given its increasing demand for labor, San Martín del Tabacal purchased old haciendas in the highlands of Salta and Jujuy and forced their peasants, many of them Kollas, to pay rent by working in the cane harvest. In the 1930s the plantation also began recruiting workers from the provinces of Catamarca and La Rioja and, initially to a lesser degree, Bolivia (Rutledge 1987:198–99, 205–6). The heterogeneity of the labor force is an important subject in current memories. As we shall see, it was through workers from other regions that most Toba learned about the struggles transforming the country, such as those associated with the figure of Juan Domingo Perón.

Patrón Costas was indirectly entangled with Perón's political ascendancy. While the Argentinean elites saw San Martín del Tabacal and its main administrator as symbols of progress and order, Colonel Perón referred publicly to them as "big exploiters" and remnants of "feudal" relations (Luca de Tena, Calvo, and Peicovich 1976:34). The 1943 military coup, in which Perón participated, was in fact partially designed to prevent Patrón Costas — about to be nominated presidential candidate — from becoming president of Argentina through the electoral fraud conservatives relied on. This coup symbolized the end of the political prominence of the land-owning aristocracy and the beginning of a new era marked by the rise of populism; it also signaled the end of Patrón Costas's political career and the beginning of Perón's, who was elected Argentina's president in 1946.

Most Toba, paradoxically, do not remember Perón and the boss of San Martín del Tabacal as men opposed to each other; rather, many see them as related figures worthy of respect. In what is probably the clearest illustration of this imaginary bond, Mariano told me that Evita (Eva Duarte), Perón's wife and the most prominent symbol of his government until her death in 1952, was the "daughter" of Patrón Costas. This kinship connection expresses, primarily, what many Toba read as a class bond between figures of similar power and stature. Most people remember Perón and Patrón Costas as wealthy, powerful, and protective men and the memory of the social benefits brought by Perón is often hard to distinguish from that of the commodities made available by Patrón Costas.

The social and political changes brought by the 1943–46 military government and the first presidencies of Perón (1946–55) had an important impact on the San Francisco River Valley. The government passed an *estatuto del peón* (statute of the rural worker) that ameliorated labor conditions, especially among permanent workers, and abolished land rent in labor services in the highlands (Rutledge 1987:112, 219–22; Bisio and Forni 1976:26). Despite these changes, the sugar barons' power was not significantly curbed. Patrón Costas continued leading San Martín del Tabacal and this plantation remained one of the most powerful in Argentina. But this took place in a context in which the changing dynamics of class struggle induced further transformations in the labor force. In the 1940s and 1950s, unions launched frequent strikes and the administration responded by sending more labor recruiters to Bolivia to hire men without working permits and weaken the union's power. The 1955 military coup that toppled Perón accentuated this trend (Whiteford 1981:22, 24–25). By the late 1950s, a period of temporary retreat for the labor movement, Bolivians at Tabacal constituted over 50 percent of seasonal workers (Bisio and Forni 1976:49).

These changes gradually eclipsed the role that the Chaco indigenous groups had played in the initial expansion of the sugar industry. By the 1930s, these groups were no longer employed as cane cutters and Ledesma and La Esperanza gradually discontinued hiring them. Yet thousands of Toba, Wichí, Nivaclé, Chorote, and Pilagá continued migrating to San Martín del Tabacal for several decades, where they became a floating mass of unskilled workers employed in tasks complementary to the harvest. This pattern continued until the late 1960s, when, in a new period of social unrest in Argentina and economic crisis for the sugar industry, the administration put into practice a mechanization plan that dramatically reduced its demand for unskilled indigenous labor.[3] In 1969 San Martín del Tabacal recruited Toba on a massive scale for the last time.[4]

Many Toba remember that during their last journeys to the cane fields the ingenio was going through significant spatial changes, which included new machines in the fields and a more intense deforestation rate. Tabacal was becoming a different place; so different that soon it did not need their labor anymore. People remember that at one moment the contractors simply stopped coming. A whole period in Toba historical experience had come to an end. Only when I asked about it, people speculated, imprecisely and without conviction, about the year of the last migration. When remembering the end of their labor in San Martín del Tabacal, what mattered to them was that they were severed from a *place* that had been central to their experiences and memories since the times of the ancient ones.

For the elites who had recruited Toba labor, the ingenios were also symbolically potent places. Political leaders, officials, and administrators have for decades regarded them as nurturing places emitting light into the Chaco wilderness. In 1921 Emilio Schleh wrote that the "civilizing and beneficial work of the factories reached the jungles of Chaco and Formosa" and that, by way of the plantations, the "wretched Indian masses" were able to "recover from their corporal misery, returning to their homes with the necessary fortitude to sustain themselves until the following harvest" (Beck 1994:179–80). In the late 1990s, with the golden age of the sugar industry long gone and Argentina immersed in a deep socioeconomic crisis, some authors resurrected similar, utopian portrayals of the early days of La Esperanza and San Martín del Tabacal (see Sierra e Iglesias 1998; Sweeny and Benavides 1998). In these accounts, as earlier in the century, the ingenios are portrayed as healing places where indigenous masses recovered from life in the bush. These views reverse and silence the experience of thousands of men, women, and children who every year left their sweat, and often their lives, in the sugar cane fields.

8

"It Seemed Like We Lived There"

> It is obvious that, even though the Indians are sometimes
> away from the Chaco as long as ten months a year, it is the
> Chaco that they regard as their home. — Winifred Revill,
> *South American Missionary Society Magazine*

At three in the morning, the head foreman rang the bell. His assistants began walking between the Toba's huts, shouting *"¡Arriba! ¡Arriba!"* "Get up! Get up!" It was utterly dark and freezing in the winter. Men and women sat around the fires that lit the huts' interiors all night long, illuminating the lote with dozens of trembling lights. Warm mates passed from one hand to another. Some people prayed, almost whispering, as the missionaries had taught them. Others shook their gourds, the poketá, and sang monotonous, wordless songs that filled up the air before the break of dawn. Still in darkness, people gathered at the lote's warehouse around the *capataz mayor* (head foreman). Under the light of lanterns, the capataz instructed the Toba interpreter, the lenguaraz, of the tasks of the day and decreed how many people were needed. The lenguaraz then translated the instructions to men, women, and youngsters. Axes, shovels, hoes, pickaxes, machetes, and knives were taken out of the warehouse and distributed, according to the task, to the work gangs. Before dawn, led by other foremen and taking their tools with them, the different groups walked to their assigned work sites, sometimes up to ten kilometers away.[1] When the sun emerged, on a clear day illuminating the mountains, men, women, and boys were already cutting trees, wood, weeds, or cane. Another day in San Martín del Tabacal.

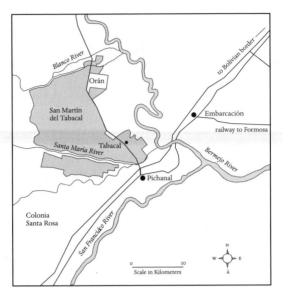

Map 6. San Martín del Tabacal

The Journey to Kol'eá

People remember that the contractors arrived at Misión El Toba some-time between March and April, depending on the changing demand for labor at the plantation.[2] The mission was the point of convergence for those willing to go to kahogonaGá, a location that reinforced its local prominence. The arrival of the mayordomos provoked a great deal of anxiety and was followed by negotiations with the capitanes — the leaders in charge of mediating the relationship with the ingenio — regarding the type and amount of goods to be distributed in advance. The mayordomos' promises often made people forget previous experiences of exploitation. In 1938, for instance, most Toba had decided not to go to the ingenio be-cause of bad experiences the previous year, "but the promise of money in advance, new clothes, and good food on the journey made them think again" (Tebboth 1938b:113). Missionary reports indicate that between half and three-quarters of the total Toba population left for the plantations every year: 300 to 500 people.[3] As a result of the human fluctuation that linked the banks of the Pilcomayo to the foot of the Andes, the mission and the villages were left semideserted for many months.

With the inauguration of the railway Embarcación-Formosa, the long journeys on foot were abandoned and large numbers of Toba and Wichí arrived at Ingeniero Juárez to board a train reserved by San Martín del Tabacal to pick up its workers along the line. In a few hours, large groups of Toba, Pilagá, Nivaclé, and Wichí arrived in Embarcación. There they boarded another train and shortly after were in San Martín del Tabacal, where foremen often split the Toba in smaller groups and distributed them to different lotes, the units of agricultural management and residence.⁴ These Toba subgroups shared their living space with Wichí, Chorote, Nivaclé, or Pilagá and their daily interactions gave rise to new identities, as we shall see. The lotes were named after female relatives of Patrón Costas: "Magdalena," "Delia," "Cecilia," "Sarita," and "Mercedes" (among others). This practice reaffirmed that Tabacal was not a faceless company but an entity strongly personalized around its owner, who directed and named the ingenio's geography as if it were a feminized, domestic domain (one of the lotes, "Doña Pancha," was named after Patrón Costas's maid). The Toba built huts with whatever materials were at hand: boughs, grass, and cane leaves. From their new dwellings, they could see on a clear day the plantation landmarks: to the north, the low, densely forested hill near the town of Tabacal, marked during harvest time by columns of smoke emerging from the factory; to the east and south, the flat landscapes stretching toward the Chaco and toward the valley's wide interior; to the west, the mountain range of Zenta and San Andrés, which absorbed much of the semantic density of the ingenio, its dangers and mysteries. These dangers, explored in chapter 9, were an indissoluble component of the experiences and memories I analyze in this chapter: the labor practices, forms of payment, living conditions, and fields of power that made the plantation a place defined in tension with Misión El Toba and the bush.

The Making of Ethnicity

Most Toba remember Tabacal as a place that attracted people from the most diverse backgrounds, languages, and cultures. It was in kol'eá that they interacted for the first time with Kollas, Bolivians, Guaraní (Chiriguano), and Catamarqueños. Thus, the ingenio became a site of cultural production that fostered perceptions of ethnic difference. In fact, the Toba's current identity as Aborígenes is a direct product of their class ex-

29. Wichí workers in the sugar cane fields, 1917.
Archivo General de la Nación, Buenos Aires.

perience at the cane fields. The administration hierarchically segmented the labor force along ethnic lines and each group was assigned different tasks and paid different wages according to their alleged skills and productivity. This policy drew on older hierarchies and imageries of alterity but created an ethnic landscape linked to a new historical process of confrontation, in which diverse groupings were asymmetrically incorporated into a single political economy (cf. Bourgois 1988:328–29; Comaroff and Comaroff 1992:54, 50).

One of the most important cleavages produced by the administration was the one separating the Chaco groups, called *Indios* or *Aborígenes*, from the rest of the workers. In their memories, many Toba transmit a strong sense of being, together with the other Aborígenes, the "less valuable" workers of the plantation. In many respects, they were. They received the lowest wages and, unlike other seasonal laborers, were paid not by piecework but by *tareas* (tasks, as I will show), lived in huts, lacked social benefits, and had practically no access to the plantation hospital. In addition, they performed tasks that set them apart from cane cutters and permanent workers. Re-created every year, this ethnicized class experience created a strong sense among Toba, Wichí, Chorote, Nivaclé, and Pilagá workers that they belonged to a same grouping: the Aborígenes. This identity merged people with heterogeneous linguistic, cultural, and historical backgrounds. The awareness of this heterogeneity did not disappear, and some Toba are quick to point out that they are "cleaner" or "harder working" than the Wichí.[5] Yet these groups began defining themselves under a term previously alien to them: an identity with a spatial anchor, the Chaco, they all shared. This was the same geographical reference the administration relied on to justify their lowly status: the fact that they were "bush people."

In the 1990s most Toba had internalized these hierarchies and remembered other workers' higher status and wages as a natural outcome of their cultural attributes. The permanent Criollo workers were at the top of the labor hierarchy. Coming from Salta, Jujuy, Catamarca, La Rioja, and Santiago del Estero, they gained the highest wages and were provided with housing (Vidal 1914:15–16). Most Toba remember the Criollos as politicized workers who had little interaction with Aborígenes. The Guaraní, remembered by the Toba as *Chaguancos*, occupied the highest status among indigenous workers (Bialet-Massé 1973:95; Vidal 1914:17). Originally slash-and-burn agriculturists from the Bolivian Chaco, many settled in the San Francisco River Valley on a permanent basis (Hirsch 2000). In San Martín del Tabacal, they worked as permanent field laborers (in charge of irrigation, as tractor drivers) and woodcutters who provided fuel for the factory, received basic housing, and earned salaries only slightly lower than those of the Criollos (Bialet-Massé 1973:95–96; Vidal 1914:17–19). The Toba interacted with Guaraní often and remember them as people well informed about the plantation, its secrets, and its dangers.

Yet the workers with whom Toba men and women contrast their situation most often are the cane cutters: *los peladores de caña* (or *cortadores de caña*). People associate this category primarily with the Bolivians, but cane cutting also involved Kollas from Salta and Jujuy and Criollos from Catamarca. The contrast between cane cutters and Aborígenes was for many Toba particularly apparent: the former were seasonal field workers like themselves but, unlike them, received housing and were paid by piecework. When remembering the Bolivians, people often express admiration for their status and skills. "The Bolivian worked the most," Mariano told me, "At night, the whole day. The Bolivians were paid by piecework. They were worth a lot, unlike us. The missionary used to tell us: 'You're like minors.' We didn't cut sugar cane, because the cane is very costly." The importance of each group of workers, as illustrated by this account, was defined by the relative value of the commodity they produced, sugar cane being the most costly. For that reason, Mariano reasoned, the Aborígenes were excluded from its production. As part of this sense of inferiority, many Toba emphasize that the Bolivians were "rich," had "nice houses," had *"documentos"* (ID papers), "knew how to read," and "knew how to go on strike." As we shall see in chapter 12, this perception constrained the articulation of collective struggles. These hierarchies were also anchored in the particular way through which the administration organized Toba labor as Aboriginal labor.

Tareas, Capitanes, Indios, Chinas, and Osacos

When remembering their work in Tabacal, many Toba express that their major concern was to finish the tarea, the task assigned to them at dawn. The tarea was the system through which the administration organized and paid the Aborígenes' labor. It was a fixed quota of labor that had to be completed in order to *tarjar*: to receive from the *tarjador* the daily ration (half of the daily payment) and a mark on their files that would credit the other half for the final payment.[6] Toba workers had to fulfill in a day some of the following tareas: to cut down three trees, chop and pile up five meters of firewood (one meter wide), or plant five furrows of cane (100 meters long). If a worker was unable to finish the tarea, he or she received no payment independently of how much work was completed, something that happened frequently (Zavalía 1915:40; Niklison 1989:86–87). This system was neither flexible (like piecework) nor fixed (like payment by the day); it was a highly exploitative one that forced laborers to keep a steady work pace but did not provide a reward proportional to the completed work.[7] Moreover, unlike piecework or payment by the day, by leaving people without any payment, the tarea system had often the unique feature of extracting surplus value for free.

The payment received per tarea depended on the category to which each worker belonged. The administration divided the Aborígenes in groupings according to their political status, gender, and age. This created further labor hierarchies, this time within each group. In San Martín del Tabacal, these categories were: (1) capitán (captain or leading headman); (2) lenguaraz (interpreter); (3) indio (adult male); (4) *china* (adult female); and (5) *osacos* (boys up to fifteen years of age). The highest wages were earned by capitanes and lenguaraces, even though they did not work as hard as the rest (Unsain 1914:86). Ordinary adult men made between half and two-thirds of those wages. Women and osacos usually received,

30. "Indigenous women in San Martín del Tabacal."
Archivo General de la Nación, Buenos Aires.

respectively, two-thirds and one third of the wages paid to adult men.[8] Through this system the Toba were immersed within a new taxonomy of power, which transformed preexisting cleavages of gender, age, and leadership into commodified markers of difference. These hierarchies, justified as a way of respecting indigenous "customs" (Unsain 1914:86; Niklison 1989:57), suited the administration's interests particularly well. The latter gained the allegiance of indigenous leaders and overexploited more than half of the work force, women and youngsters.

In their memories, most Toba men and women do not question the higher wages of capitanes and lenguaraces and see them as fair rewards for their higher responsibilities. Yet women are vocal in their grievances about their lower wages. Angélica remembered: "The salary they gave us wasn't enough for anything. . . . They paid a pittance. Instead of making [some money], they only gave us half a salary. It can't be that way." Trabajo at the ingenio was a contradictory experience for women, for despite being overexploited because of their gender they made money independently of their husbands. This dimension surfaces repeatedly in women's memories. I asked Marcelina, a woman in her late fifties, whether she liked going to the ingenio. "Yes, I liked it, because Patrón Costas gave work to us. We, the women, gained on our own. We bought something. We bought what we needed. Patrón Costas paid to us, because we like to work. We are women, but Patrón Costas gave us work. We made our own money, separate. Not anymore. Only men [get paid]. . . . Now, men give us food only when they are paid." These memories stress the stark contrast between the ingenio and women's current experience in their lands, when men give them store-bought food only when *they* get paid. Noticeably, many women remember San Martín del Tabacal nostalgically as the place where they gained autonomy from their husbands through Patrón Costas's intervention.

The hierarchies the administration imposed on Toba workers also created new types of leaders. During the first decades at Tabacal, some capitanes were shamans and former warriors who in their youth had gained prestige by scalping Nivaclé and Wichí men; yet they knew little Spanish. Their power was strongly mediated by a new figure created by the experience of wage labor: the lenguaraz. It was through the latter that foremen gave work instructions, capitanes channeled grievances, and people were paid. The role played by these men came to the fore when a new generation of capitanes emerged in the 1960s. The latter were no longer pioGonáq but men who spoke fluent Spanish and had negotiation skills with Criollos and administrators (Mendoza 2002; Mendoza and Gordillo 1988).

Working at Tabacal

Toba memories of the ingenio evoke a place ruled by spatially specific sets of hierarchies and discipline, very different from the ones that existed at Misión El Toba, the hamlets, and the bush. The mission was a place structured along moral codes that involved public and domestic places but where, simultaneously, the missionaries had little control over Toba labor and people were free to set out on long foraging expeditions. The ingenio, on the contrary, was a place in which strict control was imposed on their labor and where domestic spaces at the lote were places of "freedom," re-created every evening through dancing and intercourse. The control over Toba labor was apparent in the categories and forms of payment examined above; yet it was produced on a daily basis through the tasks men and women carried out under the surveillance of foremen led by the *lotero* (head of the lote) and the capataz mayor.

Labor discipline began before dawn. In 1996, while chatting next to his home, Tomás imitated how the capataz mayor gave instructions: "Thirty people to cut cane, only with machete. Twenty, twenty-five with shovels and pickaxes to make a channel two meters wide, one meter and twenty centimeters deep. Sixty women with knives to plant cane. Fifty women

31. "Of course, because of the ingenio." *Photo by author.*

only with machetes, to clear weeds." Memories like this outline a labor taxonomy that dismembered the Toba in even smaller groups, in a process in which the assigned tool (machetes, knives, shovels) objectified the social, gender, and spatial coordinates of the work to be performed.

The tasks assigned to men and women changed throughout the year, according to the administration's needs and the harvest stages. Planting cane and clearing irrigation canals were common female tasks, yet weeding was women's primary work. This is why adult women are currently very skillful at weeding their fields. In August 1997 I was at a camp near the marshlands where an extended family was practicing flood horticulture. It was close to sunset and while chatting with Marcelino I noticed that Valeria, his wife, continued working on the field, tirelessly weeding the soil with a hoe. I told Marcelino, "Valeria is a hard-worker!" He replied, casually: "Of course, because of the ingenio. There, women learned to work well." I was still thinking about the answer, its gendered overtones, and the way Marcelino immediately invoked the memory of the ingenio, when Emiliano came to visit us. A few minutes later, talking again about Valeria's skills, Emiliano made exactly the same casual comment: "Of course, because of the ingenio." Memories of the cane fields, in this regard, are such a recurrent presence among many Toba that some forms of trabajo cannot but relate to their past experiences in San Martín del Tabacal.

Many women remember that, while they were working, one of their pressing concerns was to look after their babies and children. They often tried to leave them in the lote, under the care of older siblings, but usually had to take them to the work site. Angélica, a woman in her fifties, remembered: "We suffered so much, the women, before." She pointed to her two-year-old granddaughter playing near us: "When we had two kids like this, we had to take the older on our backs and the smaller one in front. And on top of that, we had to carry the tools. . . . With the smallest kid, it was very complicated because I had to breastfeed him." Angélica then pointed to her five-year-old granddaughter standing next to her and added: "But with kids like this, you could leave them playing around there. That's the way it was when we were there. We suffered a lot. A lot of suffering." For women, the ingenio subverted any distinction between work sites and domestic spaces and forced them to re-create improvised spheres of childrearing within places of labor discipline averse to it. The suffering remembered by Angélica condenses these tensions and also counters nostalgic memories of female autonomy at the ingenio.

These gender-specific experiences are also mingled with memories that refer to tasks in which men and women complemented each other, simultaneously re-creating (through a gendered division of labor) and undermining (through cooperation) the gender hierarchies imposed on them. This was apparent during clearings, when women moved on first to clear shrubs and men followed them to cut down trees. In fact, one of the most important male tasks at San Martín del Tabacal was to clear the surrounding jungle, to the point that memories of those *desmontes* (clearings) make men feel that they were participants in the ingenio's expansion. In addition, men chopped wood to be used as fuel for the factory (and for the small trains transporting cane, called *Decauville*); they also dug irrigation canals and sugar cane furrows and covered the cane planted by their wives with soil. Many times they were also in charge of weeding. On an irregular basis, some men were sent to the factory, where they did twelve-hour shifts cleaning, sealing sugar bags, or piling them up. The Toba harvested sugar cane only when the cane cutters were on strike or when, near the end of the season, the pace of the harvest was delayed. In those cases, men cut cane and women loaded it into the *zorras* (cargo cars) of the Decauville train.

As is apparent, the ingenio was for most Toba a place structured by myriad labor practices subject to distinct disciplines and hierarchies, which made them move back and forth between the lotes and wide sets of work sites. People remember that they usually finished their tarea around noon. Foremen reviewed their work and, if the tarea was completed, gave them a *boleto* (ticket) that they took to the tarjador. The latter made a mark on their *planillas* (files) and gave them a ration in cash. Then, people bought food from the *tachera*: a Criollo woman who cooked for them. Many remember that they always ate the same food: cornmeal with a few vegetables and, if they were lucky, a cheap cut of beef. Since they had been working since dawn, in the afternoon they usually rested; but some, still hungry, went in groups to the fields to chew cane. Most Toba did not leave the lote alone and parents always kept a watchful eye on their children, for people agree that unknown dangers lurked in the area. As sunset approached, young men began decorating their bodies for the dancing that, banned at the mission station, they performed every evening with other Aborígenes. When the sun sank behind the mountains and darkness covered the cane fields, a monotonous, rhythmic collective singing emerged from the lotes, as men danced in a large circle holding each other's waists, and women surrounded them and picked a partner to spend the night with. Another night in San Martín del Tabacal.

It Seemed Like We Lived There

A major component of the Toba experience in Tabacal was that they stayed there most of the year. The harvest began in June and ended in November or December, but the Aborígenes arrived a few months earlier. When recruited in February, Toba men and women stayed in the plantation for nine or ten months. In the 1990s this spatial and temporal weight haunted people's memories. As Marcelino told me: "I always remember the San Martín plantation. It seemed like we lived there. When we came back here, we stayed only for two months." This experience created a certain acquaintance with the ingenio's spatial layout, its power structure, and its most overarching codes of discipline. Yet this did not turn "the mountains" into a place where the Toba felt at ease. An Anglican missionary who visited the ingenio noticed this: "It is obvious that, even though the Indians are sometimes away from the Chaco as long as ten months a year, it is the Chaco that they regard as their home" (Revill 1949:56).

Part of this estrangement was rooted in the living conditions at the lotes. People remember that their huts looked like "bird nests," were infested with fleas and lice, and provided no protection from cold and rain. Fleas and lice made living conditions hard to bear and left distinct marks

32. Toba men in San Martín del Tabacal.
Archivo General de la Nación, Buenos Aires.

on their bodies. Diego remembered: "It wasn't possible to sleep. You had to go to bed totally naked. If I didn't take my shirt off, the next day I had blood all over."⁹ In the lotes, drinking water was from irrigation canals. Before the advent of Peronism there was little health assistance to seasonal workers and even in the 1950s and 1960s this assistance was highly deficient. In 1962 the hospital at San Martín del Tabacal had thirty-five beds, four doctors, and one ambulance to cover 6,000 seasonal workers (Shapiro 1962:243; see Bisio and Forni 1976:18). People remember that the Aborígenes rarely had access to that hospital. "They didn't take us to the hospital," Mariano told me. "It seems that the hospital asked for documentos. We didn't have documentos. Only the shamans healed." The administration usually preferred to resort to massive and cheap preventive health measures, like applying vaccinations upon the arrival of the Aborígenes and spraying their huts and bodies with DDT. Yet most Toba remember that disease reached unparalleled proportions and, as we shall see, images of death and terror haunt their accounts of the ingenio.

While working under these conditions, many Toba spent part of their free time trying to complement their poor diets. In addition to chewing cane, some men went fishing with nylon lines, especially when their lote was near a stream. Even though some entered the jungle to gather honey and to hunt, most people feared those forests because of the presence of unknown wild animals and devils. Additionally, for some the sole idea of foraging in the plantation was an oxymoron. Tabacal was a place of tra-bajo where there was no room for marisca. Segundo, for instance, found my question about whether he went to mariscar in the ingenio totally out of place: "No, no. How are we going to mariscar if we were busy with trabajo? We worked all day, from night to day. We didn't rest." Yet people missed bush food, especially fish. In addition to fishing, many purchased fish from itinerant merchants and those who came to visit from the Pilco-mayo usually brought barbecued and sundried fish with them. When the end of the harvest approached, the work pace increased and people be-came impatient about going back home. Usually around mid-November, sometimes a few weeks later, the harvest came to an end. It was time for the event every Toba had longed for: el arreglo grande, the final payment of the salaries retained by the administration during all those months.

El Arreglo: Happiness among all the People!

Originally justified as a means of encouraging "saving habits" among in-digenous workers (Aráoz de Lamadrid 1914:41), the arreglo grande was the coronation of an already highly efficient system of extraction of sur-plus value. First, the administration received from the workers a huge interest-free credit for an extended time period (Rutledge 1987:215). Sec-ond, by postponing payment until the end of the harvest the administra-tion prevented people from returning to the Chaco. Finally, since each worker was owed a relatively large sum, by paying it all at once and in kind the arreglo gave the Aborígenes the impression that they made great gains. This is exactly how most Toba remember the arreglo: as a moment of abundance and excitement. Omar, an Anglican preacher in his mid-fifties, summarized this image when he told me: "The day of the arreglo, happiness among all the people!"

That day, men and women gathered around the lote's store early in the morning. One by one, they proceeded to the window accompanied by the lenguaraz. The employee checked their individual files and told them the balance pending. Through the translation by the lenguaraz, the worker began asking for the goods of his or her choice. The employee brought them, deducted them from the balance, and new rounds of re-quests were made. When the balance was paid in full, it was the next per-son's turn. As plantation policy, part of the balance was paid in cash and people usually used it to purchase the train ticket to Ingeniero Juárez and packaged food (bags of sugar, yerba mate, corn flour) to take home.

It was the end of a long year, and most Toba had numerous desired goods, including horses and donkeys, and were anxious to return to the Pilcomayo. In the Chaco the algarroba was already ripe and this was always a matter of concern, for if the return was delayed, the heavy December rains could spoil the harvest. People burnt their *tolderías* (huts), gathered their loads of goods, and took the train to Pichanal and Embarcación. With the donkeys and horses on the cargo cars, in Embarcación they boarded the train to Ingeniero Juárez. Since the capitanes had already telegraphed Sombrero Negro about the departure date, people from Misión El Toba went to the train station with horses and donkeys to wait for their relatives. Once in Ingeniero Juárez, the rest of the returnees hired trucks for the remainder of the trip home, for as Omar put it: "We had money to pay. We had plenty of money."

People remember that the reunion with relatives caused great excitement. More important, the massive return to the Pilcomayo made them reconnect with their lands, the river, the mission station, and the bush. The commodities brought back from the ingenio temporarily empowered them vis-à-vis the Criollos, who had little or no access to them and approached Toba villages to barter cows and horses in exchange for clothing and utensils.[10] With people eager to consume bush food, women set out to gather algarroba and other fruits and men fished in the river and conducted long foraging expeditions. The old men who had stayed and had cultivated their fields were now harvesting watermelons, pumpkins, and maize. People also had to readapt to the moral geography of Misión El Toba and, after the long absence in the cane fields, many went to church again to listen to the missionaries. Yet many people were also mourning their dead: adults, youngsters, and children killed by the scores of devils that haunted San Martín del Tabacal.

9

The Breath of the Devils

The alienation of the worker from his product means not only that
his labor becomes an object, assumes an external existence, but that it
exists independently, outside himself, and alien to him, and that it stands
opposed to him as an autonomous power. The life that he has given to
the object sets itself against him as an alien and hostile force.
—Karl Marx, *Economic and Philosophic Manuscripts*

That place is full of devils. Plenty. A lot.
It's called the Tabacal plantation.
—Segundo, 1995

In 1912 a British missionary who had just arrived at La Esperanza wrote
about the ranges rising west of the sugar plantations: "The mountains
with their ever-changing colours, the transition of light from shade on
the foliage, the glistening of the snow on the lofty peaks, are a source of
constant delight to the eyes and relief to the mind" (Hunt 1912b:71). Even
though most Toba were also impressed by that landscape, their view of
the mountains had little in common with an aesthetic contemplation, for
that place was for them the condensation of an experience of disease and
death. Early in 1996, I asked Ernesto, who went to Tabacal as a boy, why
there was so much disease in kahogonaGá. He looked at the ground as
he answered: "It's hard to describe. It was like a disease attacking. I don't
know which disease, but it was tremendous. It's like, it attacked somebody
during the day, and then the following day he was already finished off.
According to the pioGonáq, it's the devils living up in the mountains. . . .
There're plenty of devils in the mountains. When the devils saw the people
they said: 'Where do these people come from?' And then they said: 'Let's
go down there.'" Ernesto, like many others, remembered the ingenio as
a place infested with fulminating illnesses generated by scores of payák.

Confirming people's estrangement from that place, those evil spirits came down from the mountains with the explicit purpose of wiping out those who were strangers to the area.

Current memories of San Martín del Tabacal are haunted by images of disease, death, and devils. Accounts of the mountain devils are often intertwined with references to the *KiyaGaikpí*, cannibal people who wandered the area, and the Familiar, a diablo that lived in the factory basement and had a pact with Patrón Costas. In this chapter, I examine how through these narratives most Toba remember the ingenio as a place marked by dangers unknown in the Chaco and how, by doing so, they turn fear into a central component of the plantation's geography. Produced by people socialized into Anglican values, the devil symbolism of these memories also illustrates how missionization merged with prior cultural imageries to foster interpretations of an experience of alienation.

Death and the Mountain Devils

When in the mid-1990s people remembered the living conditions analyzed in the previous chapter, most were aware of their negative effect on their health.[1] Yet a salient theme that emerges from their memory is the close association between the disease tearing through their bodies and the mountain devils. Men and women alike agree that countless payák inhabited the peaks overlooking the cane fields. Invisible and like a silent breeze, they came down from those ridges and spread disease among the people. On the hills circling the plantation, they sometimes adopted the shape of short and hairy humanoids. According to Nicacio, a shaman in his eighties, disease also descended from the mountains as a hot and slow-moving fog, crawling down the slopes like a deadly breath: "There was a plague, very bad, hot. At night, the high mountain looked like a hot fire. Some people stunk. The plague came down from the hill, smoke of the devils. Many people died." In Nicacio's account, the devils' deadly force blended with the ingenio's geography, to the point that the mist often shrouding the jungle was inseparable from "the smoke of the devils."

Whenever I asked people whether there were diablos in the plantations, I was struck by their unanimous and expressive answers in the affirmative, epitomized in the exclamation "ooh!," and by the way they grounded the devils' abundance on a particular place: the mountains. Segundo remembered: "Ooh! There were many devils. Plenty of devils.

All the diseases. That's why the kids died; the grown-ups, women, girls, everybody." I asked him why there were so many devils. "We lived close to a mountain, that's why."

The towering forests on the mountains' base enhanced the abundance of payák. For most Toba, devils are particularly plentiful in thick forests, and the jungles of the San Francisco River Valley were of a density and height unparalleled by the Chaco bush. Those forests contained further dangers: large lions with hairy heads (*jauagapolio*) and tigers with black stripes (*kedokpolio*)—bigger than the pumas and jaguars of the Chaco—as well as large monkeys (*woyém*). Yet people agree that the mountain devils were the most deadly creatures in the area. In contrast with bush devils in the Chaco, no type of reciprocity connected them with humans. The mountain diablos were utterly alien and evil beings that caused unparalleled levels of death. Trying to figure out potential similarities between spirits from the two regions, I once asked Mariano whether mountain devils gave shamans healing power. "No, they didn't," he replied categorically. Later on, I rephrased the question and he insisted: "No, they only gave disease."

Disease became the embodiment of the social strains embedded in the plantation, for as Jean Comaroff argues in another context, "the signs of physical discord are simultaneously the signifiers of an aberrant world" (1985:9). The death of children is a particularly strong and painful theme in current memories. In 1996 Daniela, a woman in her late fifties, remembered: "When people went to the ingenio, almost all the children died there. And when they were back, all the women cried for the children." That children are remembered as the most likely to fall victim to the plantation's dangers highlights that this place threatened not just individual lives but also their *social* reproduction. Many people emphasize that work in Tabacal almost decimated them as a group. I once asked Andrés, a man in his fifties and today a farmer, if many people went to the ingenio. "Ooh! Many!," he answered. "That's why all the people of about my age were finished off at the San Martín plantation. That's why you see that we're very few now. For when we worked at the ingenio, when people returned all the kids died. They died. Boys, girls, grownups too."

Since the early twentieth century, numerous reports have documented the extremely high mortality rates among Aborígenes at the sugar plantations. Labor inspector José Niklison wrote in 1917: "The indigenous mortality rate during these first weeks acquires dreadful proportions. Families and tribes are wiped out. . . . 'If it would be possible to investigate how many leave their lives there — a missionary friend of mine wrote me — the numbers would be horrifying' " (1989:65). In 1958 a member of the staff at Misión El Toba visited the Toba at Tabacal and wrote: "It was distressing to see the cramped living quarters . . . [and] the number of sick persons" (Kitchin 1958:26). Other missionaries reported on the very high death toll of little children. One of them described the plantations as "the graveyard of babies" (Fox 1958:24–25).[2] In 1996 Ernesto remembered that people buried their dead in the forests surrounding the cane fields but that the following year those forests were cleared to plant sugar cane. For that reason, plowing machines often unearthed human bones. "At the ingenio," he added, "there must be many skeletons in the middle of the cane fields." References to the bones of their people scattered in the cane fields are also common in the memory of the Wichí (Segovia 1998:161, 163, 165) and are a graphic expression of the perception that the Aborígenes were leaving in the plantation their most basic possession, their own bodies, literally swallowed by vast fields of sugar cane.

The high mortality rate and the threat of devils did not seem to deter most Toba from going to the plantation every year. Many people remember the disease and death at Tabacal as a harsh but unavoidable fact of life, and some told me with resignation that there was little that could be done about it. As Marcelino put it: "When we arrived there, I don't know how many died. . . . The ingenio was awful, but we went anyway. We didn't think about dying. If somebody died, he died." The desire for commodities, enhanced by their growing inability to guarantee their social reproduction through marisca alone at home, seems to have been stronger than the risk of death. In fact, people often emphasize in their accounts the abundance of commodities at San Martín del Tabacal, somewhat obscuring the horror this place evokes in their memory, as if trying to compensate for past experiences of suffering.

The cyclical return to the cane fields did not mean that people did not try to counteract these adverse conditions through manifold means. In order to protect their children, many adults did not take them to the plantation as long as relatives at home could look after them. In the ingenio, unable to access the hospital, they also counted on the healing power of shamans. Some people remember that at night they could hear the loud healing songs of several pioGonáq treating sick people; however, they also agree that the shamans' power was only partially effective against the mountain spirits. When conditions became unbearable, some people simply dropped work. At the end of 1995, Segundo remembered his flight from the devils sweeping through his camp: "That place is full of devils. Plenty. A lot. It's called the Tabacal plantation. Many people died, because the devils killed the people, women, children. That day there were flies, black, small, coming out. There were plenty of them in the house, inside. One person died. And I fled to Orán, I didn't return to the ingenio. I dropped the ingenio. I fled, because it had many devils." This account also reveals that the disease unleashed by the devils was localized in the lotes and that Orán, only a few kilometers away, was a relatively safe place.

Yet mountain devils were not the only dangers lurking at the plantation. Many Toba remember that a particularly dangerous group of people inhabited the area. They were big and tall, had long beards, wore pieces of cloth wrapped around their heads, and were wealthy. They were also cannibals.

The KiyaGaikpí

According to many Toba, the KiyaGaikpí, or big eaters, were people living near San Martín del Tabacal whose most striking feature was that they ate human flesh.[3] The KiyaGaikpí were part of the direct experience of people who in the mid-1990s were approximately sixty-five years and older. They saw the "big eaters" when they were young and passed their memory of them on to the next generations. Thus, even though many people did not see them personally, they knew well who the KiyaGaikpí were and in the following decades were afraid of encountering them. A few young people told me that they were originally skeptical about the existence of such people but were nevertheless impressed by the stories they had heard. As Ernesto put it: "I couldn't believe it, but the old people saw them." In fact, he was the first who gave me a detailed account of the KiyaGaikpí. His father had told him several stories about them. In one of these accounts, a Toba man walking in the cane fields came across one of their camps. Ernesto explained:

> He was getting closer and a bearded man came out. He was making gestures so that he came, and the Toba was getting closer. When he saw the campsite, he saw all the flesh hanging from wires. There was the leg of a person hanging there, instead of the leg of a cow. The man escaped right away and told the others: "There's a group of bearded men with the leg of a person!" Ooh! The people didn't know what to do. They wanted to

leave. The foreman told them that they shouldn't be scared, that those people were staying over there.

Current memories about the origins, physical appearance, and wealth of the KiyaGaikpí condense many aspects of the experience at the plantations as well as its contradictions. According to most people, the Kiya-Gaikpí came from the place they feared the most: the mountains. Others argue that they also dwelled in camps located in Ledesma and La Esperanza. Old people have a detailed memory of their appearance and told me in detail about their thick beards, turbans, and dirty clothing, which was unlike anything they had seen before. Some features pertaining to the KiyaGaikpí's racial and class identity are sources of disagreement. Most people depict them as "white" or "very white," yet others claim they were "black" or "mulatto." Some argue that the KiyaGaikpí were workers at Ledesma and La Esperanza and that on several occasions they went to San Martín del Tabacal looking for work and human flesh. Others deny they were workers at all and argue that when they approached the plantations they just wanted to kill and "eat" people. Many Toba agree that the reason the KiyaGaikpí were not workers was that they were "very rich." Mariano told me that they were fearless because of their wealth: "The KiyaGaikpí looked as if they were the owners of everything. They say that they live on the other side, beyond the big mountain. They came down with trucks, for they were many. They have trucks. They're very rich. They have everything. They say that they have airplanes. . . . They have money. They have plenty of money. That's why they're not scared."

The commodification of social relations in the cane fields shaped Toba ideas about "the big eaters" in many ways: not only in that many considered them rich but also in the interpretations of the ways they killed. Nicacio told me that the KiyaGaikpí used to leave small packages of money by the road, tied with a string, as a bait to attract people. Others remembered that they used their money to buy their prey. They purchased human flesh either from other workers or, as Gervacio—a man in his thirties with some political experience—put it, "from the people who have money and contact with the authorities." Thus, those whose only commodity while at the plantations was their labor believed they were being bought and sold as a new type of commodity: meat. The attitudes projected onto these cannibals highlight the commodification associated with the plantation, where workers were reduced to consumable, disposable objects. This objectification acquires gendered dimensions in narratives common among men in which the KiyaGaikpí castrated their victims, put them inside a paddock, and fattened them "like animals."

Despite the fear evoked by these men's actions, most Toba point out that the administration protected the workers from them. People are unanimous: "the boss" Costas "didn't like" the KiyaGaikpí and "chased them away" from San Martín del Tabacal when he discovered they were "eating" his laborers. These accounts shed light, once again, on the paternalism projected onto the ingenio's patrón. Most Toba were also terrified of him, as I show below, but when they remember the "big eaters" many are quick to note that, being Patrón Costas's workers, they counted on his protection. This perception had significant spatial implications, for many saw the plantation as a relatively sheltering place in relation to the dangers lurking in the jungle and the mountains. Yet this was a contradictory, fragile security, permanently undermined by forces haunting workers from within the ingenio.

In tension with the recollection of their fear of being victims of the KiyaGaikpí, some Toba argue that these men's eating preferences often kept the Aborígenes from being killed. The main reason was that the "big eaters" thought the flesh of the Aborígenes "doesn't taste good" and preferred instead to eat Guaraní, Bolivian, Kolla, and Criollo workers. This distinction is remarkable, for it illustrates the ways in which many Toba internalized and resignified the ethnic hierarchies created in San Martín del Tabacal. They project onto the KiyaGaikpí the despising attitudes toward the Aborígenes widespread in the plantation, yet, at the same time, find elements of their aboriginality that played to their advantage. People agree that what made the flesh of the Aborígenes less appealing to these cannibals was that back in the Chaco they did not eat "nice things" but bush food. Reflecting this widespread perception, Bernardo told me: "They say they don't find the Toba's flesh tasty. That's what the old people say, because the Aborígenes don't eat nice things, they eat anything. . . . They'd much rather have white people, for whites have nice food and they find their flesh very nice." The tension between accounts like this and the remembered fear of being the KiyaGaikpí's victims reveals the dialectic of exclusion and inclusion that permeates current memories of kahogonaGá: on the one hand, the sense that they were not valuable enough because of their status as Aborígenes and, on the other hand, their feeling that their status as workers made them susceptible to the dangers they perceived within the space of the plantation as a whole. Because of this immersion, and despite being Aborígenes, most Toba remember that the fear of encountering these cannibals greatly restricted their mobility: men and women always had their children with them and avoided leaving the camp at night or alone.

When remembering the KiyaGaikpí, some people are clearly puzzled by their identity. To describe them, they often add further details collected from other people and from their own observations. Some remember that foremen called them *hindúes*, Hindus. Others told me that they did not like beef. As Segundo put it: "They didn't eat beef. If one of them ate cow, he threw up. The nicest for them was people's flesh."

In 1912 La Esperanza contracted over 100 Sikh men from India as part of an attempt to find "better" workers than the Chaco indigenous groups.[4] The presence of the Sikh at the plantation, described by an administrator as "handsome fellows with wonderful curled beards" (Muir 1947:264), added a new element to the kaleidoscope of ethnic differences produced in the cane fields. In 1914 an inspector of the Argentinean Labor Department described some of the features of the Sikh workers that had caught the Toba's attention: they wandered in groups, moved from one ingenio to the other, wore turbans and dirty clothing, saved much of their earnings in the bank of the estate, and did not eat beef (Vidal 1914:15). Two years after their arrival, there were only fifty or sixty Sikhs left in the area (Vidal 1914:15; Zavalía 1915:18). Many of them continued working in La Esperanza for several decades, especially as the Leach brothers' private servants. Whereas some returned to India after its independence in 1947, the rest stayed and settled in San Pedro de Jujuy (next to La Esperanza) and other towns of the area (Sierra e Iglesias 1998:72–73).

Toba memories of the KiyaGaikpí point to some of the disturbing experiences that shaped their labor in the plantations. The fear of cannibalism does not seem to have played an important role in their cultural practices prior to the migration to the cane fields.[5] Probably fostered by the rumors of the Sikhs' distaste for beef and an antonymic association between not eating beef and eating human flesh, the fear of the Kiya-Gaikpí seems to express a particular aspect of the Toba experience in the cane fields: the fear of losing one of the few things they still owned while working there, their own bodies, permanently consumed by exhausting work, mistreatment, disease, and death. In fact, the region surrounding the plantations has been haunted by stories of cannibalism since at least the early twentieth century.[6] This connection between capitalist exploitation and cannibalism is far from being restricted to this area, and stories about workers "consumed" or "eaten up" in estates, factories, or mines are widespread around the world (Gould 1990:29; Nash 1993:ix, 157; Stoler 1985:197–98).

Some indirect but remarkable connections exist between the plantation administration and the KiyaGaikpí's cannibalism. Even though people argue that Patrón Costas "chased the KiyaGaikpí away," they attribute to the latter features that put them remarkably close to their patrón: they were rich and (according to many) they were white and did not work. The attribution of whiteness to diabolical or dangerous creatures is widespread in Latin America (see Nash 1993:164, 191–94) and in this case is remarkable because it implies whitening the Sikhs. As part of the ingenio's ethnic and class hierarchies, most Toba see a direct continuum between wealth, whiteness, and not being a worker. In spite of the contradictions in their current characterization, the KiyaGaikpí add a fourth element to the list: the consumption of human flesh. With all its mediations and ambiguities, the memory of these people as rich, white, and nonworkers points to the cannibalistic aspect of labor exploitation: the consumption of the bodies of a social group by the hunger for profit of another group.

Patrón Costas himself was immersed in this blend of wealth, race, class, and cannibalism. His "cannibalism" was concentrated in a particularly symbolic place: the sugar-processing factory. It could not be otherwise, for as an administrator of La Esperanza put it: "The sugar mill is a huge, insatiable monster which must never be allowed to remain for a moment without food for its jaws" (Muir 1947:235).

The Devil in the Factory

The factory was one of the places in the ingenio that the Toba and other workers feared the most, because they saw it as the refuge of a diabolical creature known as *el Familiar* (the Familiar, literally "relative"). Most Toba define the Familiar as a payák entity, a diablo. Unlike the anonymous mountain diablos, the Familiar was an individual with specific traits: a nonhuman, evil, and powerful creature that lived in a confined space: the factory basement. As with the KiyaGaikpí, people portray the Familiar in heterogeneous ways, but most agree that he appeared after midnight and acquired animal and human shapes. As part of the same racialization of the "big eaters," many Toba say that when the Familiar appeared as a person he usually turned into a white man. This whiteness had a clear class

33. "There was a Familiar in the factory." *Photo by author.*

component: this man was educated and well dressed. Tomás described
the Familiar to me as follows:

> There was a Familiar in the factory. . . . The man always comes out, in
> the court of the factory. A big dog comes out, a big lion, all *bichos* [wild
> animals] to look after the factory. Sometimes he comes out wearing a
> suit and a tie, with shoes. Beautiful man. I've seen him. There's a change
> of shift, and then people know it's the time when the Familiar comes out.
> It's true. He comes out at two or three in the morning. . . . But people
> are scared of the man. He always looks after the factory. . . . Here he
> comes, and people hid, silent. Tie, suit. He has education.

The fear of the Familiar and its association with the sugar industry is
very old and widespread in northern Argentina. The term *Familiar* has its
historical roots in the Europe of the Middle Ages. It was the name then
given to the Devil (or to one of the lesser demons under his command) that
dwelled in the home of a witch (Godbeer 1992:162–68). In Argentina the
Familiar emerged as an important component of the cultural landscape
of the sugar plantations in the provinces of Tucumán, Salta, and Jujuy and
became part of the experience of the diverse populations providing the
ingenios with their labor.[7] At Tabacal, most Toba incorporated the fear
of this diablo through their interaction with other workers, especially the
Guaraní. After decades of labor migrations, the Familiar became as embedded in their experience of the ingenio as the cane fields, the mountain
devils, or their labor practices.

The Familiar is remembered as a creature defined metonymically and symbiotically with Patrón Costas and united with him through a pact. Unlike the devil pacts analyzed by Michael Taussig (1980), in this case it was not the workers but the patrón who made pacts with the devil, a notion also widespread in other regions of Latin America (Edelman 1994:62; Gould 1990:30).[8] Many people believe that Patrón Costas's power and wealth were closely intertwined with his relationship with the Familiar; they argue that the Familiar provided him with riches, looked after the factory, and made sure the sugar cane fields were always green. "That's why Patrón Costas had money," Emiliano once told me. "Not because of politics, but because he had a Familiar." As part of their pact, the boss of Tabacal was believed to feed the Familiar with workers. In relation to the commodification and objectification of workers, some argue that he used his wealth to buy the complicity of "the government" vis-à-vis those deaths and even the silence of the victims' relatives. In an account similar to the memories of the KiyaGaikpí, Patricio told me that Patrón Costas captured men, castrated them, and made them gain weight before handing them over to the Familiar. Since many people remember Patrón Costas as a protective, paternalistic figure, these memories are permeated with unresolved contradictions that indicate the respect and fear projected onto him. Shaking me from the lethargy of a hot Chaco afternoon, Tomás once told me, in a casual tone: "Patrón Costas had a Familiar. Patrón Costas was the nicest, very nice man."

Many people contend that, apart from the workers he received from Patrón Costas, the Familiar also went out to kill people by himself, usually those who came from distant regions. This selectivity reveals that the workers' estrangement from the local geography accentuated the risk of death. On occasions, the sign that this diablo had killed somebody was that the factory's siren went off. Toba memories of the Familiar, however, include the same tension evoked in the memory of the KiyaGaikpí: a tension between feeling threatened because they were workers and their simultaneous sense of being less likely to be killed because they were Aborígenes. Exactly as in the case of the KiyaGaikpí, some people told me that the Familiar "didn't like" the smell of the Aborígenes' flesh and preferred to eat Criollo workers. This, however, did not prevent most Toba from being terrified of the Familiar. Men who worked in the factory claim that they once saw the Familiar with Patrón Costas. Enrique, a man in his late fifties, remembered this encounter in detail, recalling the fear they felt at the sight of the Familiar turned into a large white man wearing a suit:

34. "We once went underneath the factory." *Photo by author.*

We once went underneath the factory. . . . There was a *jefe* (foreman) who was with us and he said: "If a fat person comes out, a person sort of red, nobody has to talk. You don't have to talk. Otherwise, something will happen." . . . [The foreman said:] "Patrón Costas is coming." And we all started sweeping, we all had brooms. . . . There they came, the engineer, Patrón Costas, and the fat man. [Patrón Costas said] "Good morning. These are my brave and strong people [*mi gente guapa*]." And he gave a cigarette to each of us and also matches. And the fat man was right beside him, with a black suit, black tie. He didn't talk, but we knew, because the foreman had explained to us. . . . Then Patrón Costas went to another corridor with that man. . . . One of us said: "Let's go! Let's go! Let's go!" We all ran. We went upstairs. We all talked about how scared we were: "I think that was the Familiar, the one who was with us! That's him!" . . . The old Naidó said: "I'll never go down there again. I'm really scared." We didn't know him, but the jefe told us that we shouldn't talk to him or get close to him, because he was the Familiar.

The memory of this encounter shows that members of the plantation administration often encouraged the fear of the Familiar. Several people told me that Criollo foremen often warned them "to be careful" with the Familiar and not to wander at night close to the factory. This construction of a climate of terror around Patrón Costas contributed to reinforcing a submission to his authority and maintaining the factory free of intruders. Yet it would be misleading to reduce the Familiar to the product of a utilitarian strategy of social control designed by the plantation administration, as Rosenzvaig (1986:249) has claimed. The manipulation of the Familiar figure by foremen seems to have been an attempt to use for their own convenience an old and widespread imagery created and re-created by workers themselves. In addition, these ideological attempts at social control were not necessarily successful. Since rumors about the Familiar saturated the factory with imageries of evil, on some occasions they catalyzed forms of critique and discontent, especially among the Criollos. Criollo workers with experience in collective struggles often tell stories of men who fought the Familiar and even killed him (Isla and Taylor 1995:318; Rosenberg 1936:135, 136–37; Vessuri 1971:62–63). Conversely, most Toba remember the Familiar in a way that seems integral to their memories of political powerlessness in the ingenio. Largely because of the ethnic segmentation of the labor force, the Aborígenes formed the less politicized segment of workers and rarely joined the strikes led by the union. Most Toba remember the Familiar as a devil so powerful that any type of resistance against him was futile. When I asked them whether it was possible "to defend yourself" from this devil, some people looked at me with a certain wonder at the extravagance of my question, before answering: "No, it's not possible."

In Toba memories, the Familiar epitomized the often paralyzing power of the plantation, a power in which nonhuman and human actors were closely intertwined. Foremen and the plantation's private police force were in charge of enforcing labor discipline, supported by the gendarmería squadron at Orán.[9] People remember these actors as closely involved with the Familiar. Unlike Criollo workers, most Toba make no explicit connection between this devil's victims and their level of political activism yet they associate this diablo with forms of repression at numerous levels. Patricio told me that when the Familiar came out of the factory he usually turned "into a gendarme or policeman." He added: "Then, when he walks inside the factory nobody recognizes him. . . . The Familiar cruises the streets on a pickup truck, in Orán." The Familiar, in other words, embodied the armed institutions of the state controlling and patrolling the area, to the point that the lines separating the two were often blurred. Mariano remembered: "We were afraid of the Familiar. And we were afraid of gendarmería as well." I asked him why. "Well, gendarmería was there because of the people who went on strike. That's what we were afraid of."

The memory of gendarmes, policías, and the Familiar as entities closely intertwined with each other is particularly noteworthy given the recent history of state terrorism in Argentina. Some of the repressive measures the armed forces unleashed in the late 1970s in the whole country had already been implemented for decades in the sugar plantations (Nelli 1988:41; see Rosenzvaig 1986:250–55, 1995:35). In the San Francisco River Valley, this amalgamation of state and capitalist terror peaked in the *"el apagón"* (blackout) of Ledesma on the night of July 27, 1976, four months after the onset of the military dictatorship. That night, a combined force of soldiers and plantation policemen acting under darkness kidnapped 300 workers from their homes (Nelli 1988:117; Rosenzvaig 1995:62). The Toba did not experience this last wave of terror, for by then they had stopped migrating to the cane fields. And since their home region was relatively marginal in terms of previous political activism, they were not directly affected by the kidnappings, torture, and murder then common in other parts of Argentina. Yet the way some people remembered the Familiar in the mid-1990s combined their previous experiences of terror in San Martín del Tabacal with what they had heard (through the media and their interaction with politicians) about the violence perpetrated by the military in the second half of the 1970s. The terminology some people use to refer to the Familiar, in this regard, is similar to that which became customary in Argentina to refer to state terrorism. In 1996 Gervacio, who went to Tabacal as a boy, told me about people who "disappeared" because of the Familiar; he also remembered rumors that attributed people's death to "electric shocks"—terms that in Argentina automatically bring to mind images of torture and state terror. Most people also remember that when the Familiar killed people the lights of the factory went off, which may indicate that blackouts to facilitate the kidnapping of workers were also undertaken at the time the Toba worked in Tabacal.

Estrangement, Fetishism, and the Places of Terror

The memories intertwining devils, death, the military, cannibals, and Patrón Costas create close yet not necessarily direct connections between terror and the plantation administration. This is particularly clear in the case of the mountain devils, which are remembered as faceless, anonymous, usually invisible forces directly responsible for most of their dead yet unconnected to the plantation's power. The KiyaGaikpí, for their part, stand in a contradictory place: they had no direct link with the administration either but were metonymically associated with racial and class features of administrators. In other words, since they are remembered as rich and white, their cannibalism indirectly pointed to the class subject position of the patrones. In the case of the Familiar, his connection with the administration was clear and unambiguous: this diablo is remembered as the embodiment of Patrón Costas and his armed forces. Despite the differences among them, a common thread articulates these devils and cannibals: they are strongly localized. They exist only in San Martín del Tabacal and its immediate surroundings and mark this place with dense images of terror, danger, and estrangement. Simultaneously, these figures produce a spatial differentiation in which some places absorb with greater force the terror latent in their surroundings. These places are the factory, the core symbol of the productive forces unleashed by the ingenio, and the mountains. The latter were part of a natural landscape seemingly unrelated to those social forces but that, being alien to the Toba's earlier experience of place, somehow symbolized the estrangement of wage labor.

For the reasons examined above, memories of the mountain devils and the Familiar are informed by what was a localized experience of alienation: the Toba's experience of feeling separated from their labor and its products (cf. Taussig 1980:17, 37).[10] This estrangement was more than the result of economic exploitation; it was also produced by the inclusion of Toba men and women within the most undervalued ethnic segment of the labor force and by their immersion within an overall climate of repression and political terror. These experiences made the plantation a place from which most people felt estranged, one where they did not control local rules. This estrangement coalescing in devils and cannibals captures one of the features Karl Marx associated with alienation: the fact that the worker feels that the product of his labor "sets itself against him as an alien and hostile force" (1964:123). Because of the connection between devils and the alienation generated by capitalist conditions of exploitation, it is important to take into consideration Terence Turner's (1986:111) argument that devil imageries represent "power" rather than capitalism. Power is certainly a critical dimension shaping these accounts; yet these devils' power is not power in the abstract. The power of the diablos at San Martín del Tabacal was a historically and spatially specific type of power: one produced by capitalist conditions of exploitation.

Prone to creating "alien and hostile forces," this spatialized estrangement is central in the fetishization of social relations created by devil imageries. Important aspects of the fetishism associated with the diablos were part of the Toba habitus prior to the experience at the plantations: a set of subjective dispositions amenable to explaining disease by forces beyond human control. In their first labor migrations, the figure of the payák provided them with the lens through which they tried to understand the disease decimating them in the cane fields. The experience of missionization charged these mountain spirits with further negative meanings, turning them into diablos that seemed to embody with particular force the imageries of evil the missionaries preached against at Misión El Toba. And the interaction with other workers expanded these meanings to include a diabolical creature new in Toba experience: the Familiar. But once produced in the plantation, these imageries mingled with the fetishism inscribed in capitalist production: the objectification of the social relation between labor and capital in entities with lives of their own, detached from their social conditions of production.

Michael Taussig was among the first to analyze the connection between commodity fetishism and devil imageries. He has been rightly criticized for relying on dualistic oppositions—between types of "exchange systems," "modes of production," and "forms of fetishism"—that oversimplify his historical and ethnographic material (Platt 1983:64; Roseberry 1989:222; Trouillot 1986:86–87; T. Turner 1986:105). Yet Taussig's argument that devil imageries merge commodity fetishism with indigenous forms of fetishism remains an insightful contribution that illuminates some of the memories of devils examined above. Among the Toba, this combined fetishization contributed to defining their material experience of San Martín del Tabacal. Jack Amariglio and Antonio Callari (1993:189) have reminded us that economist readings of commodity fetishism as "false consciousness" obscure the fact that this fetishism is an active force in the production of material conditions. In the Toba case, the fetishization crystallized in devil imageries was part of the very matrix in which the plantation was produced, reproduced, and then remembered as a place. For this reason, it would be misleading to see the memories of the mountain devils, the KiyaGaikpí, and the Familiar as veiled, distorted expressions of "real" social conditions. The fantastic monstrosity of these diablos and cannibals is inseparable from the very real, fabulous, and monstrous forms of wealth created by capitalism, a merging that Marx (1977:128) himself identified when he referred to the "phantom-like" or "ghostly" objectivity of the commodity (see Keenan 1993:157). In fact, when people remember the ingenio, they frequently intertwine images of death with dazzling accounts of wealth.

10

"We Returned Rich"

When you saw a black dog you had to escape, because it was the Familiar.
... When he wanted to, he killed people. Ooh! At that time there was a lot
of work in the ingenio. But the work was nice. It wasn't much. But when
you worked, you earned clothes, a lot of clothes, bicycles, record players,
radios, shotguns, donkeys, horses. —Marcelino, 1996

One of the events most frequently remembered by Toba adults about San
Martín del Tabacal involves a visit by President Juan Domingo Perón.
Many people describe how his train stopped at Tabacal and how he
emerged from one of the cars, as excited masses of workers, among them
the Toba, welcomed him. Perón reached for the bags carried by several
assistants and a few seconds later the air was filled with hundreds, thousands of coins, flying from his hands to the outstretched, desperate, hands
of the workers. In 1996 Diego remembered that day in the 1950s when
Perón threw money to them:

> In Tabacal, we saw him. It was him that we saw; we didn't see another
> man. In those days, he traveled by train. When Perón saw the people, he
> got off. There were many people. And all the secretaries had little bags.
> People didn't believe that he carried money in little bags like those. When
> he finished talking to all the caciques and capitanes it was only then that
> he threw the money. But coins, new ones! He threw money; he was
> throwing it like this [Diego moved his arms several times]. People were
> bumping into each other, many kids, women. Many twenty-cent coins,
> when they were worth something. Then you found quite many *pesitos*
> and bought a shirt. When he left, we never came across Perón again.

Diego and others remember that their attempt to gather those coins
caused chaotic excitement among them. Some even use metaphors that
remark the animallike or childish nature of their impulsive attempt to

35. "In Tabacal, we saw him." *Photo by author.*

gather the money. Pablo remembered: "People were like hens being fed with corn." Mariano said of the same event, which he witnessed as a teenager: "When he threw the money, the money was like candies. . . . And everybody ran, the kids, the grownups, everybody."

The shower of money created by Perón connected many Toba with the embodiment of political power in Argentina, the president of the nation himself, and briefly countered the estrangement that in those days they felt from national political events. The memory of this event also indicates that in the 1990s many people saw San Martín del Tabacal as a site of fabulous wealth, where money literally rained over them. In this chapter, I explore how these memories create a recurrent nostalgia for a lost source of trabajo, commodities, and money. I also examine how many Toba project onto "the mountains" fetishized imageries of wealth that contain an unresolved tension between their feeling of being participants of the ingenio's abundance and their memory of being alienated from it.

The Money Was Worth A Lot

In contrast with the memories of disease, suffering, and death examined in previous chapters, whenever I asked people whether they liked going to the ingenio, most would tell me that they did. Many would also emphasize, with nostalgia, "how nice" it was working there. As Pablo put it: "It was nice at the San Martín plantation. We returned rich. We bought boots, spurs, bombachas (baggy pants), hats, and revolvers. Others bought shotguns and boxes of bullets." This positive memory hinges on the large amount of commodities they were able to bring back home, such as clothes, horses, donkeys, firearms, ammunition, tools, or domestic utensils. This nostalgia is fostered by the way in which the arreglo grande was organized, as a gigantic potlatch of sorts in which people received large amounts of commodities all at once. The fact that at the arreglo people asked for the goods of their choice had a further ideological effect, for many remember the arreglo as if they were in charge of the situation and the balance of power at the plantation had been suddenly inverted. It was *they* who decided which type of goods they were going to take home. And as long as there was a balance left, they were able to do it over and over again, as if they were served, like patrons of the house, by respectful employees willing to comply with their wishes. Diego remembered: "You went to the store and they asked you: 'What do you take?' You asked what you wanted and the pile began growing: poncho, cloth for women, blanket, shoes. The bag was full like this, but there was still money left. Then, you continued asking." As part of these memories, people would give me long and detailed lists of the goods they received in the arreglo. They would recite these lists in a rhythmical tone, which gained momentum and a bizarre, dizzying strength as the number of commodities increased. Mariano described the arreglo grande as follows:

> The money was worth a lot. . . . I bought a large blanket, a shotgun, shells, gunpowder, reins, bit, spurs, dress cloth. I bought ten pieces of cloth, each one three meters long, two shirts to go out, five working shirts, cloth for bombachas, eight meters. I bought pants, bombacha, as if I were *chaqueño* [Criollo], hat, boots, shoes, a full suit for Sundays. [The employee] summed up and then there was still a bit left. Then I bought a flashlight, needle, thread, soap, mirror, handkerchiefs, socks.

These accounts reveal the bodily transformations produced by the experience of wage labor, which since the 1950s implied the increasing adoption of Criollo clothing styles (bombacha pants, shirts, wide hats). Yet what is striking about these memories is that they are about commodities that a few years earlier most Toba did not know or need, but that had gradually become useful, necessary, and desired. Indeed, it was their desire for goods and their dependence on them that made people return to kahogonaGá every year, despite the disease, the cannibals, and the diablos. On many occasions, many Toba remembered with excitement the wealth of San Martín del Tabacal right after mentioning how they feared the ingenio's dangers. I was often struck by the ease with which they were able to shift from one topic to the other, and by the way the memory of commodities often obscured that of terror. Marcelino, for instance, was telling me about the Familiar when he suddenly made a comment on how nice it was working at the plantation: "When you saw a black dog you had to escape, because it was the Familiar. . . . When he wanted to, he killed people. Ooh! At that time there was a lot of work in the ingenio. But the work was nice. It wasn't much. But when you worked, you earned clothes, a lot of clothes, bicycles, record players, radios, shotguns, donkeys, horses." As suggested in the previous chapter, commodity fetishism is part of the same thread creating devil fetishism. It was much later that I realized that in these accounts, rather than easily shifting topics, many people were remembering different aspects of the same experience of estrangement and capturing the phantasmagoric components of San Martín del Tabacal's wealth.

The fascination with commodities was particularly strong with the most unique and powerful of all: money. Coins were the first type of money the Toba interacted with, and consequently they called money *laikawá*, "metal." This means that they first saw money as its material signifier: small pieces of metal with a qualitative value but whose quantitative value was initially hard to decipher. Owing to decades of high inflation and peso devaluations in Argentina, the memory of money at the ingenio is often shaped by the different value attributed to money back then and today. Marcelino told me, referring to the ingenio: "The money was worth a lot, not like now. Even though the coin was a twenty-cent one, the cents were like American dollars." In the plantation, in other words, a few cents were not simply cents; they were comparable to *the* symbol of the power of money worldwide: U.S. dollars. Memories that ascribe a "higher value" to money in the past are common in contexts of high inflation; and they express, in the words of Brad Weiss, "a sense of loss and dismay which can be expressed in terms of the putatively 'true' value of money" (1997:349). Yet in our case it is important to note that many Toba project this "true" value of money not only into the past but also *elsewhere*: San Martín del Tabacal.

In chapter 17 we shall see how Toba experiences of money are also intertwined with shamanic practices and bush devils. Yet rather than expressing the "incorporation" of money within their "cultural matrix," as

36. "The story goes that Perón had a money factory."
Photo by author.

Jonathan Parry and Maurice Bloch (1991:1, 19, 21) would argue, Toba attitudes toward "metal" implied the production of *new* meanings: an improvised attempt to make sense of what was initially to them a fascinating yet hard to understand novelty: a universal means of exchange. And being "the supreme representation of social power in capitalist society" (Harvey 1989:102), money captured the power of the system at work in the sugar cane fields. This is why many Toba actively speculated on the actual *origins* of money and the wealth of the do'okohé. Some of these speculations were shaped by their memories of President Perón.

Money Factories

Several people told me that the reason Perón threw money away and gave away enormous amounts of goods during his government was that he owned a "money factory." In their eyes, this factory produced money in the same way the sugar mill in San Martín del Tabacal manufactured sugar: creating a commodity that was privately appropriated by its owner. Their experience at a privately owned plantation informed their perception that money *had* to be produced and appropriated according to the principles of private property. This view also implied a fetishization of "factories" as extraordinary machineries of steel that produce wealth independently of human labor. These connections between money, state power, and factories made some Toba conclude that in order to be president of Argentina it is crucial to own this money factory. Mariano narrated a particular version of Perón's political career in which this factory not only enabled him to become president but also allowed Carlos Menem (president of Argentina between 1989 and 1999) to succeed him: "The story goes that Perón had a money factory. And Perón had a lot of money. Then, when there was a vote, he was elected to be the government. Since he had that money factory, he was going to govern, to govern all the people. When he died, they say that Menem became president. They say that Menem stole that money factory from him."

A remarkable feature of these narratives is that they momentarily dispel the ideological fetishization of money as a free-floating and self-reproductive entity; rather, they tie money to *production* and also to the amalgamation between private property (the ownership of the factory) and the state (the rise to power of different presidents). Put another way, these accounts ground the power of money in a central authority outside money itself: the state (Taussig 1997:137), personified in our case in the figure of Perón. A further characteristic of these memories is that they ground money production in particular places. There is some disagreement among the Toba as to the precise location of this factory. Some people locate it in Buenos Aires yet others argue that it is "up in the mountains," near the sugar plantations. This factory was therefore part of a landscape spatially and socially distant from the Chaco and marked by the patrones' most prominent symbols of power. The refinery at Tabacal added a deadly element to this location, for it was the home of the diablo that reproduced Patrón Costas's wealth. It was also the model most Toba would use to imagine other factories. Some people, for instance, told me that the KiyaGaikpí were rich because they owned a "salt factory" in the mountains. Factories became a dazzling symbol of power, as mesmerizing as the image of Juan Domingo Perón stepping off the train and throwing away thousands of coins.

We Didn't Understand the Money

Despite people's detailed memories of that event, President Perón never visited San Martín del Tabacal. Yet in the campaign for the 1951 presidential election — when Perón was running for reelection — several trains went all around Argentina with government officials throwing money and gifts to the crowds, a practice customary during the Peronist government (Pavón Pereyra 1974:68). These officials usually combed their hair like Perón and were surrounded by impressive paraphernalia: large pictures of Perón, the symbol of the Peronist Party, and banners with the slogan *Perón Presidente*. One of these trains, called "Eva Perón Sanitary Train," arrived at San Martín del Tabacal on October 28, 1951, a few days before the election.[1]

This train's appearance most likely triggered great expectations at the chance of seeing the distant president from Buenos Aires, about whom most Toba knew very little. Tomás told me, remembering the day they saw Perón: "You know, we didn't know Perón. Perón arrived at the Tabacal plantation. I didn't know who Perón was." In fact, situations like this were then widespread in Argentina, and people often "saw" Perón and Evita in places they never went to (Eloy Martínez, personal communication 1997). The memory of Perón arriving in the ingenio is significant not because of the gap between the Toba subjective experience of the event and the identity of the man who originated that shower of coins. Memories like this are significant because of the meanings they convey to people in the present. The recollection of their desperation at reaching for those coins, the fact that they gathered them like "hens" running after "corn" or "candies," uncovers not only the wealth they associated with the plantation but also that they felt alienated from it.

Fascination and estrangement went hand in hand in the Toba experience of San Martín del Tabacal and this amalgamation was epitomized in the arreglo grande. I believe I only understood what many Toba might have felt at that moment one day in October 1995 when I was chatting with Tomás. We were drinking mate under the shade when he said, all of a sudden: "Gastón, I wanted to ask you something." I said, "Sure, go ahead." Tomás thought about the question for a few seconds: "Could you explain to me the difference between a ten peso note and a one hundred peso note?" I remember the shivers going down my spine, my initial confusion, and the disturbing, sad illumination at the taken-for-granted forms of power associated with knowledge such as this. While I clumsily tried to explain the difference, I asked Tomás : "So, what did you guys do when you were paid at the ingenio?" He replied: "Oh, we never understood how much we were being paid. That was for sure something we never understood, how much they were paying us per day, in pesos." I asked him whether the capitanes or the lenguaraces understood. "They didn't understand either. . . . But since people got many things, they were happy."

The use of money requires mastering a historically specific skill: a capacity to read its public, standard value. In the 1990s this was a skill that most Toba, especially young people, had already learned. Tomás, nonetheless, was a living reminder that decades earlier most Toba were innumerate and unable to decipher the value of money. This situation made them easy prey of the administration and the employees in charge of paying them.[2] Even though most people remember the final payment with excitement, for decades most of them did not know how much money they were being paid. The confusion they must have felt at that moment resonates with what Marx wrote in his youth about the dazzling power of money: "Since money, as the existing and active concept of value, confounds and exchanges everything, it is the universal *confusion and transposition* of all things, the inverted world, the confusion and transposition of all natural and human qualities" (1964:193, emphasis in original). The fact that most Toba were innumerate increased this "confusion and transposition" to the point that for them the peso was a unit of currency that, rather than an objectification of both quantitative and qualitative values (Weiss 1997:352), was a ghostly, obscure, disturbing entity. Segundo told me about the work at the ingenio: "They paid nicely, but we didn't understand the money. I didn't know. One month I was paid three million pesos. Another month I got five hundred." This account expresses not only that most Toba were cheated on the sum paid to them but also that at that moment they were torn between fascination ("they paid nicely") and puzzlement ("we didn't understand the money"). It also illustrates that it was hard for them to grasp the actual meaning of concepts such as "millions," "thousands," or "hundreds" and that they often confounded and intermixed them.

The fact that people remember that in those days they "didn't understand the money" marks a further aspect of their experience at the ingenio: money often seemed an entity with a life of its own, moving from one place to another and breeding more money, independently of human labor and social relations of production. As Taussig points out (1980), these narratives are common in other parts of Latin America and bring to light forms of fetishism and "magic" deeply embedded in capitalist culture. They also re-create the view that the power of money seems to emanate "not from the system . . . of circulation but from the physical substance of money itself" (Taussig 1997:133). In the Toba case, these accounts stand in tension with those of the money factories in that they *sever* money from its conditions of production. At San Martín del Tabacal, most Toba felt they were unable to have access to this type of money. Many people associate the latter, first, with white men from distant regions, "magicians" or "artists" with shamanic powers who on Sundays performed tricks to entertain workers. Their most remarkable skill involved the creation of money out of other objects or simply out of thin air. When people recall these acts, most give the impression that they watched them in awe, as perplexed and passive spectators. Ernesto did not see these "magicians" but heard about them from his father. Even though he is a teaching assistant, he expressed frustration for being "poor" and not knowing how to create money that way: "They are white people from the ingenio. They were young, some had a beard, and they say they were like magicians. . . . First, they pulled out a white paper and then they transformed it. And a brand new bank note appeared. They also took one [bill] from their sneakers. One of them put the hand there and brand-new bank notes came out. . . . They say it's all like that. . . . How come? I wish that I, being poor, could be like that. I don't know how this can be." According to other people, these men could produce peso notes out of various objects: burned paper, eggs, or playing cards. They could also make money breed more money, by turning, for instance, a simple coin into thousands of pesos. There was a further feature of this money: after a purchase, it returned to its owner, bringing more money with it.

Many Toba remember that this peculiar type of money could also be found in boxes buried in the plantation surroundings and up in the mountains. Thin yellow flames marked their location, a view widespread in the San Francisco River Valley and other parts of Latin America (cf. Crain 1991:76). People call these boxes "the gold" (el oro) and associate them with the mountain devils; they also agree that no Aborigen was ever able to find them and that only bold Criollo and Guaraní workers discovered them and "became rich." In San Martín del Tabacal, only once was a Toba man able to see, from the distance, the thin flame marking "the gold." However, when he got closer he lost sight of it. Tomás argued that no Toba ever found those fabulous boxes and added: "That's because we don't know that money of gold. We don't know it. We don't have knowledge. We don't have knowledge."

This image of money with a life of its own draws elements from capitalist culture and ideology: the idea that capital breeds capital independently of human labor. The fascination with this magical production of wealth is also the fascination with the recurrent, and recurrently postponed, promise of bourgeois ideology: that ordinary people can become rich. Yet in its implicit association with devils, this type of money has for many Toba negative, unnatural connotations. And the frustration and awe it evokes in current memories uncovers the estrangement that pervaded their work in the cane fields. In sum, despite remembering that they returned "rich" from San Martín del Tabacal, most people were aware, often under a foggy light, that the secret to the do'okohé's wealth was unknown to them. This is why many try to counter this estrangement through attempts to understand that wealth's origin: through references to Patrón Costas's pact with the Familiar, money factories, the power of white men to create money out of thin air, or boxes with money that breeds money. Yet these attempts at explanation are more often than not fetishized accounts that sever the creation of wealth from their labor and increase their sense of distance from the plantation's wealth, seemingly within their reach but shining beyond an abyss they were unable to cross. In the 1990s people also remembered that, in the midst of these experiences, every evening the Aborígenes claimed the lotes as places of their own.

II

"Dancing, Dancing, Dancing"

When we arrived at the ingenio, the dancing started right away.

—Tomás, 1996

I was sitting with five or six men, sharing a mate gourd in the shade on one of those Chaco summer afternoons swept by the oppressive heat of the north wind. We were in El Potrillo, seventy kilometers northwest of the Toba villages, where a contingent of about sixty Toba and I had gone for the weekend (on a slow journey on a tractor trailer) to participate in a religious meeting hosted by Wichí Anglicans. We were having a break from the long (and for me exhausting) meetings in the church, and a Wichí man they all knew joined our round of mates. Soon they all began remembering San Martín del Tabacal, where they had originally met and where they had worked together for many years. At one point, the Wichí man monopolized the conversation and began remembering the dancing that all of them, Wichí and Toba, performed every evening. Standing in front of us, with a smile on his face, he imitated the dancing rhythm. His arms stretched as if he were holding the waists of two other people. He then imitated somebody shaking a gourd. The laughter was general. My Toba companions, most of them in their fifties, followed the performance with spontaneous smiles. While laughing, some looked at the ground and shook their heads repeatedly. None of them said a word. They just laughed.

A special mood emerged out of that circle of men remembering a practice central in their youth but that now seemed so distant, so removed from that hot afternoon of February 1996, as they were commemorating the Christian values received from the British missionaries. It was as though the silent smiles indicated a subtle complicity with "youth sins" that were at odds with the Anglican values they were now observing and that reminded them how much they had changed since those days. That uncomfortable silence also illustrated that the nomí made the ingenio a place defined in opposition to the Christian morality that ruled Misión El Toba. The forms of contention connecting both places are this chapter's main theme.

The Dance of the Aborígenes

Most Toba remember San Martín del Tabacal as a place that produced multiple forms of excess: excess of disease, death, and terror, excess of commodities and wealth, and excess in the search of bodily pleasure, typified in the evening dances and the casual sexual intercourse that followed. Recreated within one place, these expressions of excess cannot be fully understood without reference to each other.

The dances at the lotes were not the recreation of a "traditional" Toba practice in a new place; rather, they were a product of the labor experience in kahogonaGá. The nomí was originally a Chorote dance, and, as a result of the intense interethnic socialization in the plantations, other Aborígenes soon adopted it. By the early twentieth century, most groups of the Pilcomayo practiced the nomí in the ingenios and in the Chaco. In October 1932, Bishop E. Every (1933:126) visited Misión El Toba when Alfred Leake was on leave. Probably because of Leake's absence, men danced near the station. Every described their dancing with erotic overtones, suggestive of the missionaries' fascination with the Toba and, paradoxically, with the practices they were trying to disallow: "It was a wonderful sight, these tall graceful men, in headdress, blankets, belts, anklets, moving in perfect time to rhythmical chants. A circle seemed the favourite figure. There must have been fifty or sixty taking part, and the effect in the moonlight was extraordinarily attractive, suggestive of the grace and strength of manhood."

As a result of the ban imposed by the missionaries, most Toba stopped dancing in their lands shortly after. This moral discipline at home gave new meanings to the migrations to the ingenio, for the lotes became the only place where people could dance openly and unmolested. Further, at the plantation, unlike the nomí previously conducted at home, they danced mingling with Wichí, Chorote, Nivaclé, and Pilagá men and women. Consequently, the nomí became a crucial site in the production of an ethnicized class identity. As some Toba put it, it was "the dance of the Aborígenes." Dancing was their *own* way of marking ethnic differences vis-à-vis

37. Dancing in San Martín del Tabacal.
Archivo General de la Nación, Buenos Aires.

other workers and affirming their status as Aborígenes working under similar conditions.

The main dancers were single men and the nomí was for them, first and foremost, a way of seducing females.[1] As Patricio put it: "We danced in order to make women fall in love and sleep with us." This required an aesthetic arrangement of their bodies according to ethnic markers that contrasted with the appearance of those same bodies while working in the fields. Men took off their working clothes—pants and shirts—and put on the clothing that symbolized their aboriginality: the chiripa, in itself a product of the ingenios. They painted their faces and parts of their bodies in red and black. Some rubbed their skin with the leaves of a plant known for its power to seduce members of the opposite sex. Many wore anklets and necklaces. This production and affirmation of aboriginal bodies was a remarkable counterpoint to the gradual transformation of their bodily subjectivity and their own interest in acquiring Criollo attire at the arreglo grande. More important, this affirmation of aboriginal bodies reminded people of their common origins in the Chaco; it symbolized an aboriginality produced by the class experience in the ingenio yet also anchored elsewhere: in the bush and the Anglican missions where Toba, Wichí, and some Chorote were induced to abandon those same practices.

38. "We chose. Women looked for a husband." *Photo by author.*

The nomí consisted of a group of men grabbing each other's waists and moving in circles, usually slowly and then more rapidly (see Nordenskiöld 1912:76). Sometimes they formed a straight row that moved back and forth. Dancing was accompanied with the singing of wordless songs, led by the *canchero* or person of the *cancha* (dance field). The latter was often a Chorote, a good singer who was followed by dozens, hundreds of howling throats. Women played an important role in the nomí, for they took the initiative to start intercourse. They watched the dancers, approached them from behind, and grabbed the men of their choice, dancing with them or taking them out of the round. Occasionally, women slipped in and danced side by side with men (see Nordenskiöld 1912:78; Trinchero and Maranta 1987:82–83, n. 9).

In their memories of the casual sex that followed the dancing, many Toba give the image of an uncontrolled promiscuity. This memory is often shaped by the contrast between that behavior and the more restrained sexual practices of the present. In 1996 Mariano remembered: "People danced. You grabbed a woman and slept just one night. A woman grabbed a man and they slept together one night. It wasn't like it is now. Now you live as a married person. . . . Back then, some men had two women. Some women had two or three men. And they sang and sang." The memory of one-night stands is often followed by comments on how men and women from different groups, as some put it, "got mixed up."[2] Mariana remembered how women chose their partners and got involved with men from various groups: "We chose. Women looked for a husband. If they liked someone, they caught him right there. Right there, they got married. Some women married Chorote. Some married Wichí. Some got together with Pilagá." These memories illustrate that sex in the lotes became a productive force, in a Foucauldian sense. The permanent coupling of Wichí, Toba, Pilagá, Chorote, and Nivaclé bodies blurred distinctions among them and affirmed that at the ingenio they were one and the same: Aborígenes. This making of aboriginal bodies also defied the moral values preached by the missionaries at home. This is why the nomí rapidly became a heated arena of contestation, which condensed much of the cultural and spatial politics of missionization.

Forgetting and Remembering the Mission

In the 1990s many Toba remembered dancing in the ingenio as a symbol of their disobedience of the rules demarcated by Alfred Leake. The nomí turned the plantation into a place free of missionary surveillance that countered and even erased what they had learned at Misión El Toba. Patricio told me that in the ingenio "people sang with gourd, the devil's singing. Everybody sang. Nobody remembered God, nothing, because there was no missionary." Significantly, at the ingenio "nobody remembered God" not because they had forgotten the mission but because they *remembered* the forms of control imposed on them there. As part of the tensions fostering their experiences of locality, most Toba pretended to comply with missionary standards at Misión El Toba yet in the cane fields produced what could be called a "hidden transcript" of disobedience (see Scott 1990). Late in 1995, Tomás remembered with a smile on his face how at the mission they "hid" that they had danced in the ingenio and how they "deceived" the missionaries by doing that:

> At the ingenio, people were the worst. Many people: Pilagá, Chorote, Chulupí, Mataco. They were the worst. People were all mixed up. A lot of dancing: all night long, every night. . . . We hugged. We did a large round. That's what we did when we worked. Not anymore. We're used to the church. . . . When we returned [from the ingenio] to the mission, we didn't do it anymore. You had to hide it. We hid it. When they took the people out of the mission and we arrived at the ingenio, the dancing

started right away. When we returned we hid it, because the missionary
was there already [He smiled]. People deceived the missionaries with
that, with the dancing.

The missionaries were aware that the ingenio was a place that undermined their authority and that stood in sharp contrast with the controlled
space of the mission. Missionaries complained frequently about the "negative" influence of the plantations and some even defined the latter as
"Satan's playground" (Fox 1958:24). In 1938 Dora Tebboth wrote shortly
after a massive departure for the ingenio: "I hope those Christians who
have gone will keep straight, for it is awful to hear some of the things these
Indians get up to at the cane-fields" (Makower 1989:108). Because of these
perceptions, Alfred Leake and his colleagues tried to stop the dancing in
the cane fields through different means. While the Toba were in their villages, the missionaries frequently preached about the evils of dancing and
casual sex in the ingenio. Yet people remember that this preaching was
not effective and that they would dance again as soon as they arrived in
Tabacal. The missionaries also counted on the influence of the Toba evangelists who migrated to the plantation (Tebboth 1943:37). This implied an
attempt to impose within the lotes the norms that ruled public behavior
at the mission. When remembering the evangelists' work, however, most
Toba emphasize that they simply ignored them. According to Emiliano:
"There was a preacher in the ingenio. At five in the afternoon, he rang the
bell to preach." He raised his hand and imitated somebody hitting a bell:
"Tin, tin, tin." Emiliano smiled and went on: "But not many people arrived, because they were dancing already. Only two arrived. People didn't
pay attention. They just danced; they liked it a lot. They didn't want to listen to the word of God. They were just dancing all the time. It seems that
they didn't listen to the bell." The lotes, in other words, were places so
potently immersed within their own norms and practices that any attempt
to re-create strict Anglican values within them was doomed to fail.

Facing these problems in their ability to restrain Toba bodies, every
year some missionaries visited the plantation. These trips were brief but
spatially significant; they were attempts to counter the ingenio's "lawless-
ness" through the direct presence of the authority figures that shaped daily
life at Misión El Toba. On these visits, the missionaries' commanding presence caused many Toba to approach them, greet them, and ask for news
from home (Leake 1940:9). Yet in the mid-1990s people remembered that

these visits were very short, lasting one or two days, and that at night, when the missionaries had left the lotes, they danced anyway.

This spatialized process of contestation lasted for decades and turned the plantation and the mission into places defined in contrast with each other. When hundreds of Toba arrived at the mission station after spending eight to ten months in a place free of missionary control, this contrast became particularly apparent and many found it hard to readapt to Anglican morality. The missionaries often lamented that people who left to Tabacal as "faithful Christians" returned as "sinners" who temporally tested and challenged mission rules (see Leake 1944:11).

As part of these negotiations, resistances, and adaptations, many Toba continued dancing until their last migrations to the ingenio. By then, dancing had adopted new bodily expressions. As new generations took to the dance floors, they gradually gave up body painting and the chiripa and during their last labor seasons most men danced wearing working clothes. The end of these migrations also meant the nomí's end. Dancing was by then deeply embedded in a particular place, the lotes of Tabacal, and when the migrations came to an end people lost that particular place of socialization of which the nomí was a particular product. In the early 1970s Ledesma and San Martín del Tabacal recruited small groups of Toba for only two months. Those were the last times they worked at the sugar plantations, and those who went agree that on those occasions they did not dance. Being a central component of their experience at kahogonaGá, the nomí came to an end together with that whole period in Toba historical experience.

When in the mid-1990s people remembered the dancing and casual intercourse at San Martín del Tabacal, some seemed to have mixed feelings about them. On the one hand, many people, including committed Anglicans, clearly enjoyed telling me how they danced and sang despite the missionaries' efforts to halt them. Some of them smiled at the image of themselves disobeying Alfredo in their youth, as if the nomí reminded them of their ability to create places of autonomy from him. On the other hand, most people were quick to note that the nomí was somewhat sinful and highlighted how much they had changed. As Emiliano put it: "When I was young, I did dance. Now I've already changed. I stopped drinking. I stopped talking no sense. I always pray to God. When I'm sick, I pray to God." These ambiguously repentant memories of past bodily excesses are signs of the resistances that decades ago linked the lotes to Misión El

Toba. Yet the nomí was more than an expression of rebelliousness. Anchored in San Martín del Tabacal, dancing was immersed within an overall experience of alienation, disease, and death.

Partying Until They All Die

The fact that Toba men and women danced in the same lotes where they felt haunted by diablos and where children died by the score made the nomí a practice fully immersed within a collective experience of alienation. It is certainly tempting to argue that, in addition to defying the missionaries, the nomí counteracted this alienation. After all, "the dance of the Aborígenes" was a collective assertion of vitality, sensuality, and ethnic pride that contrasted with the disease, exploitation, and ethnic denigration imposed on them. It was also a commemoration of other landscapes; a bodily statement that they did not forget they were Aborígenes. Through dancing, people also asserted relative control over the place where they temporarily lived and drew a line between the lote as a place of sexual excess and the rest of the ingenio as a place of work.

Yet this line was tenuous. The lotes' excesses were also the product of the plantation's alienating geography, and it would be misleading to see the nomí as an everyday form of resistance to exploitation. The administration tolerated the nomí and did not see it as a threat to labor discipline. People agree that they danced unmolested and many remember that foremen, administrators, and white visitors often came to "see" and "take pictures" of their dances. In the eyes of the administration, dancing most probably confirmed the Aborígenes' exoticism and sensual savagery and therefore their lowly status within the plantation's labor hierarchy. And for the Aborígenes, dancing was inseparable from their experience of trabajo. Because of the intense dancing and intercourse, people remember that they had little sleep and that the most enthusiastic dancers were unable to complete the tarea the following day. As a result, they earned few goods at the arreglo. More important, some remember that the bodily intensity that filled the lotes with sweat in the evening was part of the same movement that during daytime exhausted those same bodies in the fields. Andrés told me that when they were at Tabacal, they had "two jobs": "At the ingenio, there was dancing, dancing, dancing. That's why many times I say to my son: When I was young, when I worked in the ingenio, I had two trabajos. At night, there was dancing. At night I had another job: the nomí. We only slept for two hours. . . . Old people didn't dance. They were quieter. But since we were young, we worked again during the night. It was so incredible, che!" That unrestrained search for bodily pleasure was still part of an overall experience of labor. Andrés could not have been clearer: at night, they also worked. This metaphor suggests that, as in their tareas, there was something compulsive and repetitive about dancing. The nomí, despite its critical components, was still caught up in an overall bodily experience of estrangement.

In the late 1960s a Wichí living on the Bermejo River had an apocalyptic vision about the sugar plantations. He dreamed that the Wichí were to be taken on a final trip to the ingenios where they were to dance to death: "They will party all the time until they all die" (Pagés Larraya 1982, 2:257). This vision made explicit that those dances were not unrelated to the death toll decimating scores of Aborígenes in the cane fields. The nomí was a protest against alienation but also an expression of alienation. Toba resistance to exploitation surfaced in other, more openly political practices, through which individually or collectively, spontaneously or premeditatedly, people tried to undermine the plantation's seemingly unshakable power.

"We Didn't Go on Strike"

In reality one can "scientifically" foresee only the struggle,
but not the concrete moments of the struggle, which cannot but be
the results of opposing forces in continuous movement.
— Antonio Gramsci, *Prison Notebooks*

When Antonio Gramsci (1971:438) wrote that it is not possible to foresee the contours struggles will adopt, he nevertheless warned that one
can anticipate "the struggle": that is, that conditions of oppression will
generate forms of accommodation and resistance. This means that the
alienation examined in previous chapters did not prevent most Toba from
turning the ingenio into a contested place, the result "of opposing forces
in continuous movement." Edward Thompson (1966) has argued that
political agency is not the result of preconstituted subjects that "then"
act but, rather, that social subjects are constituted *through* struggle. Current memories of San Martín del Tabacal indicate that the Toba were
configured as Aborígenes through forms of contestation that — as Michel
Foucault (1990:95) would argue — were not in a position of exteriority to
the plantation's power; in other words, their resistances were inseparable
from their position as an ethnicized underclass and their internalization
of Patrón Costas's paternalism. This is why their political practice challenged the administration's power but also confirmed that the plantation
was a place alien to them. In this chapter, I examine how current memories illustrate this point.

The Grace of God: The Capitanes and Patrón Costas

People remember that they put forward demands to the plantation administration especially through direct interactions with Patrón Costas. These
demands took advantage of his frequent visits to the cane fields, which

led one of his biographers to write that "he was like the grace of God, for he was everywhere" (Aráoz 1966:61). Some Toba emphasize that the capitanes and lenguaraces often *made* Patrón Costas listen to their requests. Mariano remembered that a lenguaraz once made the patrón's car stop by throwing his hat on the road. Then he "talked, and talked, and talked" asking for new pieces of clothing because their working clothes were in rags. According to Mariano, "the boss" Costas replied: "All right. Tomorrow I'll send a telegram in order to give you these clothes." This type of interaction recreated the aura of benevolent paternalism associated with Patrón Costas, reinforced by the memories claiming that he protected their ancestors from the army. Some people, in this regard, take pains to exonerate their main patrón from exploitative conditions and point out that only the foremen mistreated workers. As Mariano's account reflects, some maintain that Patrón Costas was immediately willing to abide by Toba requests, as if they needed to emphasize their agency and counter their own memories of powerlessness at the ingenio.

In those days, capitanes and lenguaraces had vested interests in prioritizing these face-to-face demands over collective struggles. They benefited from a higher salary and their occasional dealings with Patrón Costas contributed to increasing their prestige. Yet when the tarea was difficult to complete they were under pressure to lead more forceful forms of protest. In these cases, people stopped working, usually only for a few hours, while the capitán and the lenguaraz complained to the administration, preferably to Patrón Costas himself. Gervacio remembered: "Sometimes we stopped working, for the work was very heavy and they paid little. It wasn't worth it for us. And we complained. But we complained directly to the patrón. The patrón said: 'Yes, no problem. We're going to pay.' Yes. They gave a raise." Once again, the patrón is remembered as casually and rapidly conforming to their demands, as if the heavy workload and little pay were simply a matter of miscommunication. Yet most Toba would not call these actions strikes. For them, a strike or *huelga* was a bolder, better-organized protest run by more knowledgeable workers.

The Rich, They Went on Strike

The internalization of the social distance separating Aborígenes from other workers severely hindered joint forms of struggle. When I asked people about huelgas in San Martín del Tabacal, most answered that they

39. "Round of Indians" in San Martín del Tabacal, 1923.
Archivo General de la Nación, Buenos Aires.

did not participate and transmitted the sense that strikes were alien to them. Tomás expressed this very clearly: "When the union protested, we the Aborígenes had nothing to do with it. We had nothing to do with it." The reason for this was almost unanimous: they did not have ID papers, documentos. Without documentos, the Toba lacked full citizenship rights and, in addition to not being registered voters, could not join the union. But people remember the lack of documentos as an ontological condition with deeper social implications, which confirmed their inferior status as Aborígenes. Because of this experience, currently many Toba fetishize documentos as state-sanctioned pieces of paper that grant not only citizenship rights but also basic human and social rights. This is why many people remember their lack of documentos as a paralyzing, disarming experience, which prevented them from having the right to protest.

Many Toba give another reason for not striking: they were too poor to afford it. Some remember strikes as a luxury of privileged workers like the Bolivians or the Criollos, who had enough money to buy food while not working. Toba men and women received money for their daily food plate only on completing their tarea, and the prospect of losing this meal was a particularly strong deterrent against strikes. This fear was clearly expressed by Mariano. He told me that they did not go on strike, and when I asked him why, he said: "Because if we went on strike, what were we going to eat? We didn't have money. The Bolivians went on strike because they have money saved. They had union. We didn't because we didn't have documentos. None of us had documentos. We were working as if we were minors." Paradoxically, Bolivian workers were not Argentinean citizens either and, as a result, also lacked documentos; further, they maintained a certain distance from the Criollo-led union (Whiteford 1981:65–67). Yet because many Toba remember the differences between Aborígenes and other workers as part of an insurmountable divide, they usually lump Bolivians and Criollos together within the same group. And they often refer to this divide using an ethnicized language of class, which separated "the poor" (the Aborígenes) from "the rich" (well-off workers).

Memories of strikes, in sum, are informed by the estrangement created by the lack of documentos and their distance from the workers who organized them. One afternoon in July 1996, as we were chatting about the ingenio, Patricio told me that the Toba "didn't go on strike" and that the Kollas did. When I asked him why, he replied: "We didn't because we're another race; because back then the Toba didn't have documentos. . . . Everybody was working as if they were ignorant. They didn't have papers. Patrón Costas taught them not to get involved, so that they were not hungry. The rich had things already. Then they went on strike. They already had something to spend." Somewhat confused by his explanation, I asked him whether the Bolivians were rich. His reply emphasized what for him was obvious: "Ooh! Not only the Bolivians! The Catamarqueños, Riojanos, Tucumanos, Santiagueños. They were the ones who went on strike." Whereas the administration produced and read differences within the work force through the lens of ethnicity, many Toba read those ethnic differences through the lens of class, capturing the class elements behind the production of ethnicity at the ingenio yet also reproducing the divisions created by the administration among workers (which in this case were also racialized; "we're another race"). Patricio's account also reveals the political implications of their respect for Patrón Costas's authority. The administration often succeeded not only in keeping the Aborígenes away from organized protests but also in using them to break huelgas. Many people remember that foremen told them to cut cane only when the cane cutters were on strike, and that, as a result, gendarmes often stood nearby "to protect them" from union activists.

Despite their unwilling role as strike breakers, many Toba remember *el sindicato*, the union, with admiration. Whereas other plantation workers saw the union as a "sold out" and bureaucratic institution (Whiteford 1981:65–67), most Toba remember it as the epitome of radicalism. Many were particularly impressed by the union's ability and boldness to challenge the administration. Hernán, a man in his forties who was in Tabacal as a boy, told me about the Bolivian cane cutters who in his eyes were part of the union: "They knew the work. They didn't forgive the government of the ingenio." In addition, the memory of huelgas takes many Toba back to the times of Juan Domingo Perón. Old men, for instance, remember the violent strikes that shook Ledesma in February 1946, weeks before Perón was first elected president and when they were working at that ingenio (Rosenzvaig 1995:35; Nelli 1988:43). Those strikes were part of the popular mobilizations that accompanied Peron's rise to power, and even though the Toba did not participate, many recall that it was then that they learned through other workers that, as Marcelino put it, "the people's government was coming." Memories of huelgas, in this regard, transport many Toba back to their first acquaintance with wider struggles in Argentina and ground their current political identity as *peronistas* in the ingenio's geography.

The respect for the union also emerges in the memory of the few occasions in which, setting their reticence aside, they joined cane cutters in their huelgas. Some remember those moments as if striking were a question of pride. As Pablo put it: "It wasn't that we worked just like that, that easily, without protesting." These huelgas were organized to oppose high prices in the stores and demand salary increases, yet many agree that they did not understand much of what was going on and that those who directed the strike were from el sindicato. I was talking in 1997 with Angélica and her husband Horacio about their experiences at San Martín del Tabacal, and she was complaining about women's low salaries. Horacio added:

> That's why we went on strike. Fortunately, there were many sindicatos.
> . . . Like the Bolivians, they had sindicato. When the Bolivians went on strike, they came where we were [and said] . . . "You have to go on strike so that we get a raise." . . . They went directly to talk to our capitán to let him know, so that people went on strike. Around eight or nine in the evening, our cacique shouted: "Tomorrow, nobody has to move! Today the sindicato came [and they told me] that there has to be a strike like theirs. They're on strike." The following day, nobody moved. If we were lucky we suffered only for one day, for we didn't eat. Or for two days. What could we do? We didn't work until they made a deal, until the Bolivians made a deal. And we did too.

For many Toba, their involvement in strikes confirmed how little they knew about them and how dependent they were on the union leadership.

This attitude was not simply the result of their "lack of consciousness," a consciousness often contrasted to an ideal type of "fully conscious" social actor that rarely exists in history (Dunk 1991; see Comaroff and Comaroff 1991:29; Malkki 1995:238, 242). On the contrary, most Toba were well aware of the ingenio's fields of power and their subordinate subject position as Aborígenes within it, as an underclass submitted to such conditions that made other workers look rich in comparison. What many Toba often found politically paralyzing was the location of this experience at a place that, even if looking "as if they lived there," was alien to them. This attitude, as we have seen, was not synonymous with inaction. Ordinary men and women regularly tested and challenged the spatial boundaries imposed by the administration through their own (if individual and fragmented) practices of resistance, independently of capitanes, lenguaraces, and sindicatos.

Challenging the Ingenio's Geography

One of the most widespread everyday forms of resistance was *el chupe de caña*, cane chewing. Already in 1889 the Salta governor complained that indigenous workers "chew cane from dawn to dusk, with the result that one fifth of the harvest is lost in the Indians' insatiable stomach" (Schleh 1945:293). In San Martín del Tabacal, cane chewing was a tense arena of contention. The administration allowed this practice during harvest time but banned it while sugar cane was growing; in order to enforce the ban it deployed armed foremen (*chacareros*) mounted on mules who made regular rounds along the *callejones*: the corridors that cut across the cane fields every 100 meters. Many Toba remember that they defied the ban on a daily basis, mostly because they were hungry; they were poorly fed and needed extra sources of calories to complete the tarea. This is why trespassing into the cane fields was a survival strategy; yet it was a politically charged strategy, which challenged private property and tested the spatial reach of the administration's power.

Men and women usually set out to the cane fields in small groups after completing their tarea. They hid from the chacareros far from the callejones, chewed as much cane as possible, and cut heavy loads to take to the lote. Yet encounters with chacareros were common and people remember that some of them led to violent incidents, in which foremen shot at them. This reveals that many Toba regularly tested the margins of labor control and that cane chewing confronted them with the low rank and most visible agents of labor control. These confrontations also illustrate that the cane fields were one of the most contested places in the plantation: difficult to police because of their sheer size and particularly symbolic because they contained the ingenio's most valuable commodity: sugar cane.

This spatialization of labor discipline, accommodation, and resistance involved further forms of contention, some of which included shamanic interventions. Old people remember that on a few occasions the pioGonáq bewitched and killed abusive administrators. These shamans countered the ingenio's geography of power through stealth attacks on their bosses' homes that temporarily erased the spatial barriers separating Aborígenes and patrones. In 1996 Patricio remembered how a pioGonáq bewitched two powerful administrators: "Two died: Teófilo and Guillermo.[1] A Toba pioGonáq killed them. He bewitched them with his payák. . . . They say that Guillermo died all of a sudden. The payák stopped his heart. Teófilo also died all of a sudden. . . . I was in the ingenio. But the doctors didn't even know who the pioGonáq was. If the doctors knew, they'd have caused much trouble to the indios. Fortunately, the doctors didn't know." The fact that shamanic power was invisible to patrones and doctors added to its strength as a form of resistance, for it protected Aborígenes from retaliation. Yet this invisibility to white observers was also its political weakness, for shamanic actions were not part of a wider social unrest and their protest was not even registered as such by the administration (Gordillo 2003). The bewitching of patrones has a further spatial component; it was an attempt to use power originated in the Chaco, granted by bush devils, to counteract the plantation's power. This latent presence of their homeland in the ingenio was also a reminder that the bush was the only place where people could find a respite from exploitation.

Eating Fish all Day

Many Toba remember that quitting work and returning to the Chaco was a recurrent aspect of their experience in kahogonaGá. This action mobilized clusters of extended families tied by kinship or groups of single work mates. When people decided to leave, the capitanes and lenguaraces tried to get the administration to pay for their train ticket to Ingeniero

Juárez, a demand that was not always met. Since abandoning work implied losing what they had saved for the arreglo, it usually did not involve all Toba workers. Yet labor conditions were sometimes so harsh that, as some put it, "people didn't care" about losing it all. In the early twentieth century, these returns were often caused by violent incidents with foremen that triggered threats of military reprisal. In the following decades, an important reason for going back home was the "heavy work" required to finish the tarea. Mariano remembered one of those experiences: "Once, I returned here and quitted work. The work wasn't what it used to be. Before then, we worked well. But we did another work that wasn't good. It was a lot, a lot of work. People quitted work. The patrón came. He didn't want us to go. He said: 'Forgive me! Come back! Don't go!' But we left anyway." This account is notable because it hinges on the sudden reversal of power triggered by the decision to leave the ingenio. Mariano emphasized that they left ignoring the patrón's demands for forgiveness and that this decision empowered them. It did so because it made clear that the administration needed their labor and that, despite their poverty, they could temporarily break away from the plantation and rely on an alternative place.

Returning home following their own decision to do so, therefore, accentuated in people's subjectivity the factors that made the two places different from each other. Diego pointed to this contract when he remembered a massive return to the bush that took place sometime in the 1960s. The foreman had ordered that their tarea was to plant twenty furrows of sugar cane instead of the customary seven. People immediately complained that this tarea was "too heavy," almost impossible to complete, and half the group decided to quit work. Diego was among those who returned home. He remembered: "Those who stayed returned naked. Over here, I was eating fish all day." This contrast between workers who stayed in Tabacal and returned "naked" and people who had refused to abide by those terms and were at home "eating fish all day" is eminently spatial; it was fostered by the tensions making the ingenio a place of exploitation and the bush and the river places of abundance. In Diego's memory, this was also a tension producing different bodies, naked in the plantation and well-fed in the Chaco.

The resistances analyzed earlier in this chapter were attempts to influence the ingenio's fields of force. Quitting work, on the contrary, implied abandoning that struggle and at least in the short run the possibility of improving labor conditions. But this action had important implications in the making of places; it accentuated the contrast between the bush and the plantation and denaturalized the suffering inscribed in the latter. Returning home expressed an inability or unwillingness to endure oppression any longer but also a partial autonomy from the administration and the reliance on a place very different from kahogonaGá.

III

Foraging

Until the End

of the World

13

"We're Not Going to Die"

Desired transformations focus upon "healing" as a mode of repairing
the tormented body and, through it, the oppressive social order itself.
—Jean Comaroff, *Body of Power, Spirit of Resistance*

When Toba men and women remember San Martín del Tabacal, they
simultaneously create and undermine the spatial distance between that
place and the bush. Those memories accentuate what is distinctive about
their lands in opposition to the death, wealth, sexual excess, and political
estrangement of the cane fields; yet these memories also turn the ingenio,
made distant in time and space, into a presence *in* the bush. Memory
permanently recreates this tension between proximity and distance as it
configures localities as unstable processes. People told me myriad stories
about "the mountains" in a place, the bush, that was already the product
of previous, spatially inscribed memories of the plantation. This was also
a place in which Misión El Toba, which for decades played such a potent
role in their experience of the cane fields, had disappeared. In the 1990s
the remembrance of the ingenio continued shaping experiences of the
bush, directly through references to kahogonaGá and indirectly through
the sedimentation of those memories within Toba experiences of place, in
a process in which the thin line separating "memory" and "culture" tended
to disappear. In the chapters that follow, I analyze how the memories just
discussed, together with the memories of the mission, have become part
of a habitus grounded in the bush and in its production.

The making of places through practice and memory was already unfolding at the time of the migrations between the Pilcomayo and San
Martín del Tabacal. Benedict Anderson (1991:53–54), drawing on Victor
Turner (1974), has argued that movement between places is a meaning-
creating experience. I would add that journeys create meanings especially
because of the dialectic of memory and place they generate. In the Toba
case, when men and women returned to the Chaco at the end of the har-

vest, their experience of the bush, the river, and the mission station was haunted by the long months spent in kahogonaGá. Since disease epitomized the social strains of the ingenio, that collective experience of ailing bodies became particularly apparent once people arrived in the bush, a place where debilitating and alienating conditions were relatively absent. Likewise, when hundreds of Toba returned to San Martín del Tabacal, the memory of health in their lands informed their experience of disease at the plantation. Decades after these seasonal migrations came to an end, those memories still shaped the constitution of the bush. In this chapter, I analyze how these memories produce imageries of health and resilience about bush food, bush devils, and healing practices based on shamanism and the legacy of Anglican missionization. First, I examine how these perceptions are connected to the mourning that followed the return from the mountains.

Places of Mourning

When people remember mourning those who died in the ingenio, most of them ground this action in time and space: the moment when they returned home. This location confirmed that the bush was free of the horrors of the lotes and provided a solace where they could let go of the pain accumulated during the previous months. This mourning was triggered by the disturbing contrast between the number of those who had left for the ingenio and those who got back. Julián remembered that this contrast made people sing songs of grief at their now semi-empty homes:

> When people went to the ingenio, they took all the family. When they came back here, one was missing. Some lacked two, dead at the work in the ingenio. . . . Some people sang with a gourd because their grandchildren had died, or because their sons or daughters had died. They remembered them and then they sang when they got back here. . . . They were sad. They were sad. They were remembering their children, their grandchildren. They saw the house and the daughter or the grandchildren weren't there anymore. Then at night, they sang. At four in the morning, they also sang.

Julián illustrates that mourning was intrinsically tied to space and memory: to the contrast between, on the one hand, the absence of deceased relatives and, on the other, the memory that those people were once present in those same places. This contrast also indicates that when people left the bush they were healthy. After telling me that work in Tabacal killed "forty percent" of those who left, Ernesto, the school teaching assistant, said: "I remember one of my nephews. He was beautiful and big. When the mayordomo came, he left. When they came back, he didn't exist anymore." Memories like this are informed by the contradiction between leaving the bush and *not* returning. They evoke the ingenio as a presence made potent by its impact in the bush; furthermore, they highlight that the bush produced healthy bodies, "beautiful and big," that left only to be obliterated in San Martín del Tabacal. These properties of the bush as a place of health are culturally produced through explicit references about this place's contrast with the ingenio. Diego told me in 1995, comparing the plantation's illnesses with their healthy lives in the bush:

> In the ingenio there were all types of diseases. You didn't lack disease: coughing, fever, smallpox. That's why every time we arrived over there, they vaccinated on us [he looked at his arm]. But people got disease anyway. That's why many kids died, many grown-ups too. . . . The disease came from the mountain. . . . Here [in the bush], there's almost no disease. There's some, but after a little while it goes away. . . . In the ingenio, there were tons of illnesses. They didn't go away. Here in the bush, the disease doesn't show up. It seems that over here we don't have what they have over there.

"Over here" and "over there" are part of the same, tense spatial embrace. The reference to a bush where diseases "don't show up" can only be understood by its contrast to the memory of an ingenio where diseases were so embedded in the landscape that they "didn't go away." Yet as a result of this dialectic of absences and presences the bush became more than a source of health; it also became a place of healing and resilience.

Foraging, the Toba Are Invincible

Jean Comaroff (1985:9) has argued that everyday efforts to cope with experiences of domination tend to involve exertions to cure the physical body. She writes: "Not surprisingly, . . . desired transformations focus upon 'healing' as a mode of repairing the tormented body and, through it, the oppressive social order itself." In the Toba case, the return from the cane fields after long months of exploitation mobilized attempts to recon-

40. "The influence of the algarroba harvest." *Photo by author.*

stitute ailing bodies. This involved, first, the consumption of the bush's
most significant product: bush food.

While people were at San Martín del Tabacal suffering disease on a
daily basis, they tried to eat bush food as often as they could, especially fish.
The consumption of barbecued fish sent by relatives from the Pilcomayo
was spatially significant, for it was an attempt to recreate within the debilitating space of the plantation the nurturing properties of food gathered
in the Chaco. In Toba memories, the anxiety to eat bush food intensified
as the departure date drew near and their bodies were feeling the burden of months of work. "Around this time of the year," Diego told me in
October 1995, "people were already feeling flabby. They wanted to come
back. They were thinking they wanted to eat fish and honey." He also remembered that in the last stage of their journey back home people began
picking and chewing algarroba pods in an old hunting ground located a
few kilometers from Sombrero Negro. He added: "And we all chewed
algarroba until we arrived at the mission." For the men and women who
had spent eight to ten months at the foot of the Andes, their first act of
bodily reencounter with their lands, even before reaching their villages,
was to eat bush food. In the weeks following their arrival, the daily consumption of wild fruits allowed adults and children to gradually recover
strength. In 1938 a missionary at Algarrobal noticed that "pale, thin, weak
looking children" who had contracted measles in the plantations were re-
covering "under the influence of the algarroba harvest" (South American

41. "Foraging, the Toba are invincible."
Photo by author.

Missionary Society 1938:39). The return from the ingenio and the drastic change in people's diets, in other words, had a direct and visible impact on their bodies.

The annual recreation of this cyclical movement between a place of illness and a place of health left a deep mark on Toba subjectivity. If there is something that people emphasize when they talk about fish, honey, wild fruits, and game meat, it is that they are their most important guarantee of collective well-being. The memory of the ancient ones further enhances the ingenio's legacy, for people remember the yagaikipí as remarkably strong, healthy, and resilient because they only ate fish, honey, game meat, and fruits. These combined memories inform the idea that bush food is not just healthy but has healing properties. On several occasions, I noticed that ill people avoided eating store-bought food and requested that their relatives bring fish, honey, and bush fruits to them. Early in 1996 I was chatting with Andrés, and since he had been a farmer for many years I asked him whether he still ate fish. "I eat fish only when I get the flu," he replied. "Then I feel like eating fish. When I had the flu, I wanted to eat fish so badly!" This assertion by somebody who rarely goes fishing but worked in Tabacal in his youth reveals how memories have become part of a collective habitus: a taken-for-granted perception that ailing bodies can often be cured simply by consuming the most enduring products of their lands.

Since bush food was able to regenerate a social reproduction threatened by the ingenio's death toll, many Toba see this food as a source of collective resilience. In 1916, while reporting on the exploitation of indigenous labor, José Niklison wrote: "Foraging, the Toba are invincible" (1990:121). Like many Toba eighty years later, he anchored their "invincibility" in a practice defined in opposition to conditions of oppression. The resilience associated with marisca is rooted, first and foremost, in the fact that fish, honey, or wild fruits are always available to those in need, a feature that has made foraging malleable to conditions of poverty in different parts of the world.[1] This availability stands in contrast with the commodified character of store-bought food. Thus, emphasizing the class component of their aboriginality, many Toba refer to marisca as "the life of the poor" and call bush food simply "the food of the poor."[2] This is a class identity produced in the cane fields that turned the Toba into Aborígenes. Yet this is also a subject position grounded in the bush.

The resilience granted by "the food of the poor," in this regard, is at the core of the Toba's identity as Aborígenes. And in the dialectic between their poverty and their aboriginality, the poorest Toba know that the latter—with the reliance on the bush it implies—provides them with a hardened capacity to cope with poverty and suffering. Pablo told me, with a particularly intense tone: "Sometimes I hear they're going to make a war to kill those who have nothing, so that the Aborígenes die of hunger. Sometimes I say: We're Aborígenes. We're not going to die because we have the food from the bush. . . . I'm poor, but I'm not going to die because I have something to fish, to gather honey. . . . Of course we're not going to die!" Grounded in the memory of past experiences of violence and death in their lands and at the foot of the Andes, the "food from the bush" is the symbol of an ethnicized class position that protects the Aborígenes not just from death but also from attempts to murder "those who have nothing." And the basis of this resilience is that in fact those who "have nothing" actually *do* have something: the bush.

The sedimented memories of suffering informing perceptions of marisca, the bush, and bush food make many people project this resilience into the future. And this is a future still grounded in their lands. In my conversations with Angel, a man in his late thirties and a regular forager, he often made reference to the importance of marisca. His home overlooks the green edges of the marshes and, as we chatted on a hot summer afternoon, his children were sitting around us eating barbecued fish. We had just returned from a fishing trip and he told me:

> The Aborígenes live just like that, because that's our custom. I don't say just like that, for I call this security. Like the old man says, ours is the life of the poor, born without anything until the end of the world. The poor person goes on foraging all year long because he has nothing, because he doesn't use money all day long. . . . We have to go to the bush, for the life of the poor is like this, like the old man says. . . . Thus, we're going to live with this because we have nothing. We're going to forage until the end of the year, until the end of the world.

Angel made clear that marisca, "the life of the poor," is partially the result of material constraints that leave many people with no other choice but to go to the bush. Yet he was also emphasizing that foraging, rather than representing a frail social condition, provides them with a "security" that will allow them to live until the end of time. This collective resilience is the product of a long history that regenerated in the bush social relations and bodies torn by labor exploitation; yet this resilience has also been sustained by interactions with diablos noticeably different from the mountain devils. It is in those differences that bush devils carry the burden of the ingenio's memory.

Healing, Reciprocity, and the Bush Devils

For those who did not migrate to San Martín del Tabacal, news from the cane fields often arrived through the intervention of nonhuman forces from the bush. In September 1995 Javier was telling me about the knowledge current generations have lost, for example, the capacity to decipher the language of animals. He illustrated his point by telling me a story about Miguel, a pioGonáq who died in the 1950s. Miguel was once hunting with a group of men across the Pilcomayo, in the Paraguayan bush, when he heard the sound made by a fox. Javier added: "It was like a letter but there was no letter. But the pioGonáq understood." The fox told Miguel some tragic news: his son had died in San Martín del Tabacal. "And right there," Javier remembered, "everybody started crying." Shocked by the news, Miguel and the other hunters set out to return to Misión El Toba. Before crossing the river, Miguel received another message, this time from a bird. The bird confirmed the news about his son, as if it were "a telephone" and "all of them cried again." When they arrived at the mission, Miguel found a letter sent from the ingenio by his relatives. Yet he had already learned about his son's death through his power to communicate with animals, a capacity granted to him by a bush payák. In a reversal of the memories of the plantation, a bush devil helped Miguel mourn, deep inside the bush, a son slain by mountain devils.

By projecting images of death onto a distant place to the west, memories of the ingenio contribute to defining the meanings of the devils that inhabit the bush. Likewise, experiences with diablos in the bush make the memories of San Martín del Tabacal particularly striking. Condensing the different conditions of labor, estrangement, and control prevalent in the two places, this localization characterizes bush and mountain devils in contrast with each other. When talking about sorcery and the spirits that inhabit the bush, many Toba are quick to characterize the latter as sources of disease and malaise. Yet when they remember the death unleashed by the mountain devils, the bush devils pale in comparison. This contrast is so sharp that when I asked men or women to compare the two places they often argued that in the bush there are actually few or no devils, as if the contrast made bush devils fade. Laura, a woman in her late twenties, told me in 1996 what she had heard from her mother about the ingenio. I asked her whether there were diablos there and she said: "Oh, yes. There were tons of devils at the ingenio, because the mountains are very close. There, it was much more dangerous than here in this zone. There, [the devils] came out during the day, during the night. It was more dangerous than here." I asked her whether devils like those existed "around here." She said: "No. There's almost nothing here. There aren't stories of somebody seeing a payák on the road. But over there, yes." I put this question comparing the diablos "from around here" with those "over there" to several people. The answers were strikingly similar in downplaying the presence of devils in the bush, even if moments earlier the same people had referred to them. When comparing the two places, some people added: "It's quiet here."

The reciprocity relations that connect the bush devils with humans, a relationship absent in the plantations, are a major source of contrast between the two. This reciprocity is intimately linked to the acquisition of bush food and the social relations involved in the constitution of the bush

42. "I'm giving you all these tools so that you don't
lack anything to eat." *Photo by author.*

as a collective place. This relationship also makes many people attribute distinctive features to particular bush devils (as we shall see), an individualization absent in memories of the mountain devils. In Toba lands, the diablos can be active anywhere yet the bulk of their interaction with humans takes place in the bush. This is why many Toba also call devils *viágahik*, "bush wanderers." Even though devils can act during the day, they are most active at night.[3] The reciprocity linking them with humans involves primarily healing power, for bush devils are those who provide this power to shamans, who are usually men.[4]

The pioGonáq's practice has been strongly shaped by the legacy of Alfred Leake. In contrast to the mountain devils, people argue that bush devils teach the pioGonáq only to heal. In 1988 Celestino, a shaman then in his late sixties, imitated how a payák would lecture a *brujo* (shaman): "Now that you've got my power, you shall help your people. If a person is sick, you have to heal. You shall not kill. You shall love each other. You shall love your brother." Paradoxically, a shaman appropriated elements of the Christian morality preached by Alfredo to frame the practice the latter had opposed in most stark terms. In this regard, bush devils are often depicted not only as sources of health but also as moral figures that preach values of reciprocity, cooperation, and sharing. Many people agree that sorcery is often the result of the shamans' misuse of this power. This is why some argue that when a pioGonáq bewitches too many people his payák "doesn't like it" and can punish him with death.

Shamanic power is often transmitted from father to son (or grandson) but some men are offered healing powers by a payák in an encounter in the bush or through dreams. In the past, shamanic initiation required a prolonged stay in the bush. Once contacted by the payák, the chosen person had to live in isolation for weeks, fasting and singing until the devil's healing songs were revealed to him (Métraux 1937:176–77). Currently, most pioGonáq do not go through such an intense phase of initiation, yet the acquisition of healing power is still deeply associated with the bush and marisca. The diablos usually approach men who are frequent foragers, for, being bush creatures, they "like" men who spend a great deal of time wandering the bush. The first sign that a payák is interested in turning a forager into a shaman is that it becomes much easier for this person to capture prey. Tomás told me how a bush devil would approach a forager, emphasizing its teaching and helping attitude:

> For example, one day I go to the bush to look for honey and iguana. If I'm not lucky, the payák is around there. It hides. I don't see it, but it sees me. I find lachiguana, extranjera [types of honey], and iguana. I find all the bichos as if they were tame. The payák gives me all those bichos. . . . That's what it teaches. . . . [Then] it shows up like a man, like us [and says]: "Look, my son. I'm giving you all these tools, which are mine, so that you don't lack anything to eat, so that you can get anything from the bush." It gives me the power to eat everything from the bush. Everything. Then I already have the secret and all the bichos are tame. When I sleep at night, the payák comes over and we chat.

In accounts like this, the bush devils' action is guided by moral principles of generosity and kindness that involve, primarily, bush food. Tomás also made clear that bush devils may engage in long conversations with soon-to-be shamans, a communicative practice that accentuates familiarity and understanding. The healing properties grounded in the bush, in this regard, mobilize not only food production but also the action of bush devils.

For decades, the shamans' healing power was regularly tested and challenged in San Martín del Tabacal. Because of the absence of other healing alternatives, the pioGonáq were the only ones trying to cure the scores of people who fell ill. It was through them that the bush and plantation devils met and, in a way, clashed. The pioGonáq drew on the power of the bush devils in the Chaco to counter, at least partially, the deadly power of the mountain devils. In this struggle, shamans aimed at counteracting the estrangement permeating the ingenio as a whole, turning their power, in Jacques Chevalier's words (1982:423), into "a means of asserting their own dominance over the otherwise uncontrollable forces of natural and cultural oppression." In a process similar to that analyzed by Michael Taussig (1987) in Colombia, the terror of the cane fields fostered the healing aura of shamanism. People remember those shamans who served as capitanes in kahogonaGá as their most powerful brujos. Yet some also remember that while in the ingenio their power rested on their capacity to communicate with the bush devils back home. Carancho, one of the most prestigious Toba shamans, passed away in San Martín del Tabacal. Marcelino, his grandson, remembered that before dying he said: "It seems that the payák doesn't answer anymore. It doesn't answer anymore." The ingenio had severed Carancho from the Chaco not just geographically but also in his ability to communicate with the devil that was the source of his power.

The end of the migrations to the San Francisco River Valley deprived shamans of the place that nurtured their role as protective healers. The long-term influence of Anglican missionization and the emergence of new generations of leaders without shamanic powers, for their part, gradually weakened their political prestige. Since shamans charge expensive goods for their services (bicycles, shotguns, or portable stereos), in the 1990s the existence of alternative healing practices that are free, such as collective healing prayers or biomedicine, further debilitated their social capital as healers. Because of these different factors, people agree that shamans are currently less powerful than those of the past. Yet shamanism still mobilizes forces originating in the bush, which are intertwined with healing practices shaped by the legacy of Misión El Toba.

The Soul of a Soulless Condition

As discussed in chapter 5, many Toba saw the British missionaries and especially Alfred Leake as powerful healers. For this reason the mission emerged not only as a shelter from state terror and a place of social control but also as a healing place, where people countered the disease and death at San Martín del Tabacal. In 1996 Mariano remembered that a very high number of children, "I don't know how many," died in the ingenio. Two of his sons once became so ill there that the following year he decided to leave his wife and children at the mission station and to go to kahogonaGá alone. He explained why: "Because in Sombrero Negro there was no disease. It was very nice. There was no disease because the missionary was always there, praying in the morning, in the afternoon. He didn't stop praying. When there was a missionary, there was no disease because he always prayed." Paradoxically, the health shield created by the missionaries' powers temporarily blended the mission compound with the bush and the river, which were also being constituted as places of health and healing in their contrast with the ingenio. The tension between the station and the bush did not disappear, but the two places became part of a single geography that regularly reconstituted bodies shattered elsewhere.

In the mid-1990s, twenty years after the Pilcomayo washed Misión El Toba away, missionaries were no longer living in the area and new Toba generations had taken over tasks once carried out by Alfredo, mingling decades of Anglican socialization with their own experiences and memories. In my first visit to the area in July 1987, I was profoundly impressed by the collective healing sessions conducted every night a few meters away from the dispensary where my companions and I were staying. The meetings attracted the village's most devoted Anglicans, who surrounded the ill person and prayed aloud and with increasing force to the power of "Jesus," "God," and "God's Spirit" (see Bargalló 1992). Those sessions had begun only a few years earlier and some Toba Anglicans from other villages were wary of their shamanic reminiscences. Yet by the late 1990s similar healing groups had emerged in other hamlets. In the largest village, some people had even joined an indigenous Pentecostal church new to the area, the *Iglesia Evangélica Unida* (United Evangelical Church), which includes in its cultos ecstatic dancing and singing, absent in the more subdued Anglican healing sessions.[5]

Even though many people consult the Toba nurses appointed in the three largest villages and occasionally go to the Ingeniero Juárez hospital, most seek shamans and these healing groups for treatment of serious illnesses, most of which are inevitably attributed to sorcery. Anglican and Pentecostal groups, despite their differences, rely on the curing power of "Jesus" and "God" and on techniques with shamanic elements conducted collectively: the recuperation of the patient's soul (held by a payák through a shaman) and/or the extraction of alien objects from the body (sent by a pioGonáq).[6] More important, these groups place healing power in the hands of ordinary men and women and challenge the individual and male-centered expertise of shamans and medical doctors. Both groups are critical of the commodification of shamanism and biomedi-

43. Dancing at a healing session of the Iglesia Unida.
Photo by author.

cine and claim to help the poorest Toba, who cannot afford a brujo or the medicines required at the hospital. They also appropriate the legacy of Alfredo's healing power by turning it into a force grounded in their own villages and no longer restricted to a place run by missionaries.

It is often forgotten that in the same paragraph where Karl Marx referred to religion as "the opium of the people" he wrote: "Religious suffering is at the same time an expression of real suffering and a protest against real suffering. Religion is the sigh of the oppressed creature, the sentiment of a heartless world, and the soul of soulless conditions" (1964:43–44). Like bush food and shamanism, the memory of Misión El Toba that many men and women invoke to alleviate "soulless conditions" is now inscribed in their lands. During my fieldwork, in the silence of the night I regularly heard collective healing prayers reverberate in the darkness. As I temporarily put down the pen on my notebook to listen, the intense chorus of voices combining Toba and Spanish expressions often made me shiver: *Dios ademége!* (God heals you!) *Jesús sanador!* (Jesus healer!) *Payák avenogonége!* (Get out, devil!) *Gloria a Dios, aleluya, es el espíritu de Dios!* (Glory to God, alleluia, it's God's Spirit!). On occasions, I could not but hear in those voices a collective lament, fostered by the pain of the living but also by the past suffering of those who have been long dead.

These practices are the most recent expression of attempts to counter a social malaise initiated by state violence, continued for decades in the sugar plantations, and currently materialized in everyday conditions of

44. "Now that people never go to the ingenio, somebody has eight, ten kids." *Photo by author.*

poverty, exploitation in faraway farms, and political deceptions (as we shall see). In conjunction with bush food, the bush devils, and shamanism, these efforts have enabled most Toba to counteract the forces that almost wiped them out as a group. Several people told me that the Toba population began growing again only when they stopped migrating to kahogonaGá. Many added that, unlike thirty or forty years earlier, one can now see plenty of children in their hamlets. As Ernesto put it: "When we went to the ingenio, a full generation of ours was diminished. If it weren't for that, we should be many more. The reason is that many died. Now that people never go to the ingenio, somebody has eight, ten kids." The recurrent death of children in the lotes, as we have seen, symbolized the threat that the sugar cane fields posed to Toba survival. By the same token, current references to the children's abundance underscore that staying in their lands enabled them to endure and expand as a collective.

The constitution of the bush as a place of health and resilience partially defined by the memory of San Martín del Tabacal leads us to tensions between spatially inscribed labor experiences. As mountain devils were part of a place produced through terror, exploitation, and estrangement, the forces projected onto bush devils are part of experiences of relative control over a place that most Toba feel they know better than anybody.

14

The Production of Local Knowledge

In the ingenio, Arnaldo wanted to go to the jungle, but we
were not from there. . . . People were afraid he'd get lost.
But when he got back here, he went to the bush . . .
and came back with everything.

—Andrés, 1999

In August 1990 I was in a hamlet near the marshlands when, while chatting
with Ramiro, a man in his fifties, I noticed a tall man coming toward us
from a bush trail. His beard, a rarity among Toba men, caught my attention. He was about forty and had the attire and body language of an experienced mariscador: axe over the shoulder, shirt and pants in rags, a chagüar
bag dripping honey, and the pace of somebody who exudes energy despite having been through demanding physical activity. He stopped about
fifteen meters away from us, next to a blanket, a small table, and two iron
pots. He left the bag on the table and half a dozen children surrounded him
to get their share of chunks of honeycomb. My host noticed my interest
in the newcomer and said: "He's Arnaldo; he lives there. He's always foraging." As if wanting to pique my interest, he added: "He doesn't speak."
Curious, I asked why. Ramiro told me that Arnaldo had lost his memory
and speaking abilities decades earlier, after an encounter with a payák.
The terror of that experience had left him mute. Ever since that moment,
Arnaldo had been a superb *epiáGayaik* (forager), spending much of his
time in the bush and the marshes. Years later, I saw Arnaldo again. This
time he was screaming aloud and making vivid gestures, as if he were
interacting with an invisible interlocutor. It was then that people told me
about other aspects of his condition. After losing his memory, he married
his own sister and they had a baby boy. Soon afterward, he killed the baby
on a honey-gathering trip. Despite that disturbing episode, people agreed

that Arnaldo was harmless and quiet. It was only then that I learned where his encounter with that payák had taken place: in San Martín del Tabacal.

In a somewhat extreme form, Arnaldo's case captures the ways in which knowledge of the bush is tied to contradictions embedded in places and in embodied memories of the sugar plantations. His estrangement from the cane fields, epitomized in the payák that took away his memory and speaking abilities, in the Chaco was transformed in its exact opposite: a detailed knowledge of the bush. This spatialized dialectic was mediated by madness, incest, and death, and marked by a new form of alienation: an estrangement from his kin and neighbors. Yet this case illuminates some of the ways in which most Toba produce local knowledge: in relation with embodied memories of San Martín del Tabacal and with the devils that contribute to, and simultaneously undermine, their mastery over the bush. In this chapter, I analyze how tropes of local knowledge gain their force through memories of unfamiliarity with other places. Since local knowledge, as Arjun Appadurai argues (1996:181), is crucial to produce reliable local subjects, I also examine how Toba discourses on mastery over the bush draw boundaries between Criollos and Aborígenes, poor and well-off people, and men and women. Finally, I analyze local knowledge as an attempt at spatial control fostered but also challenged by bush devils and simultaneously intertwined with perceptions that the bush, in contrast to other geographies, is a "quiet place."

Locations of Knowledge and Ignorance

Local knowledge is often analyzed in anthropology as the necessary, almost natural component of any spatially defined practice (see Geertz 1983:167, 215). In these pages, I explore a different route and examine how, as a marker of relative mastery over a particular place, local knowledge is produced and reproduced negatively through perceptions of ignorance of other places. In other words, I argue that local knowledge is permanently informed by the experience of *not* knowing other geographies. This means that many Toba produce knowledge of the bush, first, through their contrast with their remembered estrangement in San Martín del Tabacal and, second, through their current experience in places over which they exert little control, such as farms and cities. People also produce local knowledge as a critical counterpoint to hegemonic views about the ignorance of the Aborígenes, which played a major role in the ingenio's ethnic hierarchies and (in a different way) in Misión El Toba, where missionaries aimed at saving Toba men and women from their ignorance of Christianity.

This is why "to know the bush" is not just an intrinsic component of marisca's habitus; it is also a cultural and political discourse; or, to be more precise, an embodied practice that people regularly articulate in assertions of control over space. These claims are particularly clear among people who live in poverty. I was once talking with Diego, a reputed hunter in his youth, and he said confidently about the bush: "I know all the places. When I get inside the bush, I go from here to there, far away. In the past, I used to go far, fishing, hunting." I asked him whether he ever got lost. "Never, never, never. I was most skillful. The ancient ones were most skillful at walking, going far, and not getting lost." As Diego illustrates, current Toba assertions of local knowledge are legitimized by the memory of their ancestors' expertise as foragers. Young Toba often lament that they are not as strong as the ancient ones and that they have forgotten important elements of their wisdom and insights. Yet they also emphasize that, despite those losses, they still "know" how to forage. Foraging, in sum, is the main thread connecting the yagaikipí and the dalaGaikpí, old ones and new ones, and the practice through which members of new generations ground their knowledge of their lands.

This sense of "knowing" the bush is shaped not only by memories of estrangement at the ingenio but also by more recent perceptions of regional and national geographies. In addition to their first-hand experience of Ingeniero Juárez and (for some men) Formosa, many people incorporate images of Buenos Aires through radio broadcasts, schooling, or TV shows (watched in Pozo de Maza or Ingeniero Juárez). And some explicitly contrast their knowledge of the bush with their disorientation in the city. Enrique is one of the few Toba who has been to Buenos Aires several times, where he attended various meetings on indigenous groups. "I'm afraid of the city because I don't know it," he remembered in 1996. "But when we wander the bush, we know it. We know where we have to go. But I don't know the town because I'm not used to it, because I don't know it. . . . If a white man comes to the bush, he gets lost." Enrique emphasized that his local knowledge gains meaning and value through its contrast with those places ruled by spatial codes he ignores. The Aborígenes' despair is clear in plantations and cities but in the bush this situation is reversed: the whites' knowledge is of little value and, by contrast, indigenous knowledge prevails. Because of their political implications, claims of local knowledge are contested markers of aboriginality, class, and gender.

45. "The Criollos don't know the bush." *Photo by author.*

Debating Local Knowledge

Discourses on expertise in the bush are particularly forceful when people compare themselves with the Criollos. Even though many settlers regularly set out to the bush to hunt and gather wild fruits, most Toba argue that the Criollos "don't know the bush." Men ground this assertion in their knowledge of the bush's thickest section, the viáq ádaik, which they see as a place alien to cattle, horses, settlers, and women. Some concede that Criollos may go into the viáq ádaik looking for lost cattle; but they add that they do it on horseback and wearing *guardamonte* (leather flaps attached to the saddle) and *coleto* (a leather poncho) as protection from thorns. Toba men often point out that, unlike the Criollos, they are not "delicate" and enter the viáq ádaik on foot, just with a machete, and not minding the thorny vegetation. As Emiliano put it: "The Criollos don't know the bush. The Aborígenes are tireless. There's thick bush, but we get inside anyway." Claiming superior local knowledge became particularly important during the mobilization for the land title in the 1980s, when in order to delimit old territorial boundaries some Toba mapped the sites trekked by their ancestors. Relying on the memory of older men, this mapping systematized the names given to hundreds of sites spread over a wide territory (de la Cruz and Mendoza 1988; de la Cruz 1993). "Knowing" and naming the bush and its intricate geography, in short, became a politically charged assertion of spatial control.

Because of the class components of local forms of ethnicity, the aboriginality of this knowledge also informs debates between poor and well-off Toba. Many men hunt with rifles and shotguns, some of them brought decades ago from San Martín del Tabacal. Yet others often hunt simply with their dogs and, depending on the prey, basic weapons such as knives, sticks, or axes.[1] Men who hunt without firearms are usually too poor to afford them, and their skills at capturing prey, even if drawing on old techniques, have developed out of an experience of poverty. These men's claims of local knowledge are particularly compelling, for they are quick to point out that they can capture wild animals almost with their bare hands. These men often look down on public-sector employees who rarely forage, arguing that they "don't know the bush" and spend most of their time in the villages. "Not knowing" the bush is for them tantamount to becoming culturally, socially, and spatially closer to "white people": removed from the bush and secluded in the villages.

Claims of knowledge also are gendered. Many men argue that the bush is an eminently male place, basically because they trek it on a more regular basis than women and because entering the viáq ádaik requires, in their view, male features such as physical strength and determination. I asked Tomás whether women know the bush. "No. They don't know it. Women don't know," he replied. I pointed out that women look for fruits in the bush and he said: "But that's only for a while. When they fill up the large bag, they return right away. They don't get deep into the bush. The algarroba is in the open country [open section of the bush]. We men, do. We get deep inside the bush."

Many women challenge these claims. Even if they spend most of their time in the villages, when they set out to gather algarroba or chañar fruits they cover wide areas and when seeking chagüar plants they go farther and enter the viáq ádaik. Since in the villages socialization among women is restricted to the household space, where they are often in direct contact with men, gathering trips allow women to produce important places of autonomy from men. As Doreen Massey has argued (1994: 11, 179), women's mobility has historically posed challenges to male domination. Similarly, during the summer groups of women turn the most paradigmatic site of male ideology, the bush, into the only place where they are on their own and, hence, into a central space of female socialization. Luisa, a woman in her thirties, emphasized that these forays contest male claims of local knowledge when she told me: "Men aren't the only ones who know the bush well. Some men don't go to the bush either. They seldom go to the bush. Some men know a lot, but others don't. They go nearby and get lost right away. And some women know a lot. It depends on the woman. Some women wander a lot; they work a lot over there, during the time of the fruits. Not only men know. Women know as well." By asserting that some women know the bush better than some men, Luisa was deconstructing a clear-cut dichotomy between the way "men" and "women" experience the bush. By doing so, she was also pointing out that some women know the bush better than men with public-sector jobs who rarely leave their hamlets.

Despite men's and women's assertions, the bush is a not a place under total human control and local knowledge ultimately depends on their interactions with bush devils. This relationship is informed by the cultural sedimentation of memories of estrangement.

A Help for a Poor Person

In addition to being sources of healing power, bush devils are the "owners" (*ladípa*) of the animals and resources available in Toba lands. This means that the foragers' relative control over the bush, and their ability to confront a situation of poverty, depends on the devils' willingness to allow them to find food. The simultaneous role of payák spirits as devils and owners adds a further dimension to Toba experiences of the bush. Unlike the devils in San Martín del Tabacal, some bush devils have distinctive features and control different spatial niches. *Dáwaik*, a large red-feathered ostrich, is the "owner" of the grasslands across the marshes. The water is the domain of *noGoplé'ec*, "the person of the water." In the bush, various owners coexist. Most are the nameless protectors of different animals species but one is a female devil named *kopeletáGa*, the owner of nelomá (bola verde, the only wild fruit with an owner). Contrary to what this description may suggest, people do not experience these devils as members of a coherent, neatly segmented pantheon. This experience is part of what Pierre Bourdieu (1977:19) has called "a mode of practical knowledge not comprising knowledge of its own principles." As a result, there is a great degree of variation and inconsistency in the way people refer to them. During my fieldwork, most people made general statements of the sort of "every animal has an owner" and looked confused when I pressed them to provide a more coherent picture.[2] Influenced by decades of missionization, some Toba also argue that, even if diablos are active in the bush, "God" is the actual owner of all animals. What is critical to note is that, in contrast with the mountain devils, many Toba see the bush devils as potent yet often dormant entities that have distinctive traits and, more important, engage in reciprocity relations with humans.

As part of this reciprocity, diablos allow foragers to obtain bush food, regardless of its quantity, provided that they are careful with it and do not throw it away. People agree that if they do not comply the owners will "get upset" and make it impossible for them to find game or fish in the future.[3] In exchange for these precautions, the devils allow foragers to capture the species and resources under their control. Since this practice is part of a taken-for-granted habitus, foragers do not articulate this concern explicitly while in the bush.[4] They forage guided by practical needs, in a process in which the bush owners are part of their subjective, and not necessarily conscious, dispositions for action. Every time I accompanied Toba men on their hunting and fishing expeditions, my companions were focused on the practicalities of marisca and never expressed direct or indirect concerns about devils (cf. Métraux 1946a:16). Antonio, who on other occasions had described the owners in detail, told me once: "When I go to mariscar, I don't think about the owners." Bourdieu (1977:114–15) examined a similar type of practical subjectivity:

> Understanding ritual practice is not a question of decoding the internal logic of a symbolism but of restoring its practical necessity by relating it to the real conditions of its genesis, that is, to the conditions in which its functions, and the means it uses to attain them, are defined. . . . By cutting practices off from their real conditions of existence, in order to credit them with alien intentions, by a false generosity conductive to stylistic effects, the exaltation of lost wisdom dispossesses them, as surely as its opposite, of everything that constitutes their reason and their *raison d'être*, and locks them into the eternal essence of "mentality."

Similarly, devils are not part of a "mythical mentality" but of real conditions of existence. For this reason, foragers do not throw away food because, first and foremost, in a context of poverty it would be unthinkable to do so. In April 1991 I asked Diego whether people refrain from throwing away fish out of fear of offending the "owner of the water." His reply made me feel clumsy and insensitive: "People don't throw away fish because they're hungry." On other occasions, Diego had told me about the owners and his caution when handling fish, but my objectification of that explanation forced him to remind me of the hardships of an experience of poverty. On other occasions, my similar, abstract questions about

46. Local knowledge in action. *Photo by author.*

animal owners also made people emphasize the practical importance of food. I once naively asked Pablo: "What happens if you throw away the fish?" His sharp response pointed, first, to the value of food and then to the reciprocity linking foragers with "God": "What do you want the fish for? Why do you look for fish? Why do you want to eat fish? You wanted to find fish very badly, to catch a lot of fish, and now you want to throw it away! That's not good. If you look for fish, you have to be careful with it. . . . You don't have to throw it away, for it's good nourishment. Besides, later on you won't have luck. It seems that God hides it, because you don't comply, because you aren't careful."

Practical concerns over food acquisition, in sum, are intertwined with the relations of reciprocity defining interactions with diablos or, in this case, "God." And one aspect cannot be fully separated from the other. This reciprocity acquires part of its meaning through the memory of the death unleashed by the mountain devils, a particularly potent symbol of the hostile and purely negative interactions between Aborígenes and devils at the ingenio. And this reciprocity is ultimately inseparable from the social relations and sharing networks among households that provide people in poverty with foodstuffs vital to their subsistence. As a result of this convergence between devil imageries and historical practice, some people see the bush devils as one of the forces that alleviate their poverty. As Hugo put it: "The owner is like a help for a poor person. It shows him things so that he can live. It helps the person who doesn't have a job, so that he can live with honey, so that he has something to eat, so that he doesn't go out to steal." Hugo emphasized that this "help" involves not just anybody but a "poor person," specifically someone without a public-sector job. He also presented the bush devils as moral, generous figures concerned about people being forced to "steal." Yet despite these benevolent dimensions, bush devils are ultimately unpredictable, whimsical beings that not only facilitate Toba control over the bush but also erode it.

The Making of Safe and Unsafe Places

People remember that prior to the 1975 flooding the Pilcomayo River was a relatively safe place and that most local dangers concentrated in the *viáq hakoiwók*, or bad bush. The latter was full of jaguars — which occasionally injured and even killed foragers — devils, and giant snakes called *nanaikpólio*, described as thirty meters long and one meter wide. That place was also the home of wosáq, a payák creature that triggered storms and adopted the shape of the rainbow. Yet people agree that because of the opening of roads and trails and the impact of logging in the 1970s, the viáq hakoiwók has now disappeared. These changes in the regional landscape made nanaikpólio, jaguars, and wosáq abandon their lands and find refuge in the Paraguayan bush, thus transporting the relative risk posed by their presence across the international border. At the local level, the depletion of the bad bush and the formation of marshes gradually reversed the geographical distribution of places of danger, redirecting danger away from the bush and toward the new landscape created by the Pilcomayo.

The emergence of marshlands, in this regard, stimulated an intense process of cultural production. Most people agree that whereas the bush is currently free of dangers, the marshes harbor treacherous creatures, especially when they "come down" with the annual floods. This perception implies that many people see these beings as originally alien to the region. In fact, some claim that it was rare to see them "at the time of the river." These marsh creatures are, first, two types of giant snakes: *cháiq*, a long water snake (similar to nanaikpólio), and lék, the thick and short snake that can open the earth with its head (and the one most distinctly tied to the Pilcomayo); second, animals of payák nature: the *pegakpólio* (large horse), *wakapólio* (large cow), and *ketagapólio* (large goat). These beasts are much bigger than regular horses, cows, and goats and often walk on water; noticeably, they mimic animals originally alien to the Chaco that symbolize wealth, as if their presence embodied the intrusion of foreign, alienating forces into their lands. Expressing this view of the marshes, Tomás told me: "The marshes are the worst. All types of mean bichos live there." Even though most foragers rarely come across these creatures, I heard several stories of occasional encounters with them. In December 1999, at the beginning of the flooding season, a man on a fishing trip trying to cross a stream disappeared in front of his companions, swallowed by a whirlpool. His body was never found and most people concluded that a giant snake had killed him. For several weeks, some men avoided entering the marshes, and when I visited the Toba villages six months later people still talked about the incident.

These dangers and the way they produce distinctions between safe and unsafe spaces are shaped along gender lines. Unlike men, most women see the bush as a relatively feared place because of the presence of men and, secondly, wild animals. This perception includes Criollos, Toba, and Wichí men and hence makes gender cleavages more important than ethnic distinctions. I asked Fabiana, a woman in her fifties, whether it was dangerous to go into the bush. "When you go alone, maybe you'll find a man who bothers you," she replied. "Then you don't go to the bush. You're afraid of the bush. . . . If you go with all the family, then it's quiet. You're not afraid. Then you go far into the bush, with other women, and you're not afraid." Fabiana made a significant distinction: individual women are "afraid of the bush" because of the unwanted attention they may get from men; but women are able to counteract this fear by getting together and pushing for a collective appropriation of the bush, in a process in which they neutralize fear and in fact turn the bush into a "quiet" place where they "are not afraid." Memory potently informs this perception, for many women claim that the bush is not as dangerous as it was decades earlier. Old women remember that in their youth they feared the giant snakes smelling their menstrual blood and that this fear anchored them in the villages while they were menstruating. Similar menstrual taboos involved the action of wosáq.[5] Since the nanaikpólio and "rainbow" have fled to the Paraguayan Chaco, currently most women enter the bush in groups even if menstruating, an experience that accentuates their feelings of control and knowledge of the bush.

These perceptions do not alter men's and women's awareness that one place may involve risks: the viáq ádaik. The most serious hazard is to get lost, especially during the dry season, when most hinterland ponds have no water and a person lost for several days can die of thirst. Since the sun is the most important point of reference, men and women agree that it can be risky to hunt, gather fruits, or collect chagüar in the viáq ádaik on a cloudy or rainy day. Still, people agree, losing the sense of direction is ultimately caused not by human miscalculations but by bush devils. Even expert mariscadores can get lost simply because a payák decided to make them feel dizzy or scared. I asked Martín whether he ever got lost in the bush:

> Yes, many times. I don't know how is it when you get lost over here. It seems that your head is bothered by anything. Maybe it's the payák. Or maybe it's our head. It seems that we can't see, that we can't think. . . . For instance, I bump into my own footprints and go in circles. . . . Maybe it's the payák. Because my grandfather told me: "If you walk close to where a payák is, it immediately makes you get lost." It seems that the payák gives you a power so that you forget where you're coming from.

These tricks also affect women. When they split up to gather fruits they usually whistle as a way of orientation. KopeletáGa (the owner of nelomá) often imitates this whistling in order to guide women in the wrong direction and make them get lost.[6] Bush diablos can go one step further and turn disorientation into a temporary state of madness, called *nahalágaiki*. This is the result of sudden and intense fear, *nocolánaga* (or *do'é*) and *susto* in Spanish, which makes one lose his or her soul (temporarily captured by a payák). There are many cases of men and women known to have lost their consciousness, memory, or ability to speak for hours, weeks, or months. Arnaldo's case, discussed earlier, is an example of nahalágaiki turned into a permanent condition. This affliction, regardless of its duration, is strongly localized in the bush. Osvaldo, a man in his thirties, emphasized this location when he told me: "The little I know about it is that it always takes place in the bush." Further, people affected by this condition feel attracted to the bush, wander aimlessly, or (like Arnaldo) become expert foragers. Paradoxically, the only way people can acquire almost complete mastery over the bush is by giving up their consciousness to bush devils.

This spatially grounded condition, even if drawing on a cultural habitus prior to the migrations to the sugar plantations, embodies memories of recent historical experiences. Susto as a malady related to fear is common throughout Latin America. As Linda Green has pointed out (1999:120–22), among indigenous women victims of state terror in Guatemala, susto inscribes in their bodies their own memories of suffering and violence. Similarly, the fear triggered by a payák is part of a complexly embodied memory of terror and estrangement, differently produced in the bush and the plantations. This condition is also connected to the spatialization of ignorance and knowledge. In May 1999 Andrés remembered that when Arnaldo lost his consciousness in San Martín del Tabacal he permanently wandered the jungle and got lost several times. He did not know the place, and the appropriation of his consciousness by a mountain payák accentuated his disconnect with that geography. Andrés told me: "When his disease came, Arnaldo wanted to go to the jungle. But we weren't from there. If we had been in this area, he could have gone for a walk. But in those years, because of the mountains at the San Martín plantation, people were afraid he'd get lost." It was because of the location of that condition, at a place they did not know, that they could not let him go for a walk. Andrés emphasized that "in this area," back in the bush, it would have been different. And it was. When they got home, Arnaldo "changed" and was able to forage alone. "He went to the bush and came back late. And he came back with everything." This explicit contraposition between different places illuminates the spatialized tensions producing senses of ignorance and knowledge. Arnaldo's madness originated in the ingenio but in the bush led to an increased capacity to obtain "everything," fostering a productive appropriation of space in which local knowledge was increased rather than diminished. This means that despite their power, the diablos' mastery over the bush is not complete and that foragers have the skills to temporarily wrest this place away from them.

The Reassertion of Local Knowledge

Whereas in their memories of the mountain devils, the KiyaGaikpí, or the Familiar, many Toba transmit images of despair, in their lands they count on their local knowledge to counter devils. Many agree that while in the bush it is important to control any expression of fear, for a payák can turn fear into dizziness, disease, or eventually nahalágaiki (temporary madness). Thus, counteracting bush devils requires the conscious avoidance of the bodily experience, fear, that once pervaded their labor in kahogonaGá. The legacy of Anglican missionization also left a mark on attempts at countering bush diablos. Some people told me that when they perceive a potential danger, for instance while spending the night in the bush, they keep devils at bay by praying to God or singing. Hugo told me that he once got a headache while fishing and, since he thought a payák was the cause, he began singing the Anglican religious songs he learned at the Sunday culto: "Then the headache was gone. It seems that the devil got scared." Hugo scared a devil away by invoking markers of Christianity that are grounded in the villages and particularly in the Anglican churches. Yet the legacy of missionization has become part of a habitus also invoked in the bush to offset the forces once condemned by Alfred Leake.

When somebody gets lost in the bush, he or she also resorts to local knowledge to neutralize potential dangers: by tracing back their footprints, climbing up a tall tree in order to search for familiar signs in the distance, or following the dogs they may have with them. But the most pressing concern is to find the way out of the bush before sunset, for devils are particularly active at night. Those who cannot leave the bush by sunset climb up a tall tree as a protective measure. Men and women alike agree that at night a payák may make strange noises (like somebody axing a tree) or imitate human voices to scare people. Toba who get lost also count on an unexpected ally: those whom many look down on as knowing "nothing" about the bush: the Criollos. Since many settlers live in isolated puestos deep inside the bush, far from the Toba hamlets, this is not a coincidence. Accordingly, when a Toba gets lost, he or she follows the tracks left by cattle, in the hope of coming across a puesto. Despite the tensions between Criollos and Aborígenes, these tracks and this assistance illustrate that both actors are coparticipants in the physical making of the bush and that local knowledge does not exclude cooperation with settlers.

A Quiet Place

The claims of local knowledge examined in this chapter reinforce the perception that the risks posed by the bush can be contained and that, in turn, faraway places include dangers much more disturbing than those that exist in the Chaco interior. When people remember San Martín del Tabacal or imagine other geographies, the potential perils they may encounter in their lands pale in comparison and this contrast makes many feel that the bush is, after all, a quiet place. Due to the local interpretation of news broadcast on radio or TV, the places that accentuate this calmness often reach planetary proportions. When I returned to the Toba villages in May 1999, after an absence of twenty months, I visited Bernardo, who lives with his extended family near the marshes at a relatively isolated site. After chatting for a while, Bernardo told me he was happy to see me again for he was wondering whether I was still alive. Surprised, I asked why. His answer startled me. Those were the days of the NATO air strikes against Serb forces in Kosovo and Yugoslavia and Bernardo had been listening on national radio about "the war in Yugoslavia." The war was then a common topic of conversation in the villages and, drawing on the (for them confusing) pieces of information received locally, many people referred to it as "the war of the rich." Bernardo thought the bombing was also reaching "Canadá," where he knew I was living at the time. This is why, he said, he had worried about my safety. As I tried to explain that "Canadá" and "Yugoslavia" were very distant from each other, and that only the latter was object of attacks, I suddenly remembered that years earlier some Toba had made very similar comments. That recollection was a shock and an illumination. In April 1991 I went to the field soon after the Gulf War, which many Toba had also followed on the radio. On my arrival, some people had told me they had wondered whether I had been killed by "the war in Iraq." And in those days I was living in Buenos Aires! At that moment, I found those comments fascinating and intriguing but did not make much of them. But on that day in May 1999 I realized that the geographical connections people made between distant wars were indicative of a radical form of space compression. On hearing enigmatic news about places and wars they knew nothing about, many people compacted disparate geographies into *one single place* engulfed by an all-encompassing violence. Indeed, for many Toba there is little difference between Buenos Aires, Yugoslavia, the Persian Gulf, or Canada. All these places are, in their eyes, equally distant from the Chaco interior and equally alien to their experience. For this reason, some people amalgamate them in a single landscape of violence fractured by a clear class marker that further distanced it from them: "the wars of the rich."[7]

These perceptions contribute to defining the bush as a place of peace, tranquility, and silence. A few days after visiting Bernardo, Eduardo and I were talking next to his household and he repeatedly asked me about Buenos Aires and the war in Yugoslavia. "Here, it's quiet," he said at one point. "It's quiet here. . . . At least we have health. There's no crime. . . . At least we live a quiet life. Because this area where we live is bush." Sitting next to his home, Eduardo subsumed his village within the potent presence of the bush as "the area where we live." His account illustrates how perceptions of other places are part of the material sediment through which people construct local landscapes. Memories of the clashes between the yagaikipí and the army are particularly important in this regard; they make people sensitive to news about wars and make them remember the military as a destructive force that came from *elsewhere* and eventually left the area following the emergence of Misión El Toba as a refuge from state terror. The bush, in other words, is currently considered a quiet place mainly because at one point it was *not*. These perceptions are also grounded in the memory of the Aborígenes who left their bones in distant lands, slain by forces that do not exist in the Chaco interior. In this regard, references to the "silence" of the bush are informed by these memories and by the opposition between their lands as a place they "know" and the violence and alienation of distant geographies. And those landscapes of despair reassert the importance of people's control over the bush. A similar blending of place, history, and memory emerges in the ways in which people draw on the ingenio's legacy to account for local experiences of poverty.

15

"With the Fish, We're Rich"

People are hungry. In the bush there's no food.
—Gregorio, 1996

When the payák gives [shamanic] power to a person . . .
it gives him everything it has. When the man forages over
there, he finds honey. . . . He finds everything he wants.
He becomes rich. —Diego, 1997

When men and women remembered with nostalgia the wealth of the
ingenio, the arreglo grande, or the money thrown away by President
Perón, they produced those memories at a particular time and place: a moment, the mid and late 1990s, when they felt particularly estranged from
trabajo, and a place, the Chaco interior, which lacked significant sources of
commodities and money. Raymond Williams wrote that the nostalgia for
other places arises out of a state of unease with, and alienation from, the
place where those nostalgic memories are produced (1971:298). Similarly,
the memories of wealth analyzed in chapter 10 are informed by people's
partial estrangement from their own lands. The location and sedimentation of those memories have made most Toba conceive of wealth as an
attribute of distant lands such as San Martín del Tabacal and, more recently, Buenos Aires. By the same token, this sedimentation makes most
people see their lands as a place of poverty and unsatisfied necessities.
In this chapter I examine how the memory of San Martín del Tabacal
grounds poverty in the bush and how, at the same time, other experiences
and memories counter this perception. The nostalgia for the ingenio's
commodities, as we have seen, is regularly haunted by memories of estrangement from that wealth and of the dangers attached to it, a perception recently reinforced by views of "the wars of the rich" unfolding in
remote geographies. Likewise, in the pages that follow I explore how the

memory of estrangement in the cane fields and the resilience and local knowledge in Toba lands also constitute the bush as a site of alternative forms of abundance.

A Place of Poverty

Most Toba understand their poverty (*nachoGodék*) first and foremost as a condition defined by unsatisfied material necessities (involving clothing, food, and shelter), a condition they often summarize with the expression "we have nothing." Likewise, many equate being "rich" (*newoyáq*) with "having everything." In addition to framing these conditions in terms of absolute possession and dispossession, many associate poverty with ignorance (as we shall see). But more important, most Toba conceive of poverty in spatial terms: as a condition almost intrinsically inscribed in the Chaco interior. Their partial exclusion from the main circuits of labor migration, new unrewarding forms of trabajo, and the ecological depletion that in the past decades has affected the bush are all factors that inform this spatialized notion of poverty. Yet the memory of the ingenio frequently overflows these perceptions. Many Toba capture this view with the expression "here there's no trabajo" and add that in kahogonaGá they were employed for almost the whole year. As Patricio put it: "Here in this zone nobody has trabajo like we did in the ingenio. Here, there's nothing." Even young people refer nostalgically to their parents' work in San Martín del Tabacal and, by doing so, project wealth elsewhere.

The practice that best symbolizes the spatial dimension of poverty is marisca, but in a way that counters the meanings of resilience analyzed in chapter 13. For many Toba foraging alleviates their poverty but it is also characterized by conditions of mere subsistence, for beyond the occasional sale of animal skins or rhea feathers this practice does not provide the money and commodities granted by trabajo. People's estrangement from San Martín del Tabacal was the result of their lack of control over their labor and their immersion within an overall climate of disease and fear. In the bush, by contrast, people exert relative control over the pace of domestic production; yet they do not control their social reproduction: that is, they need to obtain commodities — clothes (blue jeans, shirts, T-shirts, sneakers, cloth), domestic utensils, blankets, mosquito nets — elsewhere and under conditions that are not of their own making. In July 1996, while making a tour by bicycle of several hamlets, I arrived at the

47. Boiling wild fruits (stored in the
summer) during the scarcity months,
August 1992. *Photo by author.*

household of Amancio, a man in his late fifties often surrounded by his
numerous grandchildren. This time, I noticed he was alone with his elder
daughter. After leaning my bike on a tree and shaking hands with him, I
asked him where everybody was. "They've all gone to the bean harvest,"
he told me, and added: "The necessity. A lot of necessity." In order to highlight the constraints that forced most of his family to migrate for work,
Amancio used the concept that, more than a century earlier, European
thinkers had defined as the opposite of freedom. "The realm of freedom
really begins only where labor determined by necessity and external ex-
pediency ends," Karl Marx wrote in volume three of *Capital* (1981:958–59).
In the 1990s "the necessity" was a phrase commonly used in Toba villages
to refer to local conditions of poverty and was also the main force that
continued pulling men and women out of their lands (as we shall see in
chapter 16).

These material constraints shaping their everyday practice make many
Toba feel partially estranged from the bush. Public-sector employees feel

alienated from this place becau t of their time in the
villages and rarely forage. Yet ers also see the bush
in a negative light, especially b al depletion of its resources and the uncertainty and efforts they associate with foraging trips.
Gregorio, a man in his late twenties, complained: "People are hungry. In
the bush, there is no food. There's almost no honey or fish. . . . Going to
the bush is a lot of work. I leave early. There's almost no honey. . . . Then,
I walk all day long and I'm tired. . . . What am I going to eat the next
morning? Nothing. . . . Then, we have to look for bush fruits. Just that.
No fat. No salt. Nothing."

The memory of what happened decades earlier with the goods brought
back from San Martín del Tabacal accentuates this view of the bush as
a place of scarcity. People remember that on returning home they sold
pieces of clothing, riding gear, or utensils to the Criollos in exchange for
beef and horses. They also distributed these goods to relatives and neighbors, some of whom had stayed home and demanded a share. Soon after
the return from kahogonaGá, people agree, they had bartered or given
away most of what they had earned in the arreglo grande. Currently, several people express frustration at their own "ignorance" on how to save
those goods and prosper. Late in 1995 Enrique visited me from another
village. As we were having lunch, I asked him why, according to him, most
Toba were poor. He replied: "Because we, Toba Aborígenes, don't know
how to handle things so that we don't lack anything. . . . We earn money,
we earn clothes. What happens? When we come over here, we don't even
think about starting a business, we don't even think about having a store.
We just spend money all the time. . . . I wonder why people don't understand. I don't understand anything. I only understand when it's over, because the life of the Toba Aborigen is to be poor. It's not like the whites."
This naturalization of poverty as a condition of their aboriginality contributes to the cultural sedimentation of "the necessity" in their lands, as
a force destined to mark "the life of the Toba." And the memory that the
commodities brought back from the ingenio just slipped through their
fingers turns the bush into a place with a corrosive, dissolving effect on
the wealth obtained elsewhere.

In the 1990s, with commercial hunting and craftsmanship in decline as
income sources, public-sector jobs were the only important local source
of cash.[1] The existence of clusters of better-off households was producing
spatial fractures. Yet when people compare their lands with distant places
defined by fabulous riches, these local niches of relative affluence become

in their eyes negligible. This is why most Toba still see "the bush" as a place where "the poor" (*pioGokpí*) live, a perception that incorporates Wichí and Criollos as people who, despite their differences, share with them a similar social landscape of unsatisfied necessities.[2]

Because of the decline of seasonal wage labor, Buenos Aires has emerged as a major point of reference in this cartography of poverty and wealth. Many Toba imagine this city as the natural repository of the country's riches and a place where most of its inhabitants, by the mere fact of living there, are rich. Mariano told me about the image he had of Buenos Aires, which he fashioned by watching TV at a diner in Ingeniero Juárez: "People have everything there. It's such a big city. It never ends. . . . They're all the time in their houses. They don't go to work. They are only on the streets, in trucks, cars, like ants. . . . You never see the workers. They have everything. They don't lack anything inside [their houses]. . . . I saw it on TV." Like Mariano, many people imagine Buenos Aires through the lens of class, as a place full of rich, idle people who "have everything" and where there is no trace of workers. This is particularly important among young people who have never been to San Martín del Tabacal. But this geographical perception of wealth also relates to people's view that they have been unable to retain or create wealth in their own lands.

The Elusive Knowledge of Wealth

In tension with discourses about their knowledge and mastery of the bush, many Toba argue that they lack the knowledge to produce wealth. Evoking the money factories associated with the ingenio, several people told me that this condition responds to their ignorance on how to "manufacture money."[3] The spatial dimensions of these perceptions are particularly apparent in local stories about hidden treasures. Most people argue that "gold boxes" exist only near the ingenio and the bean farms; the few who told me that these boxes also exist in the bush agreed that no Toba ever found them. Martín recounted that he was once riding his bicycle on a bush trail when he suddenly saw two pale flames in the distance. He immediately remembered that in San Martín del Tabacal those flames signaled the site of "gold boxes." He got off his bike but when he got closer the lights disappeared. "I thought it was the gold," he told me. "But it seems that . . . I don't know, I don't know. I don't understand that fire."

48. "We're born with nothing, just like this, poor."
Photo by author.

Martín then recalled that decades earlier, Moreno, his grandfather and
a powerful pioGonáq, also saw those yellow flames in the bush. However, he ignored them for he thought they were made by a payák. Moreno
learned that those flames marked the location of "the gold" only when
a white man arrived looking for them. The man found the treasure, sold
it elsewhere, and became rich. Martín commented: "It turned out that
those lights were the gold. Gold, silver: the knowledge of the whites. But
since we didn't know, the white man found the light. . . . We don't know
where that is." By emphasizing the frustrations resulting from their inca-
pacity to discover riches, narratives like this contribute to making people
feel estranged from their own lands. Toba living in poverty may master the
skills to produce bush food, but when it comes to producing money and
discovering "gold boxes" that knowledge is worthless. This is "the whites'
knowledge," even when it involves locating treasures buried in Toba lands.

   Local accounts about elusive sources of wealth also involve bush diablos. Like the mountain devils, some bush devils control riches and money.
But unlike the former, they are willing to share them with shamans. Several people told me that decades earlier devils had offered some shamans
fabulous riches. In 1996 Enrique told me that Chileno, a pioGonáq and
capitán at San Martín del Tabacal, was once foraging when he found a
shack in the viáq ádaik. The place was full of money, firearms, knives,
clothes, tables, and rolls of wire. A short man, a payák, came out and told

him he could ask for anything. Yet Chileno, dazzled by the offer, left without uttering a word. When he returned the following morning, the hut and those riches were all gone. Enrique imitated what Chileno, in his frustration, said to himself: "That was a mistake. I was wrong. How come I didn't ask him for those rifles! How come I didn't ask him to be rich! How come I didn't ask him so that I don't lack any money! How come I didn't ask him so that I don't lack clothes!" Noticeably, the mysterious shack was located in the viáq ádaik, a place accessible only to experienced hunters. That payák created an extraordinary site of money and commodities in the heart of a place of marisca; but since Chileno was not quick enough to grab them, the devil made them vanish. The following day, the bush was just bush.

Similar frustrations involve accounts about shamans who successfully replicated in the bush one of the most treasured features of the whites' knowledge: money production. Some people argue that decades earlier Carancho was one of the few shamans able to create money this way. In 1996, while we were chatting at a farming camp near the marshes, Marcelino, one of his grandsons, told me that Carancho was once drinking aloja with other men and decided to call his payák to get money in order to buy wine. Marcelino mimicked his grandfather extending his arms to grab loads of money materializing in front of him. Like the money created by "white magicians" in San Martín del Tabacal, this money had a life of its own: once spent, it returned to him. Yet Carancho never used that money to accumulate wealth. When I asked Marcelino whether Carancho became rich, he answered: "No, he didn't. He only asked for five pesos. . . . The old man only needed it to have a drink. Not much. Five pesos, but exactly like the five-peso note from the factory: with all the numbers, everything, everything, as if it were from the factory. . . . I saw it. . . . But he didn't ask for a one hundred-peso note. . . . Just a one peso-note, *centavos* [cents], when he needed tobacco." Marcelino emphasized that Carancho had been able to replicate in precise details, and in the Chaco, the power of the money factories: the capacity to create bank notes "with all the numbers, everything." This mimesis, nonetheless, did not reproduce a capitalist logic of accumulation. Carancho was happy with a few pesos to buy his basic "vices" and never bothered asking for more. Despite his remarkable powers, which currently no pioGonáq can replicate, he died as poor as other Toba. His shamanic knowledge was powerful enough to obtain money out of thin air but useless to accumulate riches.

49. The wealth of the ancient ones.
Cahenacachigi returning from the river,
ca. 1930s. *Courtesy of David Leake.*

The memory of these failed attempts by shamans to access wealth is another expression of how, for many people, poverty has become part of their aboriginality and the local landscape, as a condition that not even shamans can escape.

Yet this spatial inscription of poverty is unstable and contradictory. Even those who attribute their poverty to their ignorance are more than just passively internalizing hegemonic discourses; they are also expressing their feeling that the capacity of the do'okohé to produce immense riches requires a power beyond their comprehension. Additionally, many people intertwine explanations that naturalize their poverty as a condition of their aboriginality with accounts that, on the contrary, blame it on the relations of domination imposed on them by "the rich" or "the whites," which for most Toba are synonymous. These perceptions are informed by the memory of a past of independence and by the resilience and local knowledge that people living in poverty produce in the bush.

With the Fish, We're Rich

In contrast with some of the preceding interpretations, many Toba articulate memories that historicize and hence denaturalize poverty. Thus, it is common to hear people argue that their real poverty only began with the disappearance of the river. Eduardo and I were once talking about current afflictions in the Toba villages and he evoked, as counterpoint, the memory of the river: "In those days, they say that our parents didn't feel the poverty, because they had a lot of food, in the river, the fields, the mariscal. When this part was flooded, people's suffering began." These memories locate the origin of poverty not only in time but also in space: in the deep geographical changes stirred by the disappearance of the Pilcomayo. Some people project that transition from plenty to poverty farther back in time and space: onto those grasslands once inhabited by fiercely independent ancient ones. These memories further denaturalize current conditions of poverty, to the extent that, when remembering those times, some people emphasize that the yagaikipí were not poor at all; rather, they were "rich," owned large numbers of goats, sheep, and horses, and had plenty of bush food. People define this abundance through local markers of wealth (such as goats and sheep) and through the food that symbolizes the aboriginality and resilience of *both* ancient ones and new ones. The current importance of bush food, in short, materializes *in the present* some of the memories of abundance and well-being projected onto the past.

This experience often counters the sense that theirs is a land of hardship and in fact makes many people talk about "the bush" as a place of plenty. This abundance is grounded in particular sites: the *viáq ónaGaik* or nice bush — sections with large quantities of animals, fruits, and honey — and the marshlands. But more often than not, many people project this abundance onto "the bush" as generic container of all local spaces and emphasize the wide variety of resources still available in their lands by reciting long lists of animals, fish, fruits, and varieties of honey. As Tomás put it: "I like the bush. It has everything. It has many things: honey, yana, extranjera, lachiguana, bala [different honey types], rabbit, viscacha, deer, birds, fish." These lists are a subtle yet telling counterpoint to the memory of the seemingly endless commodities obtained in the arreglo grande in San Martín del Tabacal. Many people in fact compare bush food to *mercaderías* (store-bought food) and argue that the bush provides them with resources comparable to the latter but with one crucial advantage: they

50. The mercaderías of the bush. *Photo by author.*

are available to everybody at no cost. Some even compare their lands with an enormous store where people can just help themselves. "Fish is almost the same as the mercadería in the store," Bernardo told me. "When you don't look for it, you don't eat. But when you look for it, you eat and you're at ease." Accounts like this reinforce the sense that "the bush" is a presence that is always there, regardless of the mood of those who may temporarily stop foraging and feel attracted by other places, such as the villages or Pozo de Maza.

Through the metaphor of the bush as a store of sorts, people appropriate a symbol of commodities and money to account for a different type of abundance and also to delimit a noncommodified place of autonomy in relation to well-off paisanos, who purchase mercaderías at actual stores. As part of local forms of contestation opposing contrasting visions of poverty and wealth, Toba living in poverty often turn these images of abundance into metaphors of wealth, in which the latter is defined by non-commodified criteria. In February 1996 Roberto, a man in his thirties, was telling me about the belated arrival of the marshes' floods, which ended a long drought and increased the productivity of fishing. Wrapping up his argument, he said: "With the fish, we're rich." This view of bush food as a source of wealth, as a resource that makes the Aborígenes rich, is also connected to the knowledge required to be a successful forager: a skill that counters what many perceive as their ignorance of how to manufacture money.

Bush devils are also behind people's access to this wealth. In 1997 Diego

told me how a payák would approach a man in the bush to give him shamanic power. He said that the man first notices that his foraging skills
improve significantly: "The payák gives him everything he has. It gives
him power. When he forages over there, he finds honey. When he goes
over there, he finds whatever he wants. He becomes rich. . . . It gives
him the complete thing. Everything, everything, everything." The riches
and money that bush devils occasionally offered shamans did not change
the conditions of poverty in which they lived; yet when they offer the
skills to obtain bush food, this time people can become "rich" and get
"everything."

The nostalgic memory of the plantation's wealth does not change the
fact that ultimately most people saw those riches as alien to them. By
the same token, it would be misleading to dismiss the imageries analyzed
above as ideological mystifications of conditions of dispossession. People's
perception that the bush is an alternative source of wealth does not change
their acute awareness of their poverty; it simply asserts their refusal to ac-
cept that there is only one criterion, that of money and commodities, to
measure collective well-being.

16

Journeys to Strange Lands

We were talking [about the bean farms] and saying to each other:
"What a strange land. All the bad things come out."
—Antonio, 2000

The dimensions of the bush examined in previous chapters are linked not only to the memory of kahogonaGá and to current social practices but also to the labor migrations that, from the 1970s onward, have taken Toba men and women to new geographies. Work on distant farms has recreated the spatialized forms of estrangement produced at the ingenio and given new meanings to the healing, resilience, local knowledge, poverty, and noncommodified abundance embedded in the bush. Experiences of wage labor at these farms are also informed by memories of San Martín del Tabacal, through the sedimentation of those memories in notions of locality and through perceptions of the contrasts that make the ingenio and the farms different from each other. Some aspects of Tabacal's weight in current labor migrations emerged one evening in June 2000, as Antonio and I were chatting under the pale light of a kerosene lantern and he was telling me about his recent trip to a bean farm near Embarcación, a few dozen kilometers northeast of Tabacal. Once the group of about seventy men and women stepped out of the truck that brought them there, he told me, they spread out in smaller groups to set up their camps near densely forested hills. Antonio, his wife, and another couple set theirs very close to the hill. He said that he felt uneasy about the location but, tired from the trip, they all slept well the first night. The following morning, a cold south wind caused Antonio to enter the forest, looking for firewood. He felt a strange presence and suspected that a ghost, a *nepakál*, was near. That night, as they were in their shack, they heard strange noises. Antonio remembered:

I had a flashlight and so did my *compañero* [companion]. And we heard a noise. The other chango [guy] saw a . . . [he paused for a few seconds]. He thought it was an animal that turned into another animal. First, it was a tiger. . . . My compañero saw one that looked like a big tiger. . . . We got scared and my wife said: "Let's get out of here! Let's go where the other people are!" I pointed the flashlight to where the animal was and it looked like an African lion. It had long hair, like this [he moved his hands around his head]. It turned out it had become that animal, but it was a soul. It chased us away. We left the camp and all our clothes stayed there.

The next morning, news about the nepakál, the African lion, and the tiger spread quickly to the other camps and most people felt ill at ease. Three pioGonáq were in the group and they all said they had dreamed about the soul. They announced that it belonged to a Toba man, himself a shaman, who had died in those forests many years earlier. They said that the soul told them, as Antonio put it, "that all the Toba would die here." Since a young man had already fallen sick, quickly interpreted as a bad omen, many wanted to quit work. "We were demanding that we had to go back," Antonio related. "People said that we had to return. But the patrón didn't want to, because he needed the people. Everybody wanted to come back. We were afraid someone would die." Others, however, opposed the idea. Ramón was one of them. He was also scared but preferred to stay, for he could not afford to return home empty-handed. "I didn't get that idea of coming back because of the necessity," he told me a few days after Antonio had described the incident. He added: "What was I going to earn if I returned? I'd earn nothing." In the end, under the assurance they would be transferred to another finca, people decided to stay. Antonio, his wife, and his companions dismantled their shack and built a new one farther from the hills and deeper into the farm.

A few days after I talked with Antonio and Ramón, I raised the topic with Emiliano. We were at his household and I commented that it looked as if the nepakál in the bean farm was that of a Toba man, a paisano. He did not look surprised and immediately evoked San Martín del Tabacal: "Yes," he told me, "he was a paisano, because in those years many people died when we went to the ingenio. People died a lot, over there in the ingenio. The mountains. Ooh! A lot of people died." The memory of the ingenio impregnates Toba work in the bean farms in myriad ways: in souls that evoke the horrors of past generations and also, as we shall see, in the devils that inhabit the hills overlooking the farms and in stories about human bones scattered in much of the area. Memories of kahogonaGá also project glimpses of the ingenio's wealth onto those hills and shape sexual imageries associated with the farms. In this chapter, I draw on these dimensions to examine how these workplaces are socially and culturally configured in tense relationship with the bush and the memory of the sugar plantations. The analysis of the new patterns of labor migration takes us, first, back to the processes that followed the mechanization of Tabacal and their social and spatial impact on Toba social practice.

The Return to the Bush and the Remaking of the Hinterland

People in their fifties and sixties argue that they were never warned that the migrations to San Martín del Tabacal were coming to an end. One year, they agree, the mayordomos simply stopped coming. As Enrique put it, reflecting the frustration they may have felt back then: "They forgot the people." Many Toba talk about that moment as if the administration had broken a moral pact that for decades had firmly integrated them within the ingenio's geography. Their substitution for bulldozers, tractors, and digging machines confirmed that their labor was not needed anymore. The sense of being workers of little value now led to the perception that they were not valuable at all. Once severed from that center of power and wealth that had so potently molded their subjectivity, the Toba had to stay in their lands and search for alternative sources of commodities. But their lands were becoming a different place. The destruction of the mission and the formation of the marshes added a new spatial dimension to the end of their work in kahogonaGá. For decades the Pilcomayo River, Misión El Toba, and San Martín del Tabacal had been part of the same spatial, cultural, and historical ensemble. They had emerged as meaningful locales in close interconnection with each other, and the dismemberment of this spatial pattern in a relatively brief time span was parallel to the rise of new social forces in the area.

In the 1960s and 1970s the production of fence posts out of quebracho colorado trees (*Schinopsis quebracho colorado*) became a booming local industry. Merchants and wealthy Criollos set up mobile camps or *obrajes* that brought about an important spatial and social reconfiguration in the Chaco interior. In a few years the obrajes depleted quebracho colorado trees in the entire region and by the late 1970s post production was in decline.[1] Yet for several years large numbers of Aborígenes who had until then been employed by San Martín del Tabacal worked for these obra-jeros as *hacheros* (post cutters). The obrajes generated a selective depletion of the bush and took groups of hacheros and their families to densely forested, uninhabited hinterland areas. This labor experience was signifi-cantly different from that at the cane fields. These work sites were located not in faraway lands but in the Chaco interior; they were also small pro-ductive units that consisted of a *provedería* (a store where people obtained packaged food), a water tank, and a camp. Toba men worked in small groups spread over a wide area and were paid by piecework according to the posts' size and quality.[2] For the first time in decades, women were not hired, which made them dependent on their husbands' income. Having to adapt to a labor situation that relegated them to household tasks, women usually moved with their men to the obrajes, where they prepared food, looked for firewood, and looked after children.

The obrajes turned the bush into a contradictory geography. They pulled people out of their hamlets and took them to the place that epito-mized their aboriginality. Yet this bush was a place different from the one trekked through marisca trips. Obrajes were located deep in the cen-tral Chaco, in state-owned lands where the provincial government had granted logging permits (*guías*) to private obrajeros. Most Toba had never been to these places and, even though men set out to hunt and women to gather fruits, they never felt entirely at ease. Further, social relations dif-ferent from the ones defining the bush at home structured these places. The obrajes produced a new type of bush fractured between markers of aboriginality, such as hunting and gathering, and exploitative conditions, in a contradictory process that combined estrangement and local knowl-edge. People remember that, not being familiar with those places, it was common to get lost, a symbol of the diablos' prevalence over human skills. Indeed, bush devils were a recurrent presence in those areas and many people remember that at night one could hear strange, disturbing noises, such as the distant echo of somebody hitting a pole, as if devils were paro-dying human labor. These diablos were responsible for various forms of physical harm. I once asked Tomás whether there were diablos near the obrajes and he touched his waist as he nodded and answered: "That's why I got a disease in my waist. Ooh! We were working in the bush for so many months. That bush payák got me. I had a fever. I was in bed for several days. My waist ached a lot. . . . It wasn't just any type of disease, like cough or fever, but the devil's. That's what got me." As they did at the ingenio, many people read afflictions related to labor exploitation through a habitus that connects the aching body with hostile entities and a hostile landscape.

The obrajes, however, left a profound scar on the almost undisputed hegemony previously held by devils in those areas. By penetrating the thickest sections of bush, hacheros wrestled control over those places from nonhuman beings. They trimmed dense sections of forest and contributed to scaring away the giant snakes and creatures like wosáq, especially in areas of viáq hakoiwók (bad bush) previously feared by foragers. Therefore, current Toba perceptions that the bush is a place free of past dangers are partially the outcome of marks left by their own labor on the local geography.

Oil exploration in the 1980s further transformed and trimmed the formerly thick hinterland, for teams working for the old state petroleum company (YPF) cleared a grid of trails parallel and perpendicular to each other (roughly every five kilometers) all over northwestern Formosa.[3] By the 1990s, obrajes and oil exploration were part of the past, yet their presence had contributed to defining the bush's physical layout as a place deprived of past mysteries.

Another sector that began hiring Toba men were the cattle ranches located thirty to forty kilometers away, across the marshes in *chaatá*, the north, as many people call the Paraguayan Chaco. These estancias had already hired men in the 1960s and when the cycle of obrajes came to a close they were the nearest source of seasonal wage labor. Work in the ranches transformed perceptions of locality by opening a new (if meager) source of commodities not far from the villages but across an international border. Small groups of men cross the border usually between July and September, when the marshlands recede and the cooler weather is more conducive to intense physical labor.[4] Despite weak controls by the Argentinean and Paraguayan gendarmerías, the border crossing defines much of this labor experience, for the estrangement many men feel at the estancias is partially grounded in their location in another national geography. In the ingenio, as we have seen, the lack of ID papers made many Toba feel that even Bolivian workers had more status and power than they. By the 1990s, in contrast, most Toba had documentos and young men's labor in Paraguay reinforced their Argentinean identity and the notion that citizenship rights are spatially defined. Some men feel that as Argentinean citizens in chaatá they are more vulnerable to abuses, and they tell stories of mistreatment by armed foremen and of their powerlessness to complain to Paraguayan authorities. Since people get paid in Paraguayan currency, they spend their earnings before returning home, which further affirms the territorial cleavage created by the border. Eighty years after the army forced their ancestors to be immersed within the Argentinean nation-state, many Toba see the border as a divide that *produces* different rights and particular risks and that reinforces a national identity that was for decades both imposed on them (through violence) and denied to them (through their status as noncitizens).

Foremen in the ranches usually send Toba men to work in densely forested areas, where they make clearings, weed fences, and occasionally cut posts (paid by the day). As in the obrajes, men work in the bush yet in places unknown to them and haunted by payák forces. Amalio remembered how he and his companions were harassed by diablos while working in Paraguay: "What's dangerous over there is the diablo payák, which lives in the thick bush in that estancia. Sometimes we were working deep inside the bush, sleeping, and this payák appeared. It was all hairy and a little short. That was dangerous, because it got close to us and bothered us. Some guys were sleeping and the payák came and grabbed them, touched them. You woke up and saw it, but it disappeared right away." I asked him whether devils like those exist near the Toba villages. "No. I never saw them around here. Many times I got deep inside the bush at the time of the iguanas and never found anything. Over there, there are diablos. But over here, it's quieter." As part of the same dialectic of memory and place examined in previous chapters, many people feel that the devils in Paraguay overshadow with their intrusive presence those at home and that, like the mountain devils, they do not establish relations of reciprocity with humans. This contrast illustrates that the devils' action in Toba lands is not simply the result of their location within a generic "bush." Devils in obrajes and estancias inhabit the forests of the Chaco interior but have alienating and debilitating features. In Toba habitus, what defines these devils' engagement with humans is their immersion within a moral geography constituted by particular social relations and practices.

Geographical Dispersion and Time-Space Compression

New perceptions of place resulting from labor in Paraguay expanded in the 1970s and 1980s with the arrival of contractors sent by sectors anchored in other regions: the bean farms located in tadéwo (the west) and the cotton farms in the east of Formosa, *tayíñi* (the east).[5] This labor demand is noticeably different from the one that once originated in the San Francisco River Valley; it created more dispersed patterns of migration that broke with the previous concentration of the Toba's labor in a single locale to which they returned every year. The spatial and cultural implications of this change were profound. The new migrations took Toba men and women to farms that on occasions would not recruit them the following year, an irregularity that significantly decreased their acquaintance with these places. And whereas until the 1960s the sugar plantations were people's main point of reference outside their lands, in the 1990s they had new parameters of orientation: first, the axis opposing tadéwo and tayíñi, the west and the east, along the road connecting Formosa to Embarcación, and second the axis uniting their hamlets and the estancias across the border.

The speed involved in labor migrations has also decreased perceptions of the distance separating the bush from other places. The time-space compression analyzed by David Harvey (1989) as a distinctive feature of capitalism's geopolitics, in other words, also reached the Chaco interior. In the early twentieth century, the journey on foot to the ingenios took up to two months. In the 1930s, once Toba migrants began boarding the train in Ingeniero Juárez, travel time was reduced to three or four days. In the 1980s, with the construction of new roads and the use of trucks, contractors took people to their destination in a matter of hours. This compression and the dispersion of Toba laborers in myriad places make the farms in the west and the east much less commanding in their physical and social presence than the ingenio, especially because their capacity to absorb laborers is also much lower. Whereas between 60 or 70 percent of the total Toba population regularly migrated to San Martín del Tabacal, only 10 or 15 percent currently go to the farms (even less to the estancias). Additionally, people work four to six weeks in tadéwo (in May–June) and two or three months in tayíñi (between February/March and April/May) and in any given year those who work at one harvest often do not at the other. As a result, people stay most of the year in their lands, which has strengthened the force of the bush in everyday practices, imageries, and political struggles.

Currently, most young people see the bean farms in the west as their main source of items such as clothing, blankets, or radios. The recurrent crisis of cotton production in eastern Formosa has significantly deteriorated working conditions there and by the mid-1990s farms from that region had almost stopped recruiting Toba harvesters.[6] The memory of the sugar plantations permanently informs people's assessment of these places. Marcelina, who worked in Tabacal as a teenager, told me about her negative experience in a cotton farm near the town of Pirané: "It's not worth it, because you earn nothing. The ingenio was worth it, in the past, because you earned money. In Pirané, it's only hunger." The memory of San Martín del Tabacal makes women particularly critical of the farms, for contractors include their work within a family account administered by their husbands. The ingenio's mechanization, in this regard, meant the end of the only trabajo in which women were paid separately. Young men and women who have never been to the ingenio also compare what they have heard about it with their current experience of earning just a few staples in the east or the west. Memory haunts these labor experiences in further ways.

A Strange Land

Tayíñi and tadéwo are regions with distinctive landscapes, histories, and agricultural sectors. Even though in both places people are paid by piece-work (per hectare in the bean harvest and per kilo in the cotton harvest) and work in teams formed by friends or family members, the different geographies in which these farms are immersed and the memories they evoke create distinctive perceptions of place.[7]

The cotton farms hiring Toba men and women are small and medium-size units that, unlike other *colonias* (farms) in the region, are not mechanized. They are located in totally flat extensions of campo, cleared out in the early and mid-twentieth century. This is a region to which few Toba had been prior to the 1970s. Because of this and the intermittent character of their work as cotton harvesters, most people feel little connection with the area. Even though some Toba occasionally see lights moving on the cotton fields, often interpreted as payák, most agree that it is rare to encounter devils, souls, or dangerous animals. When I asked why, most explained that the area is nónaGa: flat, treeless extensions of open country. In other words, in their explanations most Toba grounded their perceptions of danger (or lack thereof) in the landscape.

Tadéwo, on the contrary, is part of a geography directly related to Toba history and memories. Hills dominate the farms to the west and thick and tall forests cover part of the region. These farms are run by large companies that have semimechanized the harvest: men and women line up (pre-

51. Working in the bean fields, 1996. *Photo by author.*

viously cut) bean plants so that threshing machines gather them. While
people bow down to do their work, the memories evoked by kahogonaGá weigh heavily on them. Devils and other dangers are plentiful there,
people agree, "because of the hills." The past horrors of the cane fields
sometimes materialize in the souls of dead Toba that adopt the shape of
African lions and Bengali tigers. Old people claim having seen these animals—the "big puma" and "big jaguar"—in the jungles surrounding San
Martín del Tabacal. Some people comment that they also saw them at
a circus in Ingeniero Juárez. These animals symbolize a wild nature coalescing in creatures that, by being alien to the Chaco (and, in fact, to
the American continent), epitomize all that is strange, foreign, and potent
about the landscape surrounding the ingenio and the bean farms.

As part of this sedimentation of memories, many Toba claim that at
night in tadéwo one can hear voices emerging from bones scattered in
the area. In 1999 I was talking with Antonio about his experience at a
farm near Embarcación. "When the weather changes," he said, "all the
voices come out. Everybody was scared. . . . Over there, you can hear
many people who died. You find the bones and they scream." Many Toba
explain the appearance of souls or devils in changes of weather, a storm
approaching or cold wind suddenly blowing from the south, as if these
atmospheric variations would awaken old memories buried in the geography. In this case, when I asked Antonio whose remains they were, his
answer was ambiguous: they belonged, he told me, to "people who died
in the forests." Yet those bones are not unrelated to the collective mem-

ory of the ingenio; they are echoes of past horrors that left traces in space: human remains that have become a physical component of those places.

The hills of tadéwo are also the home, people agree, of countless devils that share many features with those of the ingenio: they are faceless, evil spirits whose actions are aimed primarily at causing physical harm. The overwhelming levels of disease and death that characterized San Martín del Tabacal are absent but people claim that these devils make them ill and that, occasionally, they also kill. At night, they approach the workers' camps as moving lights, hairy humanoids, or wild animals. They also materialize as naked men or women who try to seduce harvesters. According to Fernando: "If they hug you at night, you're going to die." In this regard, in the bean farms the action of devils has sexual overtones absent in memories of the mountain devils. While chatting at his home, Luis told me about the dangers of working at night in the west:

> Some people work at night, but it's very dangerous. There're many diablos payák over there. One of them is like a female devil. She does things in order to kill a man. That's why we don't work at night. A Wichí friend died because he worked at night. He didn't have a knife wound, nothing. Maybe a payák did it. . . . Many people died. It's very dangerous. We always pray to have the strength to keep on working. . . . We always sleep together. At night, this payák makes noises like voices.

Luis feminized this devil as a stealthy, deadly presence that forces some workers to stay at night in their camps. He also pointed out that some people try to counter fear by praying, as some foragers do in the Chaco, invoking the legacy of Anglican missionization. Shamans working on the farms try to keep devils at bay through their dreams but most Toba feel that the best protection is just caution. Even though on clear nights some people work to maximize their earnings, many others do not leave their camps until dawn. As Antonio put it: "At that time we couldn't leave. We couldn't leave. Around five or six in the evening we stopped working, because we were scared." Workmates sharing the same shack often take shifts to warn of anything unusual. Several people told me that at night they often hear diablos singing like Criollos or screaming like wild animals. These spirits often leave marks of their presence in the camps, such as knife cuts on people's clothes. Unlike bush devils in the Chaco, which rarely invade domestic spaces, diablos in tadéwo undermine the boundaries between domestic and work spaces and immerse the camps within the climate of apprehension involving the farms as a whole.

Influenced by the stories their parents and grandparents told them about riches buried near San Martín del Tabacal, young people argue that the hills west of the farms are full of treasures. Yet whereas the "gold boxes" in kahogonaGá were semantically linked to the ingenio's wealth, riches in tadéwo are physically and socially removed from the farms. More so than in the ingenio, where people felt they benefited at least partially from its wealth, this separation often turns these riches into unreachable entities. This gap is recreated by devils. Some people claim that harvesters can access these treasures only if kidnapped by a payák. Stories with sexual overtones about female devils abducting men in the bean farms are relatively widespread in the Toba villages. Hugo told me about a payaGó, a female devil and "a beautiful woman" who kidnapped a boy from the bean fields:

> Over there, there's a woman who snatches people. . . . She grabbed a boy and took him to the cerro [hill]. She took him there and showed him her house. She showed him all the things. She has everything. They say the woman has a lot of money. They say they got together as if he were her husband. She was a beautiful woman. They say they had two kids, like these [he pointed to his little children], but they were monkeys. . . . The boy had long hair and hands like this, with long nails. This is the story of all the cerro. The cerro has everything. There's everything over there.

This narrative brings to light some of the spatialized perceptions of riches examined in the previous chapter: the notion that wealth implies "having everything" and that this is the attribute of distant places, in this case the hills near Embarcación. But because these riches are controlled by devils, they are alienating and ultimately dehumanizing forces that turn people into animallike creatures. Many Toba express their estrangement from this wealth, once again, in perceptions of knowledge and ignorance. As in the ingenio, many people argue they cannot reach those treasures because they "don't know" the place. A similar attitude is conveyed in stories about men who come down from the hills to offer workers the chance "to get rich." According to Antonio, one night he and his workmates saw an old man with a suitcase wandering the bean fields. The following day, a Guaraní worker explained to them that the suitcase was "full of money" and that the old man would share it if they left an offering of coca leaves, wine, and cigarettes. I asked Antonio whether they left the offering. "N ̣ " he said. "Only the Chaguanco [Guaraní] did. Since we're not used to t we didn't leave coca or wine. In this area of ours, we don't see thing

52. Proveduría at a bean farm, 1996. *Photo by author.*

that." He added that after listening to the Guaraní man, they said to each other: "What a strange land. All the bad things come out."

This view of the farms as strange lands explicitly defined in contrast with home turns them into places ruled by negative forces ("bad things") that the Toba ignore ("we're not used to that"). As in kahogonaGá, this estrangement has political implications. Men and women challenge exploitation and put limits on labor discipline on a daily basis: by handling bean plants with little care when the contractor is not watching, cooking beans to save money at the proveduría, taking large (sixty kilos) bean bags home at the end of the harvest, or putting pressure on the contractor through individual demands (for instance, to bring in more drinking water, take ill people to the nearest dispensary, or lower prices at the proveduría). Yet many Toba argue that when confronted with systematic abuse they "don't know" how to go on strike. When strikes do occur, they are usually led by Criollos or Guaraní to demand a wage increase or lower mercadería prices. This dependence on other workers' leadership reinforces the sense that tadéwo is a place ruled by fields of force different from those of the Chaco, where many Toba have been more confident in articulating assertive forms of contention.

These localized forms of estrangement are parallel to, and stand in tension with, attempts to turn the farms into places of relative autonomy from the moral rules that dominate some Toba villages through the *Consejos de la Iglesia* (Church Councils). Formed by men and women usually over fifty years of age, these village-based councils try hard to keep the missionaries' legacy alive and pursue a strict agenda against "vices" (drinking and chewing coca leaves), brujos, and practices perceived as immoral. Tomás, a council member, once told me about their tasks, half jokingly and half seriously: "We're like policemen." Single men and women are the primary target of the councils' action and for this reason many among them see the farms as relative shelters from this control. Current labor migrations thus produce a spatialized politics similar to the one that once opposed Misión El Toba to the ingenio, and some youngsters go to the west and the east with the aim of drinking wine, chewing coca leaves, and having casual intercourse. As Antonio summarized it: "In the place we were at, there was a lot of action." The eroticization of devils examined above is not unrelated to this experience. As in San Martín del Tabacal, "the action" involves socializing with other workers: Criollos, Guaraní, and especially Wichí (in the cotton farms, only the latter), who usually conduct the same tasks and get paid the same wages as the Toba do. Intercourse is not associated with the exuberant bodily performances once mobilized by the nomí, but "the action" and "the vices" remind young people of what they heard from their parents and grandparents about San Martín del Tabacal. In the winter of 1996, I was talking with Martín about the farms and he described how he and his friends walked at night between camps searching for women. "It was the same as in the ingenio," he said. References to the sugar plantations remind young people that, despite conditions of exploitation, distant places can provide them with niches of partial autonomy also sought out by their ancestors.

The fact that some people wander at night to find sexual partners while others stay in their camps to avoid diablos illustrates the tense entanglement of work, estrangement, fear, and sexuality characterizing Toba experiences at the farms. In one of the lengthy conversations I shared with Antonio about tadéwo, his memories captured some of these tensions. "I liked it there," he said of the west. "I almost didn't want to come back." I asked him why. "Because of the vices. We also have them here but over there there's work. Besides, the patrón didn't let us come back because we're hardworking. . . . But in the end, we missed our families, because after a long time you feel homesick." I asked him whether he was considering going back to tadéwo. "No, I'm not. I don't know how it is that I don't even think about going back there." The west was for Antonio many things at the same time: a place he liked because of the "vices" and the trabajo available there, a place ruled by the patrón, and a place he did not plan on returning to.

We're Happy Because We Got Back Here

The dispersion of Toba labor in the west, the east, and the north has made the opposition between the bush and work sites more diffusive than the one that existed at the time of the ingenio. Yet labor migrations begin and end at the same place, "the bush," and these journeys continue to produce meanings about home. The presence of threatening, debilitating, and at points deadly devils in bean farms and ranches informs the perception that the bush in their lands is a "quiet place," where devils contribute to reproducing healing forces and access to bush food. The trips to "strange lands" that they "don't know," defined by the lack of control over the pace and products of their labor, shape the notion that the bush is a place they *do* know. The commodities earned on farms and ranches and the riches hidden in tadéwo further reproduce local views of wealth as a spatialized social condition distant from the Chaco interior. Yet the unreachable, alienating nature of these riches and the meager staples brought back home also shape the perception that the bush contains a different, non-commodified abundance. In short, these labor experiences also contribute to delimiting the bush's spatial and cultural configuration.

As occurred when their parents returned from San Martín del Tabacal to mourn their dead, the contrasts mentioned above become particularly apparent when people return home. In August 1997, as darkness was falling on our village, Kiko, a seventeen-year-old, dropped by for a visit. He had just returned from Embarcación and was eager to talk about the experience. Sitting across a table illuminated by candles and full of notebooks and tapes, he told me the contractor had refused to take him and two other Toba men back home. He left them instead, with a group of Wichí, in El Potrillo (seventy kilometers away), which meant they had to pay a Criollo to drive them home. When they finally arrived, Kiko had with him a large bean bag, a few oranges, a portable stereo, and no cash. That was all he brought back from the west. He then told me, as the candles' light illuminated his smiling eyes: "When we got here we were happy, because we got here. It's not like when we were over there in tadéwo. We're happy because we got back here."

17

Locations of Contention and Hegemony

Is it conceivable that the exercise of hegemony might leave space
untouched? — Henri Lefebvre, *The Production of Space*

In my exploration of the memories and practices that come together to
constitute the bush, I have emphasized the malleability of places but put
temporarily aside most of the struggles that make the bush a contested
locality. At this point, it is important to turn to this political dimension and
examine how most Toba asserted control over the bush while migrating
to the ingenios and, more recently, while working in the farms and facing
the challenges posed by the presence of state resources in their villages.
The bush was never simply "there," as a given entity, for people living
in poverty to benefit from. Most people had to struggle to secure access
to its resources, confirming David Harvey's (1989:237–38) point that any
struggle over power relations is also a struggle over space. These forms of
contention have opposed Toba and Criollo settlers but also people living
in poverty and well-off leaders. In this chapter I analyze how local conflicts have revolved around the reproduction of collective relations of production and how they have recently become enmeshed in party politics,
the internalization of the ideology of trabajo, and the demand for public-
sector jobs. These hegemonic fields of contention, I argue, are mobilizing,
straining, and politicizing the places and memories analyzed in previous
chapters.

The Making of a Collective Place

The current perception of Toba men and women that they have a *right*
to make use of the bush, and that this collective right is fundamental in
the resilience granted by marisca, is the historical result of decades of ten-

sions with settlers over land use and of their work in places organized along capitalist relations of production. The collective *use* of land certainly existed prior to those experiences; but this practice gained force in its tension with the forms of private ownership brought by a new political economy. When many Toba remember that their ancestors did not know that cattle "had an owner" they shed light on a clash between different types of ownership, a clash that was absent from their previous territorial confrontations with the Wichí and Nivaclé. It was through this dialectic that people developed, first, the notion of the bush as a place collectively shared by all Toba, and, second, the perception that this collective use had to be *defended* from new actors. These struggles were simultaneously spurred by the debilitating and destructive forces haunting them in kahogonaGá, which made it crucial to secure the bush as a place of relative autonomy from labor exploitation.

During most of the twentieth century, these territories in the western Chaco were government lands over which no local actor had legal entitlement and most Toba challenged the settlers' presence through the everyday use of local spaces. Competition over land was exacerbated by the seasonal absence of the hundreds of men, women, and children who went to the ingenios, which facilitated the occupation of land by settlers. As a result, the return from the cane fields often entailed conflicts over new paddocks or puestos built by Criollos. The mobility of extended families through foraging trips over wide areas was one of the main means of challenging the settlers' presence. As Anna Tsing has observed (1993:150), this type of mobility is far from being part of a repetitive, tradition-bound pattern; rather, it is connected to the expansion of social spaces and the political negotiation of local fields of power (see Massey 1994:150; Harvey 1989:234). Mobility enabled many Toba to dispute the Criollos' use of their lands and re-create the bush as a practiced place: a space claimed as a locality of their own. In 1942 Dora Tebboth noted that in a short stretch of time Toba villages had multiplied from four to nine. She added: "These small groups are continuously clashing with the local settlers, scenes arise and we can never get at the truth" (1989:134). Tebboth was bringing to light the political dimensions of Toba mobility and illustrating that these groups had conflicts with the settlers because they were *moving* to new sites. For several decades, conflicts sporadically involved cattle killing, a practice that revived memories of violence and asserted control over land by openly challenging Criollo notions of private property. Currently, mobility has been restricted by the construction of schools, dispensaries, water pumps, and brick houses but conflicts with settlers continue involving mobile forms of appropriation of space.[1]

Patterns of movement, as we saw in chapter 6, also opposed Misión El Toba and the bush as sites ruled by different moral economies. By the 1960s, however, the initial zeal of the first generation of missionaries was winding down. In 1957 Alfred Leake left for Britain for five years and, affected by a shortage of staff, direct missionary presence among the Toba became intermittent (Makower 1989:135–36). Even though Leake returned and stayed in the area until his 1971 retirement (when he and his wife went back to England), the mission was gradually becoming a different place. The new generations of Anglican missionaries were more concerned with development and social justice than with immorality and heathenism. By the time Leake left, staff at Misión El Toba was organizing a (short-lived) logging cooperative, offering technical assistance in farming, and further encouraging handicraft commercialization. Most Toba had also changed. By then, adults in their thirties and forties had been born after Alfredo's arrival and had been socialized within the parameters of the Anglican mission. Even though pockets of dissatisfaction persisted, in the early 1970s the bush camps were losing their aura as sites where people defied Anglican codes of morality. When floods destroyed Misión El Toba, the missionaries withdrew to Ingeniero Juárez and lost the direct presence they had constructed among the Toba for over four decades. The 1982 Malvinas War between Argentina and Britain caused most missionaries to abandon the country for several years, which further debilitated the Anglican presence in the area.

The floods radically transformed the local institutional geography. The destruction of Sombrero Negro and Puerto Yrigoyen (upstream) forced state agencies such as gendarmería to move their local bases to new sites, among them the cluster of ranchos known as Pozo de Maza, which also attracted Wichí groups displaced by the marshes. Most adult Toba had obtained their documentos a few years earlier.[2] With their ID papers, people became more visible within the optics of state bureaucracy but also citizens with formal sets of rights, a status that ended their long political despair over being undocumented Aborígenes in the ingenio. The military dictatorship ruling Argentina from 1976 to 1983, nonetheless, hindered political activism in the area. In those days, *la política* (politics), as people currently define their involvement in party politics, did not exist in their villages as yet. Teodoro remembered: "In the past, I was thinking: 'What's this thing about la política?' We knew nothing about that." All

53. Meeting with government officials, 1997. *Photo by author.*

this changed when in December 1983 new democratically elected governments took office in Argentina and Formosa. State agencies significantly
expanded their presence in Pozo de Maza and the recently relocated Toba
villages, marking the beginning of la política and people's first regular engagement in elections. A 1984 provincial law on indigenous rights gave im-
petus to land claims all over Formosa. Given the missionaries' withdrawal,
the Toba now had to engage the state on their own, without mediators,
and learn a new political language. The struggle over the bush moved to
new fronts and new places.

Prior to the struggle for land titling, Toba leaders (most of them forged
as capitanes in San Martín del Tabacal) had little or no experience in negotiations with state institutions. The land claim significantly expanded their
political experience and their geographical points of reference. Following
strategies debated in assemblies, leaders began traveling to Formosa to
meet government officials and get acquainted with the legal procedures
associated with the claim. This demand led in 1986 to the legal recognition of the western Toba villages as a single *asociación civil* (civil association).[3] The parallel involvement in electoral politics further removed
the struggle with the settlers away from the bush. Leaders began nego-
tiating the electoral support of the Toba villages with members of the
Partido Justicialista (Peronist Party), hegemonic in Formosa, and this increased their bargaining power. Unlike the days of political estrangement
at the ingenio, this momentum paid off. In May 1989 the asociación rep-

resenting the Toba hamlets obtained collective title over 35,000 hectares: an area of roughly fifteen kilometers in width and twenty kilometers in length. Even though the asociación had demanded a larger territory, men and women continue hunting, fishing, and gathering over wide areas outside these boundaries (mostly government-owned lands that are not fenced).

The granting of the title made most Toba gain confidence in their control over local spaces and confirmed they were able to strengthen and reproduce collective access to them. Spatially and politically dispersed and with few votes to offer, the dozen Criollo families living inside Toba lands have not secured land titles in other areas yet and the asociación has forced them to stop constructing paddocks and cutting down trees, a sign of the Toba's new capacity to assert control over the bush.[4]

With the title secured and new state resources arriving in the villages, "the land" gradually lost the political salience of previous years. The rise of la política and the consolidation of the Pozo de Maza municipality as a new gravitational center transformed the local political landscape. The unrewarding trabajo in farms and ranches and the ecological degradation and poverty associated with the bush were further factors causing many people to seek resources and jobs from *el gobierno* (the government). Men grew increasingly concerned about the lack of trabajo in the area and articulated new types of mobilizations. These demands would have a deep impact on the production of meanings about the bush.

The Struggle for Trabajo: Hegemony and Political Subjectivity

Drawing on the memory of the ingenios, the legacy of Anglican socialization, and the influence of government discourses, by the late 1980s the valorization of trabajo had become pivotal to Toba political strategies. Many men see a job in state agencies as an asset associated with the security of a regular source of cash (a *sueldo* or salary) and easy labor tasks carried out in their own hamlets or Pozo de Maza. Among women, concerns over trabajo focus on craftsmanship, an exclusively female arena and one of the few forms of "work" that allows them to obtain goods independently of their husbands (only a handful of women, midwives and teaching assistants, hold public-sector jobs). Since the main crafts buyer is the ICA, women also consider that their trabajo is deeply connected to la política and put permanent pressure on their husbands to demand better conditions of commercialization.

The growing force of the ideology of trabajo in Toba everyday life accentuated the negotiations for jobs and resources in la comuna, an institution particularly malleable to local political pressure. These negotiations peak in the months preceding municipal elections, when the posts of *intendente* (mayor) and *concejales* (the four elective representatives in the municipal council) are at stake. Candidates from different factions (*lemas*) of the Partido Justicialista create webs of supporters through patron-client relationships, in which the distribution of jobs and mercaderías plays a crucial role. By giving away trabajo and store-bought food, Criollo leaders often gain clusters of followers in Toba and Wichí villages. Bernardo articulated the logic of these relations when, in 1997, he justified his support for the Criollo mayor: "Since the man helps me a lot, I have to support him as well. That's why we want to support him as candidate for mayor. . . . If he has something, he'll give me something, at least mercadería." This patronage undermines the salience of markers such as "Toba" and "Wichí" at the time of elections and subsumes them within hegemonic fields linked to party factionalism. As a result, rather than aiming at forming a unified "Toba" political block, Toba leaders and their followers usually confront each other and strike alliances with Criollo and Wichí leaders from different Peronist factions. In each local election, this situation creates a fragmented political landscape of Toba candidates who (in addition to their Toba followers) have clusters of Wichí supporters, Wichí candidates who have clusters of Toba supporters, and Criollo candidates who have followers in both groups. These divisions create recurrent conflicts in the Toba villages. Eduardo captured these strains when he told me, right before an election: "Our ancestors had the war, with spears and knives. We, the new ones, have la política." Party politics, in other words, is often seen as a vicious and wide-ranging arena of confrontation that evokes the violent lifestyles of the ancient ones.

Ernesto Laclau and Chantal Mouffe (1985:58, 85) have argued that hegemony determines the identity of social actors as a plurality of subject positions. Similarly, in the Toba hamlets hegemony produces political identities shaped by manifold fields of antagonism that merge aboriginality, gender, class, and party factionalism. Yet this heterogeneity does not mean, as Laclau and Mouffe claim, that no subject position is more significant than others (1985:36, 84). The predominance of one position over

54. Election day in Pozo de Maza, October 1995. *Photo by author.*

others is not pregiven but situational and as a result *temporal* and *spatial*: that is, the result of the prevalence of one antagonism over others at particular moments and places. During electoral periods, subject positions related to party affiliation assume a dominant force but tend to recede in the intervals (usually two years) that separate elections. And this subject position is permanently molded by people's identity as Aborígenes, which colors party factionalism through the accentuation of divisions between "poor" voters and "rich" leaders. Since for ordinary Toba aboriginality is indissolubly linked to poverty, many of them are critical of well-off leaders who benefit from la política and argue that they see little difference between a Criollo candidate and a "rich" Toba who does not live and behave like "a true Aborigen." Many agree that if they receive more benefits from a Criollo, they have no problems backing him. Paradoxically, people's identity as Aborígenes accentuates the criticism of indigenous leaders, contributes to the support of nonindigenous candidates, and reinforces subject positions linked to party factionalism.

These fields of negotiation and contention had profound implications in the distribution of trabajo in the area. By the early 1990s, several Toba men had gained considerable power within la comuna: including administrative posts and two of the four positions as concejales. In 1992 over sixty men in the three largest hamlets (out of a combined population of about 900) were municipality employees. Most of these jobs (making adobe bricks, clearing bushes, or doing miscellaneous repairs) were part-time, paid very low wages, and were not even registered in the payroll office, but their existence expressed the balance of power reached between ordinary people, indigenous leaders, and Criollo leaders at the municipality.

Yet this balance was unstable, and the neoliberal budget cuts then sweeping through Argentina eventually undermined it. In December 1995 a new Criollo mayor took office in la comuna and, under pressure from the provincial government, laid off most of the part-time employees. Confirming how important the jobs had become as a source of livelihood and how deeply the valorization of trabajo was embedded in people's subjectivity, the layoffs triggered a heated mobilization that momentarily galvanized previously dispersed political energies. When in July 1996 the Formosa governor toured the Toba hamlets in a caravan of four-wheel drives, a group of the laid-off employees did something previously unheard of in the region: they displayed a rudimentary but large sign by the road that read *"Peronistas sin trabajo,"* Peronists without jobs. The display of this sign captured the dialectic of inclusion and exclusion experienced by these men; it highlighted the contradiction between, on the one hand, their identity as peronistas and their previous support of Peronist candidates and, on the other hand, the fact that they had lost what until then had been their reward for their party loyalty: their trabajo.

This protest also underscored one of the paradoxical features of hegemony. William Roseberry (1994) has rightly argued that the concept of hegemony should be used to examine not consent but forms of struggle: the ways in which the images and symbols that subordinate groups use to resist their domination are shaped by the process of domination itself. This is clear in the Toba's struggle for trabajo: a demand that challenges a neoliberal agenda aimed at cutting public spending but is simultaneously caught up in the productive values and ideology inculcated by state institutions. These mobilizations also show that hegemony, as Gavin Smith points out (1999:243, 245), is not something that people simply consume; rather it is a process in which they are active participants in *creating* and reproducing. But more important, the immersion of these struggles within hegemonic fields contributed to the remaking of the local geography, confirming Lefebvre's (1991:11) point that the exercise of hegemony does not leave space untouched.

We're Forgetting the Bush

The mobilizations and negotiations over jobs and resources turned Pozo de Maza into the political and economic center of gravity of the region. Whereas a few decades earlier this site was just an overnight stopover for hundreds of Toba on their way to San Martín del Tabacal, in the 1990s it had grown to absorb local expectations about "the government." A totally new place emerged in the area, entangling the Toba villages and the bush in new sets of relations and conflicts. In the hamlets, everyday conversations include discussions or comments about la comuna, the mayor, or the concejales. And on the local dirt road, one can regularly see pickup trucks and men on bicycles going to and from Pozo de Maza several times a day. By capturing the resources, tensions, and imageries associated with state power, la comuna is gradually devaluating the political and cultural weight of the bush, a situation particularly clear among political leaders and public-sector employees.

In 1995, when he was a part-time employee at the municipality, Tomás told me that it had been more than a year since he had last eaten iguana meat. He added: "Now, we're forgetting the bush. We're getting used to the government. Some women also get used to the government things. Sometimes, the government sends food and women stay here. They don't go to look for food." This account indicates that the dependence on "the government" changed not only patterns of consumption but also patterns of mobility. Tomás highlighted the spatial *fixity* associated with trabajo and state assistance: the fact that it tends to ground people in their hamlets and limit their foraging trips. He also gendered the households' links to the bush by projecting them onto women's foraging practices, a paradoxical point given that many men claim that the bush is a male domain. The value of trabajo has accentuated the images of poverty associated with the bush, and many young men look at marisca in a negative light. While we were chatting next to his rudimentary dwelling at the edge of the bush, Amalio, a man in his mid-thirties and one of the laid-off employees, told me in 1996: "In the past, we suffered so much, when I had to go into the bush, everywhere. It was a lot of effort. When I wasn't lucky, it was worse. I had to return hungry. . . . It's not possible to be like that, without a trabajo. . . . Now I'm thinking about having a trabajo. That's more secure." For Amalio, in sum, the bush is a place of suffering, poverty, and

55. Municipality employees at work, 1992. *Photo by author.*

uncertainty, defined in opposition to the places—the villages and Pozo de Maza—where one can benefit from the regular cash flow of a public-sector job.

The expansion of flood farming in the 1990s, also related to the political and cultural salience of trabajo, was a further force pulling some households away from the bush. Early in 1996 I was talking with Andrés next to his four-hectare field near the marshes. He began telling me how he had gradually abandoned marisca to consolidate his trabajo as a farmer. "Until '87," he said, "I think I was still foraging. I continued foraging. I knew how to look for honey. And the following year, I couldn't go out anymore because I already had trabajo. I already produced my trabajo. Then, I finished. Up to now, I don't forage anymore. . . . I know how to mariscar, but since I have my trabajo, my trabajo helps me out." Like many others, Andrés sees marisca and trabajo as mutually exclusive practices. His account also indicates that his trabajo is strong enough to neutralize marisca even though he "knows" the bush.

These experiences are weakening the bush as an everyday point of reference, increasing the weight of fields and hamlets, and altering previous perceptions of regional geographies of power and wealth. The relative availability of jobs and other resources in Pozo de Maza is also restricting participation in seasonal labor migrations. Since most men feel that trabajo at la comuna is more rewarding than labor on the bean farms, many have redirected their expectations of material progress away from the west and toward Pozo de Maza. Some people point to the contrast between this focalization of their practices on a nearby place and their past experiences as highly mobile workers. Rodolfo, a man in his sixties who regularly works for a Criollo merchant, remembered when people worked all over northeast Formosa at the times of the obrajes: "In those days, we left and worked everywhere. Now it seems that people don't leave anymore because the governor helps us a little. It's not like before when we didn't have documentos. Before, we almost didn't live here. We searched for work." This account illustrates that public-sector jobs and state assistance are retaining many Toba in their lands and curbing the forces that for decades, when they were undocumented Aborígenes deprived of political rights, made them search for work elsewhere.

There is one faraway place, however, that has gained prominence with la política: the east. The trips to Formosa regularly conducted by leaders and their followers have expanded local senses of place to a city that only a few decades earlier was alien to their experience. This has created greater awareness that the provincial center of power is located in tayíñi, a process that is reconfiguring the cartography of wealth and power created by the migrations to San Martín del Tabacal. Unlike the time of the ingenio, this geopolitics is based not on capitalist bosses (such as Patrón Costas) but on politicians and state bureaucracies.

The struggles and expectations through which people weave together these geographies, nonetheless, is not a one-way movement leading toward the gradual demise of the bush; rather, it is a contradictory process that generates multiple tensions and resistances. People living in poverty continue to rely on marisca and continue migrating to the farms and, less significantly, the cattle ranches. Despite the pull toward the villages, Pozo de Maza, and the fields, many do not have other choices. The attempt to adapt to the values and places sanctioned as positive by the state is permanently reshaped by these constraints and by the resilience grounded in marisca and reproduced, this time, by the strains of la política.

At Least We Have the Bush

The manipulations and deception associated with local elections and party factionalism have made most Toba critical and wary of "politics." Many people remember with nostalgia the struggle for the land title, when "the Toba were all united," and complain that nowadays, because of la política, "we're all divided." This longing for a time prior to la política is also closely associated with the memory of the semifull employment granted by San Martín del Tabacal. "At the time of the ingenio, money was worth it," Gervacio once told me. "Now it's very different. Everything is política. Some people wait in order to see if they'll get trabajo, but they wait for nothing. When people went to the ingenio, everybody brought things back. Now with la política it's never enough. It's not like before." In this regard, people invoke the memory of the ingenio's abundance to criticize current conditions of poverty and the false promises aroused by la política, which often seem to reduce life in the villages to an endless game of negotiations and manipulations ("everything is política").

Yet resistance to la política is more often than not anchored in the place that, unlike the ingenio, is more clearly defined as alternative to the sites of trabajo: the bush. Countering the forces examined earlier in this chapter, criticisms of party politics usually draw people's attention away from Pozo de Maza, the hamlets, and the fields and toward the bush. During the periods of increased tensions preceding local elections, it is common to hear people living in poverty argue that once the elections are over, once the mercaderías distributed to buy their votes stop coming, what they will still have is "the bush." These perceptions draw on the memory that this place has been a shelter from state violence, missionary discipline, and labor exploitation. La política thus reconfigures in new ways the autonomy, local knowledge, and resilience sedimented in their lands. In 1995 Tomás had a job at la comuna and had told me that people were "forgetting the bush." Four years later, he had lost his trabajo and was foraging again. In those days, illustrating how senses of place change according to shifting experiences, he told me: "I don't have trabajo but I can go to the bush and get food. Even if we don't have trabajo, at least we have the bush." This reference to people "at least" having the bush highlights that this safeguard is the result of adverse conditions that turn their lands into a place that is their last resort but also one they can always count on.

Those who rely extensively on marisca often make more openly political statements about the relative autonomy granted by the bush from party factionalism. In 1999 I was with Roberto in his small hamlet on the shores of the Pilcomayo marshes, a place relatively removed from roads and rarely visited by political candidates. He emphasized the autonomy that marisca, "the life of the Aborigen," provides poor people from the deceptions by politicians: "This is the life of the Aborigen. When he has nothing, when he has no money, he lives off marisca. . . . I think people aren't interested in politics anymore, because they know well that the poli-

56. Bush resources and "women's work":
preparing chagüar fibers. *Photo by author.*

ticians are liars. When they take on their *cargo* [political appointment],
they forget the things they promised. . . . That's why people get closer to
the shores of the marshlands, because the food is here. There're things to
eat. . . . Since I don't have a sueldo I have to live here, until I die." Roberto
grounded resistance to la política in the practices and places that best capture their subject position as Aborígenes. This position outlines an ethnicity linked to poverty and foraging and defined in tension with those
who have cargos. This critique also involves a temporal and spatial fluctuation: on the one hand, the cycle of promises and deceptions involved
in every election and, on the other hand, people's response to this cycle
by moving, *literally* in Roberto's quote, from one place to another: away
from la comuna and closer to the marshes.

Among women from households living in poverty, frustrations with
"politics" are connected to the especially acute lack of trabajo available
for them. Whereas in their critique of la política men invoke a gender-
free notion of aboriginality, many women usually anchor their critique in
their situation as aboriginal *women*. The fact that they refer to their trabajo as "women's work" illustrates that they aim to carve out a place of
autonomy not only from la política but also from "men's work." As part
of this experience, for many women the bush also evokes meanings of
autonomy, yet for different reasons than for men. Unlike men's trabajo,
spatially secluded from the bush, craftsmanship requires women to foray
in the bush in search of fibers (used to manufacture bags) and natural

colorants (used to dye fiber bags and wool tapestry). Thus, even though women make crafts in the space of their households, their most important trabajo implies going to the bush and relying on its resources. Consequently, the bush allows them to sustain a female "work" alternative to the male-dominated trabajo available at la comuna. By doing so, they create a place of autonomy from men and from the male domain, la política, that saturates public debates in their hamlets.

These tensions between la comuna and the bush also involve employees actively involved in political negotiations at Pozo de Maza. Even if they rarely forage, these men consume bush food often through relatives and neighbors and also participate of the collective memories that make the bush a place of health and resilience. In moments of political conflict, it is not rare to hear these men also refer to the bush as a place that protects them from the negative aspects of la política. When, in December 1995, the Criollo mayor laid off dozens of employees, Eulogio, a nurse in his mid-thirties, emerged as one of the leaders of the mobilization for trabajo. Because of Eulogio's activism, a white leader of the Partido Justicialista threatened to take away his job. At a meeting in a Toba village, Eulogio said aloud to this politician: "If you want to take my sueldo away from me, just do it! Who cares! I like eating chañar. I like eating fish. That's what I always ate when I was a kid. Who cares, I never got used to that money anyway." In the following months, I heard several people commenting on the boldness and rightfulness of this intervention, and this support may explain why in the end Eulogio did not lose his job. His outspoken position was a public declaration that, unlike other Toba, he had not been spoiled by his trabajo. More important, he made the point that many Aborígenes, even those with jobs, still counted on the bush as a place of their own: a place that could enable them to sever or at least limit their dependence on political patronage. Critical stances such as this have not changed the fact that trabajo is still strongly embedded in local values, practices, and expectations. Yet these experiences contribute to creating counterhegemonic values: they denaturalize the idea that trabajo is the only viable productive alternative in the region; and they do so by constructing values, practices, and places alternative to it.

This production of the bush as a site of resistance to party politics is inseparable from ongoing tensions with the Criollos over land use and from attempts to reproduce a collective appropriation of space. The granting of the land title, in this regard, did not stop the bush from being a contested terrain.

The Political Remaking of the Bush

As part of the arenas of contention examined above, men living in poverty have tried to counter the influence of Pozo de Maza by redirecting disputes over power relations back to the bush, the place in which they feel most confident. This has fostered conflicts with settlers and well-off leaders. Between 1996 and 1998, aiming at halting trespassing and illegal logging, the Toba made an unambiguous assertion of spatial control by building a wire fence around the eastern limit of their lands. This fence cut off settlers living within the perimeter, who responded by surreptitiously cutting sections of wire and moving cattle in and out. This triggered a long war of attrition in which, for three years, both sides tested the limits of each other's actions. In January 1999, tired of replacing cut wires, Toba men armed with rifles and shotguns stormed a hut recently built by settlers in their lands. The Criollos fled and declared at a police station that the Toba "wanted to kill them all." This incident revived memories of the bloodshed in 1917 and greatly increased local tensions between Aborígenes and Criollos. Yet many ordinary Toba also criticized some of their leaders and accused them of receiving cattle from settlers in exchange for a verbal authorization to stay in Toba lands. This was seen as a serious infringement of the collective appropriation of the bush. At a heated assembly, these accusations were made public and those leaders vehemently denied the charges. This pressure succeeded in forcing the negotiation of a public agreement with the settlers, signed in February 1999, which stated that the latter were to pay for land use with head of cattle to be held collectively by all Toba hamlets.

These struggles are illustrative of the practices countering the pull toward la comuna and indicate that ordinary Toba have been relatively successful in reproducing the bush as a collective place.[5] Gramsci's point that struggles are "the result of opposing forces in continuous movement" (1971:438) stresses that these processes' partial moments are the unpredictable outcome of fields of contention. Yet the continuous movement Gramsci alludes to can also be read spatially: as a process in which political actors *position* themselves simultaneously in different places (see Gordillo 2002c). In the area of Pozo de Maza, this shifting positionality between the bush, the villages, and la comuna is a source of meanings and actions that are further altering the local geography. And these are actions through which Toba living in poverty seek to construct a secure place from the historical forces imposed on them. This is why, as Donald Moore observes (1998:351–52), forms of contestation such as these do not originate from a place of relative autonomy located "outside" power relations. Most Toba have resisted giving up the bush *because* this place has been historically immersed within larger fields of power, those that made them Aborígenes.

The niches of partial autonomy carved out in the bush have so far not challenged local and regional relations of domination; but these are places that people painfully and painstakingly *gained* from those relations. For this reason, these sites help foster dreams of freedom complexly intertwined with the presence of yet another place. This is a place that, in the last stage of our journey, reflects back on Toba lands what they were like in the past.

18

The Other Side

Hope is memory that desires.
—Honoré de Balzac, *A Prince of Bohemia*

If the river returns, people are going to get closer to the river.
They're going to eat fish and won't come back. They won't come back.
—Pablo, 1996

"The other side," laheGó, is a latent yet often potent presence in the Toba villages. When people remember the times prior to the 1975 flooding, they evoke places currently located across the marshes—and therefore project their past elsewhere. This projection is particularly forceful because those sparsely populated stretches of grasslands and thick bush are reminiscent of past landscapes once roamed by the ancient ones. This spatial and temporal cleavage creates a further set of tensions configuring Toba lands; it highlights that the bush is an impoverished place depleted of resources, and it accentuates the image of natural exuberance associated with the other side. In this chapter I examine how people perceive laheGó through the memories evoked by the marshes, the international border, and the old river. I also analyze how in 1995–96 a severe drought caused many Toba to project brief yet intense expectations onto the other side through rumors about the "return of the river."

The Making of the Other Side

The notion of "the other side" is a product of the constitution of the border along the Pilcomayo. In the early twentieth century, the Toba made use of both banks of the river and did not see the ñachi (the river) as a limit between different territories (Mendoza 2002; Gordillo and Leguizamón 2002:35–37). In those days, spatial orientation was primarily based on the distinction between upstream and downstream and the river and the hinterland.[1] When Bolivian and then Argentinean troops arrived in the area, they enforced the river as the borderline and changed this spatial pattern by confining Toba hamlets on the Argentinean bank. In the early 1930s the growing tensions between Bolivia and Paraguay over the control of the territories north of the Pilcomayo River led to a large-scale military confrontation. With about 100,000 casualties, the Chaco War (1932–35) became the bloodiest war between nation-states in twentieth-century Latin America. This level of violence unfolding on the Pilcomayo's left bank strengthened the awareness that the invisible line traced by the do'okohé along the river had a powerful effect on the events unfolding on one side and the other. In 1934 the Paraguayan army launched a sweeping offensive along the Pilcomayo and forced Nivaclé groups and Argentinean Criollos living near Bolivian forts to flee the area. This displacement created further spatial changes. In 1939, four years after the end of the war, Alfred Métraux (1978:82) was in San Andrés, upstream from Sombrero Negro, and wrote, "The Bolivian bank used to be well populated. Today, there is nobody there." Métraux noticed that the other side had emerged after the bloodshed of the war, like the calm after the storm, as a semideserted wilderness, the product of the removal of the local population through state violence.

Under Paraguayan sovereignty, laheGó was subjected to a dynamic of spatial appropriation significantly different from that on the Argentinean side. By employing few people, the estancias reproduced those lands as uninhabited thick bush. The continuing depletion of the more densely populated Argentinean side by Toba, Wichí, and Criollos accentuated the contrast between the two riverbanks. "The forest on the Paraguayan bank is greener, thicker, than on our bank," Métraux (1978:82, 83) wrote, noticing that the international border was producing a different landscape on each side of the river. For decades most Toba experienced this contrast on a daily basis: they could see the other side from their hamlets; and many men and women regularly crossed the river to hunt and gather honey, fruits, and chagüar. After the 1975 floods, with the new villages resettled farther south, this proximity was lost but the other side continued guiding Toba perceptions of their lands.

The memory of the Chaco War is an important component of this spatialized contrast, fostered by the detritus left by the war in the cattle

57. Soldiers from Fortín Magariños on the Bolivian bank
of the Pilcomayo, across the river from Toba lands, 1912.
Archivo General de la Nación, Buenos Aires.

ranches across the border. On February 7, 1934, the commander in chief
of the Paraguayan Army, Mariscal José Félix Estigarribia (1969:126), reported to the Ministry of Defense: "Those prisoners declared that a great
number of their companions have perished, principally from thirst. All the
road covered by the enemy in his retirement is strewed with corpses, and
some of them were burned—killed by their officers because they refused
to continue the march." Estigarribia was referring to the Bolivian troops
that had just fled Fort Magariños, across the river from Sombrero Negro.
Most of those soldiers had died not far from the Toba villages. Sixty-one
years later, I was talking with Tomás about the Paraguayan bush. He had
never been deep inside those lands, but had heard from other people that it
is easy to come across human bones and rusty weapons. Those places, he
added, are also haunted by souls: "In Paraguay, there're plenty of bullets,
skulls, bones of the Bolivians. At night, you hear screams, people screaming over there. . . . All the campo is full of arms, some in good shape:
rifles, carbines, everything. Trucks, plenty of trucks, left out there in the
bush." Several men related similar accounts about the bones and material
remains that impregnate the Paraguayan bush with living echoes of the
Chaco War. In those places, memory seems to be eternally inscribed in
space, erasing historical time and making old battles linger indefinitely.

Diego remembered that when they were back from San Martín del Taba-cal, he and other men crossed the river to hunt iguanas. During these expeditions, they were haunted by the sounds of a war that had ended decades earlier:

> We went to Toba Quemado to look for iguanas. . . . We went for about twelve days, with many people. We went there and asked for permission at the estancia. At night, we arrived at Toba Quemado. We slept there. And we heard the noise of trucks, as if they were very close. [We said:] "What's that?" And the noise stopped. It wasn't there anymore. Then, we heard screams of men, shots. But it wasn't true. We only heard them. We also heard the noise of an airplane. Over there, we saw many bones. It's full of bones. The bullets are there. Over there, there's the head, the feet, everything. We were watching. But there were many iguanas.

These intermittent yet vivid sounds of violence fix the memory of battles in the Paraguayan bush. This memory is also part of the experi-ence of young men who work at the cattle ranches. Several men told me that when they rest at night in the estancias they often hear screams, gunshots, and explosions. Those sounds, they add, are often intertwined with the distinctive sound of devils hitting hollow trees or imitating the voice of Criollos. People who told me about the "war noises" in Para-guay usually expressed a mixture of perplexity and detachment. When, after describing the skeleton of a Bolivian soldier, Diego added "but there were many iguanas," he made clear that those remains did not distract him from his main goal: to hunt. After all, the men who fought and died in that war were not Aborígenes and were alien to the Chaco. Yet the memories fostered by the sight of human remains are not unrelated to the Toba's own historical experience. Those screaming bones remind them of the bones of their ancestors scattered elsewhere, hundreds of kilo-meters to the west. And that history of violence is constitutive of the other side as a place of natural exuberance. Nature and history have fed each other in laheGó, where marks of state violence are scattered next to the signs of wilderness that attract Toba hunters. Produced by state violence and the international border, the other side has become the last refuge of animals and creatures that inhabited the area at the time of the an-cient ones.

A *Contradictory Wilderness*

When I was in laheGó in June 2000, my companions stopped numerous times to show me footprints of animals rarely seen on their lands, such as pumas and tapirs. They were reiterating what I had repeatedly heard before: that the farther one moves from the marshes into Paraguay, the thicker the bush and the more numerous the animals that have almost disappeared on the Argentinean side. This includes extraordinary creatures such as the giant snakes. As Mariano put it: "They went over where it's quieter. They don't like the noise of trucks." Another bush creature that has vanished from Toba lands and settled in the Paraguayan bush is "rainbow." I once asked Omar whether people see wosáq. "Not here," he replied, "but when the weather is cloudy or rainy, we see it from the distance." He pointed to the north: "We see the sun and we see wosáq coming out over there. Not here, but we see it over there, in Paraguay." Men who go to laheGó to hunt or work in the estancias often see "rainbow" on those lands and agree that it now lives there "because it's quieter."

These creatures' flight across the international border highlights the depth of the changes that have affected the local geography. In their dislike for Criollos, noise, cattle, roads, and trucks, wosáq and the giant snakes symbolize the world as the ancient ones knew it: free of settlers, cattle, and state agencies. They also reflect an eagerness to reconstitute that past *elsewhere*, far from the impoverished bush the Toba currently know. These changes mean that no viáq hakoiwók (bad bush) under the control of dangerous creatures is left on the Argentinean side. Only in Paraguay, people agree, can one find sections of bad bush, and this displacement has completed the transformation of their lands into a pale expression of what they once were. The constitution of laheGó as a "quieter place" illustrates that even if the bush in Toba lands looks quiet compared to San Martín del Tabacal or Buenos Aires, it is still marked by trails, roads, and cattle.

The Paraguayan bush, however, is a contradictory wilderness. Private estancias own most of those lands and as a result their resources are not readily available to the Toba. Hunters are permanently confronted by this contradiction and have to seek permission from foremen before beginning a foraging expedition. Martín remembered how he and three friends were once denied permission to hunt iguanas on the land of a ranch. Since one of Martín's friends, Amalio, had worked at that ranch the year be-

58. Ostrich hunting on "the other side." *Photo by author.*

fore, he talked to the patrón. Martín recalled the dialogue and pointed out the contradiction between their aim to *iguanear* (hunt iguanas) and the patrón's emphasis that they had to trabajar: "We told him that we wanted to iguanear. He said: 'No problem. But first you have to trabajar.' But Amalio didn't want to trabajar. He just wanted to iguanear. But the man got angry. Amalio told him: 'No, I came to iguanear.' The man got upset: 'Then, get out of here! I don't like men looking for iguanas around here.' " This incident sheds light on a tension central to the experience of Toba men in laheGó: the fact that there they conduct practices that stand in opposition to each other, marisca and trabajo. Furthermore, the private ownership of land in the Paraguayan Chaco ensures that this tension has to be negotiated at each ranch. After the incident with the patrón of the first ranch, Martín and his friends went to another estancia. This time, the capataz authorized them to kill as many iguanas as they wanted. Iguanas were so abundant that in a couple of days Martín captured a dozen and ate a lot of barbecued meat. "There were many iguanas, because nobody lives there," he told me. He added that he brought back twelve skins, meat, honey, and mercaderías bartered at the estancia. Martín and his companions re-created the bush on the other side as a place of abundance: abundance of bush food and also commodities such as iguana skins. During these marisca expeditions, the fear and estrangement evoked by the Paraguayan bush tends to dissipate. For example, Martín had told me several times that those who work at the estancias are haunted by scores of payák. Yet when I asked him about diablos during their hunting trip, he

59. Remembering the Pilcomayo on the Paraguayan
bank of the old river. *Photo by author.*

said: "We didn't hear anything. Silence. We heard nothing. We just saw
the tracks of bush animals."

The other side as a place of natural exuberance "where nobody lives"
makes the bush in Toba lands look like its reverse: a place drained of creatures, secrets, and animals and full of people, villages, and trails. Mariano
told me how the bad bush that once covered part of their lands had disappeared: "It seems that there's no more bad bush, because there's a road
that goes to Pocitos. There's a road that goes to Churcal. There's a road
that goes to Algodón. There's a road that goes to Rinconada. There's a
road that comes from Perdida. There're roads everywhere in the bush.
Then it seems that the bush is not the bush." Mariano was emphasizing
that by being traversed by roads and trails connecting myriad sites and by
being drained of its old dangers, the bush had lost some of its defining
features qua bush. The "real bush," he and many others would agree, is
in Paraguay.

These perceptions contrasting the other side with Toba lands are mediated by the marshlands, the place that stands between the two. Like
the bush on the Argentinean side, the marshes are a recent and impoverished version of a prior place, the river; like the Paraguayan bush, they
harbor potentially dangerous beings. This situation makes the marshes a
borderline of sorts between the Toba's home and the other side as a place
inhabited by creatures of the past. The marshes are also the reminder of

the river, whose vestiges I was finally able to see with my own eyes in those days of June 2000. On the third day of our expedition in laheGó, my six companions and I reached the old river. It was an impressive sight: the old banks formed steep bluffs clearly visible across the flat geography. Carving through the two banks, the dry riverbed was covered with lush vegetation and tall trees. We stood in reverent silence on the top of the Paraguayan bank, observing what was left of the Pilcomayo, as the oldest hunter told us how that place looked in his youth. As I listened, I tried to imagine water flowing a few meters below us. I was trying to visualize the place that, only a few years earlier, many Toba had hoped would materialize again.

The Return of the River

In 1991 the governments of Argentina and Paraguay began constructing two canals on the Pilcomayo 100 kilometers upstream from the Toba villages. The aim was to stop the gradual dissolution of the river into marshlands and guarantee an even flow of water to both sides of the international border (Gordillo and Leguizamón 2002). Yet as a result of technical miscalculations and intense sedimentation in the Argentinean canal, in 1995 the Paraguayan canal was absorbing most of the water flow. In a few months, large floods covered the Paraguayan Chaco and the marshes in Formosa dried up almost completely. By December 1995 there was almost no surface water near the Toba villages. The recent layoffs at la comuna further worsened the scenario. With no fish, people lived for several months in precarious conditions, gathering wild fruits, gradually harvesting their fields, and hunting alligators stranded in shallow ponds. The sudden lack of fish enhanced the value of marisca even among public-sector employees and farmers. Hernán, who in another moment had told me that he had "dropped the bush" because of his trabajo in horticulture, told me during the worst moment of the drought: "In the marshes we have the fish, the fruits. If we don't have fish, how are we going to feed our kids? Without the food of our own we're screwed."

For several weeks the drought became the most pressing local concern and the most recurrent topic of conversation. Yet initially people had little information about the canals and most of them created interpretations and rumors at odds with official explanations. As James Scott points out (1990:145), rumors are not produced randomly: "As a rumor travels it is altered in a fashion that brings it more closely into line with the hopes, fears, and worldview of those who hear it and retell it." The rumors produced by many Toba about the drought were molded by their memory of the river, their perceptions of the other side, and their distrust of state agencies, accentuated in those days by the conflicts at Pozo de Maza. Further, some people interpreted the drought in terms of the state violence once unleashed in their lands and of the death toll that almost decimated them in San Martín del Tabacal. In February 1996 I was talking with Pablo about the drought and he told me, in a casual tone: "Maybe it's the government that wants to kill us." I asked him who wanted to kill them. "I don't know, someone toward Bolivia. Maybe the government did business with Bolivia, with Paraguay. That's why the water has gone to Paraguay. . . . They say they closed the river, I don't know where in Bolivia. . . . We're saying that the government is very bad. They want to kill us."

In those days, interpretations like this were ubiquitous. Nobody seemed to believe that the drought was the unintentional result of the canals' sedimentation. Rather, most Toba agreed that "the government" had deliberately deviated the Pilcomayo River, either to "kill" the Aborígenes or "do business" with the Bolivian and Paraguayan governments. Eduardo told me that (the then Argentinean president) Carlos Menem had "sold" the river to Paraguay because the Aborígenes eat fish only for subsistence purposes. "That's what people are commenting," he added. "The government says that it's better if the river passes over there, that over there they're going to sell the fish. It seems they're going to harvest money. And the Paraguayans will send part of the money [to the Argentinean government]. Because if the river passes over here, we're going to fish all day and they won't make any money. Because we eat, we don't sell." This interpretation emphasized that the river and the marshes are noncommodified places in the hands of Aborígenes but also sites threatened by several states' attempts to seize them according to a capitalist rationality. This seizure would require taking the Pilcomayo *away* from the Aborígenes and moving it elsewhere, where obscure actors would "sell fish" and "harvest money."

Simultaneously with these rumors, and in tension with them, many people created other interpretations about the possible outcome of the drought, involving a radical transformation of the regional landscape but in a way more favorable to the Aborígenes. According to one rumor, the river was to return to its old course along the border and flow again *as a river*, resuscitating the landscape that disappeared in the mid-1970s. Some people speculated that heavy machinery, the same used to dig up the canals upstream, would open up the old riverbed. Yet many others told me that the riverbed would probably be carved again by lék, the giant serpent responsible for its origin in mythical times. These interpretations reasserted the inscription of Toba social memory in space, for the force that would re-create a place of the past was a creature from the times of the yagaikipí.

But the most significant aspect of these rumors was the dramatic social implication of the river's return. Many Toba agreed that if the Pilcomayo flowed again along the old course, the poorest among them would abandon their hamlets and settle in laheGó, next to the river, where they would live off marisca "like before." On the basis of this hope, for a few months many people projected strong images of abundance and collective well-being onto the other side. As Eduardo put it: "If the river returns we can have a quiet life. We'll gather honey every day." Among some people living in poverty, these expectations reached semiutopian dimensions potently informed by the memory of past times of abundance on the Pilcomayo. In early February 1996, during the drought's worst moment, Pablo told me that those like him who had nothing would abandon their hamlets, settle near the river, and never come back: "If there's a river like before, those who don't have sueldo will go and won't come back. They're going to live like before. . . . If the river returns, people are going to get closer to the river. They're going to eat fish and won't come back. They won't come back. . . . Those who have a *sueldito* [a little salary], who have pensions, maybe won't go. We, those who have nothing, no pension, no trabajo, we're going to go to the river."

This expectation of a collective displacement to a different place, a place of abundance and autonomy separate from current conditions of domination and political patronage, brings to light spatial dimensions common in utopian traditions worldwide, which, as David Harvey has noted, usually project their Promised Land *elsewhere* (2000:156–96). But this is a place where the Toba had *already* been, the river, which most of them remembered well and with nostalgia. Edward Casey has argued that nostalgia implies a particularly intense spatialization of memory: "Nostalgia leads to invoke the following principle: *in remembering we can be thrust back, transported, into the place we recall*" (1987:201, emphasis in original). During the drought, in remembering the river many Toba were transported back into that place, to the point that many believed, and hoped, that its materialization would be imminent. Paraphrasing Balzac, their

60. "They're going to eat fish and won't come back."
Photo by author.

hope was their memory of the river desiring to cease being just a memory. Yet this hope was molded along the incipient class tensions unraveling in the largest villages. Pablo made clear that the return *to* the river would exclude those with trabajo and well-off leaders. Since many people were concerned about the recent layoffs at Pozo de Maza, the memory of the river fostered the longing for a place where trabajo would no longer be needed. By making the distinction between people with "suelditos" and those who "have nothing," Pablo also pointed out that the river would be re-created as an altogether new place: an egalitarian domain where people would live off bush food. In fact, in those days people with jobs agreed that only those living in poverty would move to the other side. Some public-sector employees mentioned that, even though they would also welcome the river's return, they had too many material interests invested in their hamlets, namely their trabajo and brick houses, to abandon them.[2]

Heavy rains temporarily ameliorated the situation in the area in mid-February 1996, and in August the opening of a new canal upstream regularized the water flow. Water covered the marshes once again and the environmental and social crisis that had engulfed the region came to an end. People gradually received more information about the canals, leaders clarified in public that the government had no plans to "make the river again," and the comments about the return of the river gradually faded. But not completely. The following year, in sharp contrast to the previous year, the marshlands' annual flood brought an unprecedented amount of water that forced some families to temporarily leave their homes. In August 1997 I visited the Toba villages again and, to my surprise, found that some people were still hopeful that lék would dig up the Pilcomayo's old course. The flood's intensity, they argued, was the clearest sign that this return was possible. One of those who made this point was Andrés, a farmer whose fields had been severely affected by the drought. He told me,

> Maybe lék wants to make the river like in the past, for lék is the one who made the river. . . . Paraguay closed it in those years. That's why we were suffering. We didn't have water. . . . It's not possible that the river is the only one that saved those of us who are poor. We get the fish and we live with that. It seems that the water doesn't want to leave those who are the poorest. It seems that the water goes where the poorest live. That's my idea. . . . The water washed away what had blocked the river. . . . This is why we've seen bichos that aren't from around here, because the water came down with everything. That's why lék wants to make the river.

As part of the expectations created by the possible return of the river, Andrés saw the river as an entity with a life of its own, which had the explicit will to save "those of us who are poor." Moreover, this will made water destroy what had "blocked" the river and threatened the Aborígenes' survival. As Thomas Macaulay argued, rivers evoke, more so than other aspects of landscapes, the appearance of self-animation, "something resembling character" (Schama 1995:355). The rebellious and compassionate character that Andrés and other Toba project onto the Pilcomayo reveals a fetishization grounded in their historical memory, for this fetishization gives this river an agency that is not just random or natural but aimed at helping "the poor" and undermining state attempts to control its course. Yet these imageries also require analyzing how the memory of the river, a place that does not exist anymore, is connected to the everyday presence of the bush.

The River and the Bush

The expectations aroused by the drought capture some of the ways in which memories and places coalesce in the marshes, the bush, and the other side. The awaited return of the river turned the international border into a frontier separating a place of domination and a place of freedom. For decades the Pilcomayo River was a limit, as cultural as it was physical, between the Paraguayan bush and the depleted bush on the Argentinean bank. In 1996 the river was no longer there but the borderline *did* remain in the same place, as threshold to a region reminiscent of landscapes once solely inhabited by Aborígenes. This thick location, saturated with memories, triggered the brief hope that people could live "like before."

The river emerged, at least for a few months, as a utopia in the strict sense of the term: a nonplace projected onto a site covered with thick bush and grasslands. This view incorporated the bush in contradictory ways. On the one hand, being spatially contiguous with the old riverbed, the Paraguayan bush and the grasslands in laheGó fostered the hope of the river's return with glimpses of geographies of yesteryear. They provided the background of semiuninhabited landscapes and abundant resources onto which this return was projected. On the other hand, the place that symbolized promises of well-being was the river, not the Paraguayan bush. After all, the latter is also a place owned by cattle ranchers and haunted by devils and phantoms of the Chaco War.

But how does the river, as a utopian nonplace, relate to Toba lands? The bush that people tread on a daily basis is too close to their experience of poverty and state domination to produce dreams of freedom. Yet drained of animals and resources as it is, this place is the only thing many people have. This is not without significance, for many Toba know, and remember, that the bush is the place where they were able to endure impossible odds. The river, after all, is gone. And the bush is still there, as the place that will enable "those who have nothing" to forage until the end of the world.

Conclusions

The meaning of a word is determined entirely by its context. . . . Contexts
do not stand side by side in a row, as if unaware of one another, but are in a
state of constant tension, of incessant interaction and conflict.
— Valentin Volosinov, *Marxism and the Philosophy of Language*

It lies in the definition of negative dialectics that it will not come to
rest in itself, as if it were total. This is its form of hope.
— Theodor Adorno, *Negative Dialectics*

The primary challenge I faced in writing this book was analyzing the
patterns that constitute places while bringing to light the tensions that
permanently erode them. The bush, San Martín del Tabacal, the mission station, the lands across the marshes, and the other sites examined
in these pages are far from being well-bounded entities with straightfor-
ward meanings. They are unstable processes made and unmade through
practice and through the connections these places maintain with each
other. Memory is a major force in this integration of disparate localities
in a single historical geography. Remembering and its sedimentation in
space are constitutive of experiences of labor and locality; they guide practices, struggles, and hopes, and connect the places in which memories are
produced with vanished and contemporary landscapes. I have explored
these memories in search of the meanings and spatial tensions they convey, making the assumption that memory is as culturally constructed as
it is historically real, and that it is true *of* something.

Made historically meaningful and culturally factual through social
memory, the places explored in this book are torn by contradictions. The
ambiguity resulting from these tensions pervades these geographies with
a dizziness that dismantles any pretension to situate "culture" within a
well-bounded "place." For most Toba, the bush is a site of resilience that

has enabled them to endure state terror, capitalist exploitation, mission-ary social control, and state domination; a domain characterized by ne-cessity and material hardships; a place of health and healing that counter-acts illness and death; a source of noncommodified abundance; a depleted locality deprived of the forces and creatures of the past; a place of local knowledge and quietness where people counter the estrangement and de-spair experienced elsewhere. As part of these experiences, San Martín del Tabacal is remembered as a source of disease, death, and terror; a place of sexual excess and freedom from missionary control; an alienating place run by codes and forms of knowledge alien to the Toba; a site of wealth, money, and commodities that were nevertheless beyond their reach. The same tense polysemy is part of the production of the other places inter-twined with the bush and kahogonaGá: the mission station where men and women found shelter from state violence, guidance into a changing world, and new forms of discipline; the farms where current generations supplement the poverty of the bush with meager resources, find relief from the moral standards of their villages, and are haunted by the memo-ries of the ingenio; the Pozo de Maza municipality, which captures the expectations projected onto public-sector jobs yet also the deception of la política; the land across the marshes, which reminds many Toba of lost landscapes of abundance yet immerses them in labor exploitation and the detritus of the Chaco War. All these sites are made, unmade, and remade in their myriad interrelations and through practices and struggles intrin-sically tied to remembering.

In my attempt to make sense of these places, I learned that the pat-terns tying them together are the contradictions embedded in Toba ex-periences. I also learned that these tensions, in turn, permanently under-mine these threads. Put another way, the tensions that oppose and unite the bush, the plantations, the mission, or laheGó are the forces that pro-duce yet simultaneously destabilize their configuration. Valentin Volosi-nov (1973:79–81) wrote that meanings are shaped by the contexts of their production and that the latter "do not stand side by side in a row, as if unaware of one another, but are in a state of constant tension, of inces-sant interaction and conflict." Similarly, the places analyzed in this book were never "unaware of one another"; they were constituted *through* their permanent interaction. These interactions are eminently negative, in the sense that they are based on contrasts and oppositions. The symbolism of social healing rooted in the bush can only be fully understood in terms of the memory of unhealthy, disrupted bodies in the ingenio. The dancing in San Martín del Tabacal gained its semantic force in the alienation of the cane fields and in its contrast with the bodily and social control at Misión El Toba. Perceptions about the depletion of the bush are defined in opposition to laheGó as a place of plentiful wildlife. And so on. Since these are moments in a dialectical movement, we should add "and vice versa." In other words, death at the ingenio was made more apparent by experiences of health and healing in the bush; and the moral rules at the mission looked particularly intrusive because many people danced in the plantation's lotes and prepared aloja in bush camps.

This dialectic destabilizes any notion of meaning as an "inner" property of places, even if we take what superficially seems to be fixed about them: their spatial boundaries. People define these boundaries depending on context, hence these boundaries are highly flexible. When a public-sector employee talks about the importance of trabajo and complains about the hardships of marisca, the bush becomes a place clearly separated from the hamlet where he lives and "works." Yet when the same person compares the tranquility of "the bush" with the noise and violence of big cities, the former becomes a sheltering place that includes his hamlet within it. And when some argue that the Aborígenes will not die because they have "the food from the bush," the bush represents not just a forest but also the marshlands and their lands as a whole. The same fluidity applies to a place like San Martín del Tabacal. When people remember the dangers of the jungle surrounding the cane fields, the ingenio appears as a place delimited by human labor and separated from the forests and the mountains. But when several generations of Toba said to each other, on the arrival of the contractors, "let's go to the mountains," the ingenio was subsumed within the dominating presence of kahogonaGá.

The shifting character of places takes us to a further point. Theodor Adorno (1973:31–33) argued that a negative dialectic, a dialectic that explores contradictions until their ultimate analytic consequences, is necessarily a source of vertigo. Unlike regimented ways of thinking that demand "a frame of reference in which all things have their place," dialectical thinking necessarily fosters vertigo and flourishes with it. Part of this vertigo, the same I felt while writing this book, results from the fact that dialectical thinking implies thinking in terms of contradictions and also, as Adorno pointed out (1973:145), *against* contradictions: that is, exposing them politically as sources of social suffering and undermining their reification into "laws." Vertigo, in short, is a sign that contradictions have not been turned into rules detached from history and are, rather, tied to the absolute earthliness of social practice. This openness, as Adorno put it, is its hope (1973:406).

The production of places through contradictory relations and practices does not make them less meaningful, real, or physical. Despite a recent resurgence of interest in the concept of negativity (see Coole 2000; Fabian 2001), a pervasive view in anthropology insists that social processes should be defined "positively" rather than negatively, as if negativity would make them less substantial; or as if it were possible to make sense of something without first determining what it is *not*. The underlying fear seems to be that an emphasis on contrasts and oppositions would turn social action into a reactive phenomenon deprived of agency.[1] Even Doreen Massey (1994:169, also 121), whose ideas inspired many of these pages, somehow reproduces this position when she argues that places are constructed *not* through "negative counterpositions" *but* through "positive interrelations" with other places. In this book I have tried to show that it is through contradictions, which are not but negative relations of opposition, that subjectivities and memories gain their cultural and historical force and, for that reason, their agency. Agency is not a given quality located "within" social actors but *the act of doing*: the result of acting "outwards" vis-à-vis multiple fields of force. Negativity, in this regard, undermines the notions of boundedness and authenticity that pervade "positive" definitions of culture, place, or identity; it asserts that any dimension of practice, never exhausted within its inner limits, is defined in its myriad relations to other social fields.[2]

The multiple tensions I have tried to unravel in Toba experiences and memories confirm Gramsci's (1995:342) point that "in real history the dialectical process is separated out into innumerable partial moments." Yet this fragmentation should not obscure that some contradictions are more influential than others in the way places and subjectivities are created and recreated throughout history. My position in this book has been that labor plays a particularly important, but not unique, role in this process. We have seen that labor experiences, in particular the tension between marisca and trabajo, are a major force in the production of places and memories. The fact that most Toba refer to "the bush" as the figuration of the relations and practices defining them as foragers, and that this is informed by their memories of the sugar plantations, illustrates the salience of the practices through which people produce and reproduce their everyday life. My attempt to blend labor and culture also recovers the analytical and political force of the concept of alienation: the subjective experience of being exploited and not controlling one's labor and conditions of social reproduction. I have grounded alienation not in the separation between workers and their "human essence," as Marx (1964:126–29) originally did in his youth, but in the estrangement produced by historically specific experiences of exploitation. And I have tried to show that estrangement, rather than being simply an embodied condition, is inherently tied to the making of places.

The Toba case, nonetheless, also illustrates that labor practices do not simply "create" spatial and cultural configurations, a position that would reproduce the shortcomings of objectivist determinism. Gavin Smith (1999:250) has rightly argued that "cultural expressions become inscribed on the landscape to form the material conditions of subsequent generations." Likewise, the meanings Toba men and women project onto particular places become a material force that guide how they perceive their own labor. Since cotton farms in the east are surrounded by open country, devils are to them less tangible there than in tadéwo or Paraguay. Fear, in this case, is constituted not just by conditions of exploitation but also by a culturally constructed association between diablos and thick forests. Similarly, forested areas located in different places evoke diverse types of dangers. Thus, the jungles near the sugar cane fields fostered a terror absent in the viáq ádaik (thick bush) of the Chaco. These examples illustrate that contradictions are culturally and spatially defined and that people often experience their labor according to the memories evoked by its location.

Yet how do Toba living in poverty cope in practical circumstances with the myriad meanings of the bush, the ingenio, or la comuna? Bourdieu (1977:123) was partially right when he wrote that "a word cannot always appear with all its meanings at once without turning discourse into an endless play of words." Yet it is important to add that the multiple meanings of a place, even if not articulated all at once, always stand in a culturally productive tension with each other. Paul Ricoeur (1974:71; 1976:55) rightly held that polysemy is defined by tensions between different meanings that create further meanings and hence ambiguity. Ricoeur's phenomenology, nonetheless, is based on a dialectic removed from history. As Johannes Fabian has argued (1983:128), ambiguity is not a logical property of symbols but the result of historical confrontations. Ambiguous memories of the ingenio, in this regard, result from a contradictory experience that provided many Toba with valuable commodities but also weakened their bodies and threatened their social reproduction. When people remember one of these dimensions they usually put the other temporarily aside. But the tensions between the two are still part of their overall memory of the ingenio and are a culturally productive, and historically defined, source of ambiguity.

An important point follows from this. These contradictions are not resolved and hence do not reach closure in a synthesis. This is one of the major arenas in which a negative dialectic departs from Hegelianism and positivist Marxism, for such a synthesis could only be conceivable if the dialectic is removed from history and locked into the realm of abstract thought. Among the Toba, this means that their knowledge of the bush or their sense that fish makes them "rich" does not annul the partial estrangement from their lands created by conditions of oppression. These experiences coexist as testimony of the social contradictions that have defined their subordinate immersion in a capitalist political economy.

When in the late nineteenth century the Toba inhabited a landscape of savannas, their subjectivity and sense of locality were also defined by tensions and memories. But back then people held control over their social reproduction and their practices were not torn by labor exploitation. Their subjectivity provided them with the concepts and dispositions with which they tried to figure out their first journeys to the plantations and the arrival of new actors in their lands. This process implied more than culture informing practice; it was an active yet improvised attempt to *understand* the transformations affecting their lives. This cultural production was, to use Jean and John Comaroff's words (1991:229), part of "early pragmatic efforts to plumb the depths of the colonizing process, to capture the mysterious bases of the European production of value." What payák, foraging, or local knowledge meant prior to the migrations to kahogonaGá was redefined by the new spatial tensions in which they were reproduced. The payák figure was immersed in Christian imageries and in the cane fields it acquired alienating dimensions absent back in the Chaco. Due to these experiences at the ingenios, so were reformulated the meanings of bush devils at home, in a process also constituted by Anglican missionization and a social context of poverty. This turned bush devils into beings that, although whimsical, "help the poor."

These processes have created a spatially and culturally distinctive experience, which reformulated influences stemming from British missionaries, Criollo settlers, workers from myriad regions, foremen, and agents of the provincial and Argentinean state. Yet it would be misleading to contend, as Marshall Sahlins probably would (1981, 1985, 1993), that Toba women and men have incorporated historical change "within their cultural terms." As Volosinov pointed out (1973:84–85), interpretations such as this presuppose a dualism between "inner" and "outer" elements and the explicit primacy of the former, in which acts of cultural expression go from inside out and everything outer "is merely passive material for manipulation of the inner element." I have tried here to show that Toba subjectivity was never an "inner element" but a practice defined by its multiple connections with broader social fields. I have also tried to undermine the dualism between "material" and "symbolic" elements in Toba practice and to overcome the distinction between their "culture" and their "history." My premise has been that culture is deeply historical and history is profoundly cultural and that the notion of a dialectic between "culture" and "history" as separate entities is misleading and nondialectical in the first place. And, with Henri Lefebvre, I have tried to show that this fusion of history and culture, rather than unfolding "in" space, *produces* places.

Of the places examined in this book, the bush is the only one that Toba living in poverty have been able to produce and reproduce until the present time. The grasslands, the river, Misión El Toba, Sombrero Negro, and San Martín del Tabacal emerged as sites momentarily carved from the flow of history only to disappear later as tangible presences. Produced by the same forces that transformed the ancient ones into wageworkers and impoverished foragers, the bush nonetheless remains: deprived of resources, traversed by trails, roamed by cattle, but still fostering the Aborígenes' resilience. The devils inhabiting this landscape are probably the most significant expressions of its historicity. Their changing, malleable meanings capture the profoundly historical character of Toba constructions of locality and the culturally productive tensions tearing through them.

The devils wandering the bush bring to mind, paradoxically, old colonial mythologies about the Chaco. In 1733, relying on the writings of another Jesuit missionary, Father Pedro Lozano (1989:56–58) argued that indigenous groups turned the Chaco into their bastion only following the Devil's directives. Several Jesuits speculated that because of this region's inhospitable forests, no Indian could have lived there prior to the arrival of Europeans. Lozano wrote that before the Spanish came from Peru, the Devil summoned large masses of infidels in Tucumán, west of the Chaco, and warned them that they were about to be invaded by strangers. The newcomers would deprive them "of their land, their women, their children, and even of their own freedom." In order to avoid slavery, he told them, they should all flee to the Chaco. The Devil promised that in those forests they would live in abundance, and added: "Follow me with the assurance that I shall take you to places where you shall live free from such evil people." The Devil then turned into a hurricane and set out for the Chaco. Large masses followed him. "And the wretched are there until now buried by the darkness of infidelity, with no hope of getting out until God feels sorry for them; and this is the reason why this province is inhabited by so many people, the more people the farther one moves away from the lands of the Spanish."

Almost three centuries after Lozano wrote these lines, hundreds of Toba men, women, and children were finally pulled out of the Chaco interior. Inverting Lozano's mythical historiography, it was on a booming capitalist frontier that they were to discover, for the first time, the faces of devils. And it was on returning to their lands, against all odds, that they would attempt to create places in which to be free.

Glossary

Note on Pronunciation

I transcribed sounds in Toba, as it is spoken in the northwest of Formosa, as follows. Vowels: *a*: approximately as in *father*; *e*: approximately as in *electric*; *i*: approximately as in *feet*; *o*: somewhat as in *note*, but slightly lower; Consonants: G: voiced postvelar fricative; *h*: voiceless glottal fricative (approximately as in *home*); *k*: voiceless velar occlusive; *ñ*: voiced palatal nasal; *q*: voiceless velar occlusive; *w*: voiced bilabial semivowel. This guide is partially adapted from Métraux (1946a) and Wright (1997) and does not cover all the language tones.

Toba Terms

chaatá: the north; the Paraguayan Chaco
cháiq: giant water snake
dalaGaikpí: the new ones; current Toba generations
do'okohé: the Criollo settlers; white people in general (plural)
epiáGayaik: skillful forager
haliaganék: headman; leader with shamanic powers; boss; politician
kade'tá: "our father"; missionary; "God"
kahogonaGá: the mountains; the sugar plantations
kedokpolio: "large jaguar"
KiyaGaikpí: "the big eaters"; the cannibals of the San Francisco River Valley
kohilé'ec: Criollo settler; white person (singular)
kohodót: bush dwarf; the male partner of *kopeletáGa*
kol'eá: tobacco fields; San Martín del Tabacal
konánaGae: witch
kopeletáGa: the owner of bola verde (a wild fruit); the female partner of kohodót
laheGó: "the other side"; the lands across the marshes
lakáia: siblings and first cousins; friends; "brothers" in a Christian sense
lék: giant but short water snake that in mythical times created the Pilcomayo River

nanaikpólio: giant bush snake
nepakál: soul
népe: foraging
newoyaGák: wealth
newoyáq: rich
newoyagádipí: the rich
nimatáq: drinking feasts of aloja
noGoplé'ec: water creature; the owner of the water
nomí: collective dancing
nónaGa: open country, grasslands
ñáchi: the Pilcomayo River
payaGó: female payák
payák: evil spirit or devil. In Toba lands, they are also the "owners" of animals and natural resources. The term is also used as an adjective to refer to unknown, dangerous, and powerful nonhuman creatures.
pioGóik: poor
pioGokpí: the poor
pioGonáq: shaman
qomlé'ec: Toba
tadéwo: the west; Salta and the bean farms
tayíñi: the east; Formosa city; the cotton farms
viáq: the bush
viáq ádaik: large bush
viáq hakoiwók: bad bush; thick bush section inhabited by numerous devils and other dangerous creatures and animals
viáq ónaGaik: nice bush; bush section with abundant wildlife, honey, fruits, and hardwoods
waido'omá: labor contractor
wosáq: payák creature associated with storms and the rainbow
yagaikipí: the old ones or ancient ones

Spanish Terms (local and regional meanings)

Aborígenes: indigenous people
algarroba: edible fruit of the algarrobo tree
aloja: fermented beverage made out of algarroba or honey
antiguos, los: the ancient ones
arreglo grande; arreglo: final payment at the sugar plantations
bicho: wild animal; bug; unknown creature
boliche: rural store
bombacha: baggy pants worn by the Criollos
brujería: sorcery
brujo: shaman

cacique: indigenous headman

campo: open country; grasslands

capataz: foreman

capitán: indigenous leader and mediator with the administration at the sugar plantations

cargo: public-sector job; political appointment

cerros: mountains; hills

chaguar: plant that provides strong fibers used to make handicrafts

chango: boy; young man

chiripa: a long cloth wrapped around the waist. Between the early twentieth century and the 1960s, it was the most common garment worn by Toba men and women

Chulupí: the Nivaclé

colonia; colonia algodonera: cotton farms

comuna, la: the municipality of Pozo de Maza

concejal: elected representative at the municipality

Criollos: the nonindigenous rural population of northern Argentina; settlers in the Chaco interior

culto: Anglican service

diablo: devil, payák

documento: ID paper

estancia: cattle ranch

finca: farm

gendarmería: military border police in Argentina

hachero: wood or post cutter

huelga: strike

ICA: Instituto de Comunidades Aborígenes; agency of indigenous affairs in Formosa

ingenio: sugar mill; sugar plantation

lenguaraz: indigenous interpreter at the plantations

lote: lot; the units of management and residency at the sugar plantations

marisca: foraging

mariscador: a frequent and skillful forager

mate: a type of tea popular in Argentina, drunk from a gourd (the mate proper, where one places yerba mate and pours hot water at regular intervals) and through a metal straw (*bombilla*)

mataco: old, pejorative term to refer to the Wichí

mayordomo: labor contractor for the sugar plantations

mercadería: store-bought food

monte: the bush; forest

monte grande; monte fuerte: thick bush; large bush

obraje: mobile logging camp

obrajero: the owner or administrator of an obraje

paisano: Aborigen

patrón: boss

peronistas: members of the party founded by Juan Domingo Perón (also known as Partido Justicialista)

picada: trail

política, la: politics

proveduría: store at plantations and farms

puesto: the dwelling and corrals of settlers who look after cattle

rancho: adobe hut; rudimentary rural dwelling

sindicato: the union

sueldo: salary; public-sector job

tarea: daily task that workers had to complete to get paid at the ingenio

tarjador: employee who gave workers their daily ration in the bush

toldería: temporary indigenous hamlet; camps at the sugar plantations

trabajo: work; job

yerba mate: the herb used to drink mate

YPF: Yacimientos Petrolíferos Fiscales; the old state-owned oil company in Argentina, currently privatized and known as YPF-Repsol

zafra: sugar cane harvest

Notes

Introduction

1 See the glossary for a note on pronunciation of Toba terms.

2 This does not mean that space is absent from these analyses. The ethnographies by Thomas Abercrombie (1998:113, 179, 359), Jennifer Cole (2001:106–22), and especially Joanne Rappaport (1990:9, 11, 151–53, 155–56) do pay attention to some of the spatial coordinates of memory (see also Malkki 1995). Yet legitimately concerned with other issues, these authors do not theorize the role of places in the production of memories.

3 Certainly, phenomenology does not exhaust the growing anthropological literature incorporating space within studies of memory (see Lewis 2001; Regis 2001; Orta 2002), some of which draw on the much-cited piece by Pierre Nora (1989) on sites of commemoration. Yet phenomenology remains to date probably the most influential body of theory trying to account for the intersection of memory and place (see Riaño-Alcalá 2002).

4 Some Chaco ethnographers have argued that foraging makes indigenous groups predisposed to wage labor because the two practices are "culturally compatible" with each other. For a critique of this perspective see Gordillo 1993.

5 My perspective on experience, in this regard, differs from phenomenological approaches to the concept and in particular to experiences of place, as exemplified in the work of Fred Myers (1986), Keith Basso (1996), and Stephen Feld and Keith Basso (1996). These authors tend to analyze experiences of place as culturally given: that is, as points of departure that are only *then* situated in history. While sharing with these authors an ethnographic interest in senses of place, I conceive of experience as a historical product constrained and recreated by fields of power.

6 This view of the dialectic has become standard in anthropology. Even authors engaged in a sophisticated use of dialectical thinking in their work such as Jean and John Comaroff reproduce this notion when they happen to *define* the concept (see Comaroff and Comaroff 1997:28, 409; also Comaroff 1985:1, 6, 43). As argued, among others, by Edward Thompson (1978b:114) and David Harvey (1996:48), one of the recognized complexities of the dia-

lectic is that it is a *practice* that defies being enclosed and objectified within a narrow definition.

7 The first Andean ridges and the Paraguay and Paraná rivers mark, respectively, the western and eastern limits of the Chaco. To the north, the Chaco is limited by the hills of Chiquitos, in southeastern Bolivia. To the south, it gradually merges into the Pampas, south of the Salado River. The Gran Chaco is often divided into three large subareas: the northern Chaco (Chaco boreal), north of the Pilcomayo River; the central Chaco, between the Pilcomayo and Bermejo rivers; and the southern Chaco, south of the Bermejo.

8 Other denominations, primarily to distinguish them from the eastern Toba, are Ñachilamolék Toba (Mendoza and Gordillo 1988; Gordillo 1999), Toba of western Formosa (Mendoza 1994; de la Cruz and Mendoza 1988; Gordillo 1992, 1994, 1995b, 1996a), and Toba of Sombrero Negro (de la Cruz 1993).

9 All Toba groups are part of the Guaycurú linguistic family, which also includes the Pilagá, Mocoví, Mbayá (today Caduveo), and the now disappeared Abipón and Payaguá. Yet significant differences separate western and eastern Toba. The Toba examined in this book are linguistically closer to the so-called Bolivian Toba and the Pilagá than to the eastern Toba, to the point that it is hard for them to communicate with the latter. The close links between western Toba and Pilagá led Alfred Métraux (1937) to refer to both groups as "Toba-Pilagá," a term previously used by Erland Nordenskiöld (1912:18), Rafael Karsten (1970:6–7), and John Arnott (1934). This term, however, obscures the different histories that have constituted these groups and the fact that they have historically regarded themselves as different from each other. Métraux was aware of this and wrote: "These Indians claim the name of Toba and regard themselves as different from the Pilagá" (1946a:10, also 1937:174). Probably because of this, soon after Métraux abandoned the term "Toba-Pilagá" altogether (see 1946a; 1946b).

10 The same predominance of locality over temporal location characterizes urban, middle-class memories. As Edward Casey (1987:214) aptly put it: "We often remember ourselves in a given place; but how often do we remember ourselves as having been at a given date?" (see also Lefebvre 1991:95; Rappaport 1990:151).

11 This is the book's "ethnographic present." Yet my narrative purposely intertwines the past and present tense to avoid giving the sense that, as argued by Anna Tsing (1993:xiv–xv), local practices are either "out of history" (by overusing the present tense) or "*are* history," in the colloquial sense (by overusing the past tense).

12 The fact that memory is molded by experiences contemporary to remembering has been analyzed by numerous authors (see, among others, Cole 2001; Fentress and Whickam 1992; Gordillo 2002a, 2002b, 2002d; Malkki 1995; Sider and Smith 1997; Swedenburg 1991; and Trouillot 1995).

13 Even though devils can acquire male and female features, men and women tend to present them as male. A female devil, *payaGó*, provides healing power to the *piogonaGá*, the (currently rare) female equivalent of the *pio-Gonáq* or shaman.

1. Landmarks of Memory

1 Exogamy is defined by the prohibition to marry *laqáya* (siblings and first cousins), *laqáya's* children, and the *laqáya* of one's parents (see Mendoza and Browne 1995). Because of bilateral descent, there is no defined system of descent that privileges any one genealogical line. What brings extended families together is usually strong leadership.

2 Some people also refer to their ancestors as *toihekpí*, "very old people."

3 The first forest strip, eight to twelve meters high, comprised algarrobos (*Prosopis alba* and *nigra*), vinal (*Prosopis ruscifolia*), chañar (*Gourliea decorticans*), and tusca (*Acacia aroma*). Farther into the hinterland, tall hardwoods dominated the monte, some of them up to fifteen meters high: quebracho colorado (*Schinopsis quebracho colorado*), quebracho blanco (*Aspidosperma quebracho blanco*), urundel (*Astronium balansae*), palo santo (*Bulnesia sarmientoi*), and palo mataco (*Prosopis kuntzei*) (Morello 1970:44–46; Castañeda Vega 1920:65).

4 In 1919 Rafael Castañeda Vega (1920:21) wrote about Colonia Buenaventura: "According to the references of the settlers, ten or fifteen years ago not everything was monte as it is now: close to the river . . . everything was a wide grassland, dotted every now and then with big patches of forest."

5 Many Toba also refer to this area as *nonakapiGát*, which could be roughly translated as "a place with areas of trees and open country." The Criollos call this area *monte ralo*, "sparse bush."

6 Some Criollos living in poverty also hunt and gather wild fruits and honey. But their livelihood and identity are based on cattle raising.

7 See Luis María de la Cruz (1997:106–107) for an analysis of a similar flexibility of marisca among the Wichí.

8 Once women bring fruit loads to their homes, they prepare them for consumption or storage. They pound the algarroba pods in mortars to turn them into flour, which is then mixed with water to form *ikiénik* (*añapa* in Spanish): a sweet paste people suck and drink with one hand. They also sun dry algarroba pods and other fruits in order to place them in storage huts elevated one foot off the ground. Algarroba reserves usually last until March or April. Fruits like sachasandia, bola verde, and poroto de monte are stored primarily for the months of scarcity.

9 With the end of the gathering season, women enter the bush on a much more irregular basis. In addition to organizing expeditions to collect chaguar fiber, women enter the bush to gather fruits that ripen in the fall

(March–June): mistol (*nála, Zizyphus mistol*, of a larger variety than the summer variety), doca (*Morrenia odorata*), and tusca (*Acasia aroma*) (Gordillo 1992).

10   This is the only case in which the Toba have a mythological explanation for the origin of a particular place. Probably because of the flat Chaco geography, Toba mythical accounts are not localized in recognizable places. This marks a contrast, for instance, with some North American native groups (Basso 1996; Pryce 1999:111) and the Australian Aborigines, who see features of their land as the result of the action of mythological beings (Myers 1986:57; Povinelli 1993:136–37).

11   The uanaganaGát net consists of two flexible sticks (up to two meters long) tied from both edges. The heélaGae is made with two rigid sticks tied only from one edge. Team fishing required two groups playing complementary roles: young men with uanaganaGát nets gradually advanced downstream, fishing and pushing fish toward older men holding heélaGae nets and forming a line across the river.

12   Since nets are not suitable for fishing in shallow marshes of clear water (where fish can see and avoid men diving with their nets), some men use only a small version of the uanaganaGát net to capture small fish in muddy waters. Owing to the decrease in the productivity of fishing, people are not able to store dried fish as in the past. At most, some people keep barbecued fish for a few days.

13   The main catches are palometas (*Serrasalminae*), pacús (*Colossoma mitrei*), sábalos (*Prochilodus platensis*), surubíes (*Pseudoplatystoma coruscans*), and dorados (*Salminus maxilocus*). The productivity of fishing decreases in August and increases again in December, when the annual floods bring in new shoals.

14   Most of these fields range from a quarter hectare to two hectares, but the small group of full-time farmers works four to six hectares each. In 1997 the fields in use by all Toba near the marshes, scattered in dozens of locations, encompassed a total of eighty-six hectares.

15   People begin working the fields when the marshlands recede in May and the soil is humid. Some nuclear families and even whole households set up temporary camps near their fields (often for several months). While men and women prepare the soil for plowing, they live mostly off fishing, hunting, and gathering honey. The tractor owned by a Toba farmer plows the fields (financed by the ICA) and men and women plant in late July or early August (mostly watermelon, pumpkin, melon, and corn). People stay near their plots, weeding them on a regular basis, until December, when they harvest them before the floods cover the area again.

16   The most sought-after type of hive is that of the *konaiapolio*, "large bees" (of European origin, *Apis melifera*, called *extranjera* in Spanish). Other varieties include bala (*uaGató*), lachiguana (*katék*), moro-moro (*konoyáq*), yana (*ma'ayé*), and carana (*ne'ehal*). Hunters often go to the marshes with the

purpose of capturing prey such as ostriches (*Rhea americana*), carpinchos (water pigs, *Hydrochoerus hydrocoeris notialis*), and various types of birds.

17 By the late 1990s, a dirt road was under construction to link settlers in the area with villages farther east in Formosa.

18 The passenger train service had been terminated and freight trains derailed often because of the tracks' decrepit state.

19 Most dry beans produced in the area are white beans of the genus *Phaseolus*.

20 See *Página/12*, May 22, 1996.

2. Heaven and Hell

1 All translations from texts in Spanish and French are mine.

2 The Chaco linguistic families that include groups with a foraging tradition are: Mataco-Mataguayan (Wichí, Nivaclé, Chorote, Maká), Maskoi (Maskoi, Lengua, Sanapaná, Angaité), and Zamuco (Chamacoco, Ayoreo) (see Métraux 1946b). This list does not include the numerous groups that by the twentieth century had been wiped out by disease and violence.

3 In the early seventeenth century, for instance, the Lule of the Salado River massively fled to the Chaco interior to avoid servitude (Lozano 1989:98; Métraux 1946b:227).

4 Even though many Jesuit missions were short-lived, they played an important role in the consolidation of the frontier. Since they employed indigenous labor in different activities — especially cattle raising, the economic base of most missions — in the long run they contributed to creating a labor force for the Spanish (Gullón Abao 1993: 155, 347). After the Jesuits' expulsion, Franciscans took control of many of their missions, yet most of them were abandoned or began a period of decline.

5 Most members of this Toba group ended up moving to Argentinean territory and settling in Monte Carmelo (on the Pilcomayo), Tartagal, and Embarcación (see de la Cruz 1989:97; Mendoza 1999:82–83).

6 Whereas in Salta and Jujuy the term *ingenio* is synonymous with plantation, in the province of Tucumán the term often refers just to the sugar mill, for many sugar-processing companies (unlike those of Salta and Jujuy) do not own cane fields.

3. Places of Violence

1 Currently, people remember the names of fourteen bands. These names refer to groups that existed when the mission station was founded in 1930 but also to some that had by then dissolved. Most bands were named after animals that expressed distinctive features or eating preferences, yet without representing a totemic ancestry. For a detailed analysis of the bands'

names and approximate geographical distribution, see Gordillo 1992:75–77 and especially Mendoza 1999, 2002.

2 In 1898 a member of the border commission with Bolivia wrote that on his trips to the Pilcomayo he encountered "a migrant mass of workers" (AGN, *Archivo Roca*, Legajo 155, letter of Manuel Olascoaga to General Julio A. Roca; Thanks to Vanesa Harary for this reference). In 1903 a Toba man told Astrada he had been at Ledesma (1906:109). By 1905, various explorers had reported that Wichí, Chorote, Toba, and Pilagá groups of the Pilcomayo had been in the ingenios (see von Rosen 1904:13–14; Luna Olmos 1905:46, also 35, 47, 49, 58; Astrada 1906:105, 109, 142; Lange 1906:55).

3 In addition to kahogonaGá, some people use the term *máik lacháqa*, "the place of the sugar cane." KahogonaGá means not only "mountains" but also "thunder." Among the eastern Toba *qasogonaGá* is a figure that unleashes storms and thunders and is linked to the Andes (Miller 1975:481 and Wright 1997). Among the western Toba, the closest equivalent is *wosáq*, "rainbow," also associated with storms but not with the mountains.

4 In those years, women represented about half of the indigenous labor force, a percentage of female participation in a workforce that was among the highest in Argentina (Lagos 1995:135, 142).

5 Prior to the migrations some Toba made chiripas with wool, as Nordenskiöld (1912) noted among the Nivaclé. Yet many Toba remember that chiripas became their most important garment only when they obtained cloth at the ingenios.

4. Searching for Our Fathers

1 The Leach brothers granted the missionaries several houses at a site called Los Urundeles, one and a half kilometers from the sugar mill. This place became, as one of the missionaries put it, "our headquarters for working the Chaco tribes" (Hunt 1912b:72).

2 Yet the Franciscan order continued to be active along the western edge of the Argentinean Chaco, especially among the Guaraní.

5. A Kind of Sanctuary

1 Currently, the most common word for "God" is the Spanish term *Dios*. People use *Kade'tá* to refer to God as people do in English or Spanish: that is, as a metaphor ("our Father") that does not replace the word "God." For instance, during service, people often say *Haliaganék Dios am Kade'tá*, "Lord God, you, our Father."

2 A missionary wrote about the Toba's frustrations, clearly fostered by their view that leaders should be particularly generous: "They had expected

much in the way of material blessing, but the missionaries were not at all generous with their goods. They gave no free flour from their food store or clothes from their boxes. Things were not quite what they had expected and hoped for" (South American Missionary Society 1937:55).

3 See also Métraux 1933a:204; 1937:171 and Saint 1936, part II:244.

4 In December 1932, Alfred Métraux encountered a Pilagá group in Descanso (Estero Patiño) and wrote: "Convinced that I was an English missionary, they had celebrated my arrival as the beginning of a new era, an era in which they would be protected from the vexations of the Argentinean military authorities" (1937:172).

5 Dora Tebboth (1989:58–59, 215) wrote that a boy going from Misión Pilagá to El Toba was shot dead by settlers and that many Toba and Pilagá men were ready to take revenge. Troops arrived in Misión El Toba responding to rumors of an imminent "Toba uprising."

6 In 1944, for instance, the authorities of the National Territory of Formosa temporally banned Protestant teaching, claiming that the constitution stated that indigenous people should be taught Roman Catholicism. This temporary ban severely disrupted the activities of the Anglican stations (Makower 1989:127).

7 See AHF *Expedientes Judiciales, Cajas Aborígenes: Sumario No 5/950, "Causa: hurto reiterado, contra el indígena 'Caradura', denuncia de Don Guillermo Alfredo Leake."*

8 Further factors contributed to the mission's demise: the lagoon on which it was located had dried up and the missionary in charge, John Arnott, went back to Britain to fight in World War II. However, the missionaries acknowledged that the 1937 massacre played a decisive role in the mission's decline (Arnott 1937:112–13; Makower 1989:111–13).

6. "In the Bush, You Can Do Anything"

1 These observations come from Métraux's personal diary, published posthumously. It is worth noticing that they are at odds with the accounts he published about the Anglican missions after his first visit to the area in 1933. In a 1933 piece, capturing the initial stage of missionization, he took pains to emphasize the missionaries' respect for native customs and the positive climate that prevailed at the stations (Métraux 1933b). Despite the personal reservations that emerge from his 1939 diary, Métraux considered that the missions played an important social role protecting indigenous groups from the military and the settlers, for whom he often expressed an overt antipathy.

2 As Alfred Leake (1933:68) wrote: "Medical work is in many ways the most difficult, because of the opposition of the witch-doctors. This work has to be carried on with great caution, for the witch-doctors, although rarely

openly hostile, are quick to lay at the door of the missionary any serious sickness or death."

3 The missionaries had their own ambivalence; they were aware of the economic importance of foraging and some of them even regarded fishing, hunting, and gathering as "Toba traditions" that could be preserved (Leake 1940:8; Grubb 1965:18–19; Tebboth 1989:140). Nicacio remembered that Alfredo enjoyed eating bush food and that he encouraged people to continue doing so because, so he used to tell them, "That's the food that God made for the poor."

7. The Promised Land

1 By the time he founded Tabacal, he was national senator for Salta and had occupied key positions in various provincial governments, including that of governor between 1913 and 1916 (Luque Colombres 1991:71–75).

2 This occurred when President Ortíz resigned due to health problems. In September 1942 Patrón Costas became provisional president while President Castillo was abroad (Luque Colombres 1991:159–60).

3 Mechanization began in the mid-1960s, with the aim of reducing costs, diversifying production, and limiting the political challenge posed by large concentrations of workers (Bisio and Forni 1976:12, 15); it first involved cane loading and transportation and then, more gradually, cane cutting. Shortly after, mechanization also included the practices carried out by Chaco groups: clearing sections of forest, digging canals, and woodcutting. In 1965, the same year Robustiano Patrón Costas died, San Martín del Tabacal employed 7,291 field workers. In 1970 the number had dropped to 4,268, an over-40 percent reduction (Bisio and Forni 1976:18).

4 A few years later, Ledesma and San Martín del Tabacal recruited small groups for short time periods. The last trip took place in 1976.

8. "It Seemed Like We Lived There"

1 By the 1960s, people were taken to distant work sites by tractor trailers. In wintertime and when the work site was close to the lote, the first bell rang at four in the morning.

2 For this reason, recruitment could take place as early as in February.

3 In 1937, in the village near El Toba, 300 people migrated out of a population of about 500 (Leake 1937:127–28). In 1950, 500 out of 700 left (AHF *Expedientes Judiciales: Cajas Aborígenes; Causa: Hurto reiterado, contra el indígena "Caradura," denuncia de Don Guillermo Alfredo Leake,* page 1).

4 In turn, the lotes were grouped in *colonias* (colonies); see Bosio and Forni 1976:49.

5   The administration manipulated these differences as well. Even though all Aborígenes received similar wages, the administration regarded the Wichí as the epitome of savagery and the least productive workers; by contrast, it usually saw the Toba as "cleaner" and "more civilized" than the former (Bialet-Massé 1973:95).

6   Those who completed all their *tareas* (*tarja completa*) received extra incentives: weekly and monthly bonuses in cash and clothes in accordance to their category.

7   Because of its twofold character, some authors have argued that the tarea system represents a piecework system (Conti, de Lagos, and Lagos 1988:22; Gordillo 1995b:111; Muir 1947:235; Vidal 1914:9); others argued that it was characterized by "a fixed salary" (Beck 1994:167). It was both systems and neither of them at the same time.

8   In the early twentieth century women's salaries were higher in relative terms. In La Esperanza, men were paid 1.15 pesos a day, women 1.00, and osacos 0.50 (Zavalía 1914:52; cf. Vidal 1914:8; Unsain 1914:86–87).

9   Administrators, labor inspectors, and anthropologists have described indigenous camps in the plantations as a reproduction of the "traditional" huts in the Chaco (see Niklison 1989:69; Pagés Larraya 1982, 3:51). This analogy, in addition to being superficial, was particularly suitable to the interest of the plantation administration, which made huge savings in housing costs (Unsain 1914:46; Vidal 1914:13; Niklison 1989:88). In the lote, the Aborígenes certainly relied on techniques used at home to erect basic dwellings, yet the materials employed (mostly cane leaves), the damp weather, and the living conditions were far from those of the Chaco. In addition, by the time the Toba were migrating to Tabacal on a regular basis they had adopted the solid rancho used by settlers (supported by poles fixed to the ground and with adobe and straw walls).

10 The Toba did not keep those cows; they obtained them for their meat.

9. The Breath of the Devils

1   For instance, Horacio, a man in his fifties who has been involved in politics for many years, told me: "Many people died there, maybe because the patrón didn't look after the people. He didn't give medicines. He didn't send the doctor. He didn't give housing. He only gave [us] that toldería." Yet most Toba blame devils for the high death toll in the cane fields (and for most deaths in general). In this regard, for many Toba this explanation and the effect of poor living conditions do not exclude each other.

2   In 1967 a Toba nurse trained by the missionaries kept a record of twenty-four children and four adults who died during that year at Tabacal (out of a total of probably 300 or 400 migrants). To date, I have been unable to find other, more systematic statistics on the death toll at the ingenio. It is

very likely that the administration did not register most of these deaths (especially those of children and babies). As elsewhere in the Americas, the high mortality rate among these indigenous groups was probably related to their lack of natural defenses against new diseases. Missionary reports about the cane fields suggest that among children the most common epidemics were measles and chickenpox (South American Missionary Society 1938:69; Bradberry 1958:58). Yet my aim here is to analyze what the Toba remember of that experience and the meanings associated with it, rather than to reconstruct that experience in quantitative or biomedical terms.

3　*Kiyágaik* means "big eater" (*pí* is a suffix denoting a group). KiyáGaik is also the name given to the beetle that shamans place inside a person's body to cause a disease. The disease, and the pain resulting from it, is the result of the beetle eating flesh from within the body.

4　In addition to the Sikhs, the plantations brought from overseas small groups of Russian, Japanese, Italian, and Spanish workers (Vidal 1914:13–15).

5　The only reference to cannibalism that may have existed prior to the experience of wage labor involves a myth about the origin of tobacco. In this myth, a woman ate her husband and other people before being killed by her own children and burnt to ashes. It was from these ashes that the first tobacco plant grew. Of the dozens of interviews I conducted about the KiyaGaikpí, only Segundo made a connection between them and this myth. When I asked him whether there were KiyaGaikpí in their lands in the Chaco, he told me: "There aren't any around here. Only a long time ago, there was a woman who ate her husband. But only a woman. The tobacco plant. But a long time ago."

6　In the second decade of the century, Criollos in Ledesma were horrified at the alleged cannibalism of the "Chiriguano," who according to them had already eaten "quite many people" (González Trilla 1921:263). Around that time, the Wichí at Algarrobal—not far from San Martín del Tabacal—thought that the first Anglican missionaries, closely associated with La Esperanza, were cannibals (Makower 1989:40).

7　Depending on their geographical location, different social groups describe the Familiar in various ways. In some cases it is presented either as a large black dog (*el perro Familiar*) or a large snake (*viborón*). Yet the Familiar is often depicted as having a changing physical shape, including that of a well-dressed white man (see Rosenberg 1936: 133–37; Vessuri 1971:60–62; Rosenzvaig 1986:248; Coluccio and Coluccio 1987:50–52; Isla and Taylor 1995).

8　Other laborers, however, considered that it was possible to make deals with "the Devil" to increase productivity. This is the case of the Bolivian cane cutters, paid by piecework (Whiteford 1981:55).

9　See *La Nación*, October 23, 1946.

10 In *The Devil and Commodity Fetishism*, Taussig refers only briefly to alienation to explain devil imageries (1980:17, 37) but nevertheless maintains an overall connection between these imageries and labor conditions. In another piece (1995:398), he offered a reinterpretation of his original thesis of the devil pact in which he does not refer to labor or alienation. In this new analysis, Taussig interprets the devil contract as a phenomenon of sheer excessiveness and exuberance restricted to the sphere of *circulation*: instances of "giving without receiving."

10. "We Returned Rich"

1 *El Mundo*, October 26, 1951; November 8, 1951. Having in mind the Toba's vivid depiction of Perón throwing money at Tabacal, I devoted weeks of bibliographical research in Buenos Aires and Salta looking, without success, for any published reference to this episode. First, none of the most important biographies of Perón report a visit to the San Francisco River Valley. Second, since many Toba agreed that the train had arrived at Tabacal close to the end of the harvest (the "Eva Perón Train" arrived at that time), I reviewed the October and November issues of a mainstream newspaper during Perón's first two presidencies (1946–1955). No trip by him to Tabacal is ever mentioned. Tomás Eloy Martínez (personal communication, 1997), one of the most distinguished writers on Perón, agrees that there is no evidence of such a trip. The closest Perón seems to have been to Tabacal when he was a public figure was in his Salta and Jujuy tour during the campaign for the February 1946 presidential elections. However, he did not visit the sugar plantations. After all, the latter, and especially San Martín del Tabacal, were strongholds of his most bitter political adversaries. According to Ernest Sweeney and Alejandro Domínguez Benavides (1998:240), Perón told Patrón Costas, at a meeting held in 1943, that he had been at Tabacal as a low-ranking officer, when he was not a public figure.

2 In 1914 an inspector of the Argentinean Department of Labor wrote about the arreglo grande in Ledesma: "The employee who pays can write any type of sum, $12 or $96. The Indian will always pick up the receipt, with any type of amount written on it, because he does not know how to distinguish the numbers" (Unsain 1914:71). The same year, another inspector noted the same thing at La Esperanza; he also analyzed the files of 300 indigenous workers and found out that none received what they were owed. Furthermore, many got nothing (Zavalía 1915:50–51; see also Niklison 1989:92).

11. *"Dancing, Dancing, Dancing"*

1   Rafael Karsten (1970:27) claimed, from his 1912 fieldwork among the Bolivian Toba, that the nomí was aimed at neutralizing evil spirits. Current memories and ethnographic sources do not corroborate this assertion.

2   As a result, venereal diseases were rampant. Mariano remembered that he was accordingly careful when choosing his sexual partners: "I didn't go with women who fooled around with just anybody."

12. *"We Didn't Go on Strike"*

1   Guillermo Otero was *jefe de cultivos* (head of crops) during the early years of San Martín del Tabacal. Teófilo Mayer was administrator in the period 1923–42 (Aráoz 1966:68).

13. *"We're Not Going to Die"*

1   The so-called Kalahari Debate has partially hinged on how to account for this resilience. Whereas Edwin Wilmsen and James Denbow (Wilmsen 1989; Wilmsen and Denbow 1991) see foraging among the Kalahari San as the product of a history of marginalization, Richard Lee, Jaqueline Solway, Mathias Guenther, and Richard Daly (among others) have analyzed foraging as an old practice only recently adapted to relations of domination (Solway and Lee 1990; Lee and Guenther 1991; Lee and Daly 1999). Both sides, nonetheless, tacitly agree that the mobility, flexibility, and accessible technology associated with hunting and gathering are relatively well adapted to cope with conditions of exploitation.

2   As Nicacio put it: "The rich eat bread. We the poor eat all that food, our life, because we're not rich. The Toba eat fish, in the bush, all day long."

3   For this reason they are also called *piyágahik*, "night wanderers."

4   The female equivalent of the male shaman, the *pioGonagá*, is currently relatively rare in this group. The *konánaGae* or witch is not a healer but only a source of disease.

5   Eastern Toba in the province of Chaco founded *La Unida* in the late 1950s and its overarching principle is healing through trance (Miller 1979, 1995; Wright 1992, 1997). Whereas the Anglican healing sessions are held separately from the regular religious service, at La Unida healing is an integral component of the culto.

6   The extraction of objects, in some cases through the use of Bibles, is much more common in the Iglesia Unida. Some participants in Anglican healing

sessions have a negative view of object extractions, given their suggestion of shamanism. Yet at Anglican sessions, individual participants have nevertheless healed some people this way (see Bargalló 1992).

14. *The Production of Local Knowledge*

1 People refer to this type of hunting without firearms as *hayáGan*, a practice they distinguish from *hainaganéGe* (to shoot).

2 It would be inaccurate to attribute this attitude to a recent process of "acculturation." In the 1930s, Alfred Métraux found among the Toba a strikingly similar pattern of overlapping answers about animal owners. For instance, people gave him six different names for the "owner of the water": *saayín, soñidi, wién, noGoplé'ec*, and *lék*, a listing similar to the one I gathered in the 1990s (see Métraux 1946:6, 50, 52, 149). Some of these names, however, refer to fish (saayín) or anguilas (wién) that some people do not recognize as payák creatures.

3 With some species, these restrictions involve not only meat but also nonedible parts. The disposal of bones and internal organs is important with species seen as "delicate," like ostrich and iguana. When men set a fire in order to gather honey and neutralize bees with smoke, some try not to burn the hive. Even though wild fruits (except nelomá) do not have individual owners, women do not gather fruits they will not take with them.

4 Some Chaco ethnographers have been prone to exoticize the figure of the "owners," widespread among indigenous groups in the region, by enclosing them in a purely mythical sphere and creating what Bourdieu (1977:19) has called an intellectualist reification of native explanations. For a critique, see Gordillo (1993, 1996b; also Briones 1996; Gordillo 1996c). On North American natives, see also Paula Pryce (1999:86–89, 95) for a critique of academics "approaching aboriginal peoples with the lens of spirituality."

5 Old men and women argue that in a distant past wosáq sank a whole village with storms because a girl approached a pond while having her period.

6 *Kohodót*, a dwarf payák and the partner of kopeletáGa, is particularly prone to playing tricks on humans.

7 It is worth noticing that this spatial compression is not exclusive to the Toba. With the signs reversed, it is not dissimilar from views in North America about violence in "the Third World," according to which countries as different as (for instance) Somalia, Colombia, or the Philippines are lumped together into one generic landscape of violence ("the wars of the poor").

15. "With the Fish, We're Rich"

1   For decades, selling animal skins (carpinchos, yacarés, wildcats, foxes) was an important source of income but in the late 1980s legal regulations and market changes severely restricted its importance (Gordillo and Porini 2001). As noted in chapter 5, the missionaries at El Toba regularly purchased handicrafts. After the Anglican withdrawal, the provincial government (through the ICA) bought large loads of handicrafts for several years but by the early 1990s this purchase had become highly irregular.

2   Since settlers are not granted the forms of state assistance common in Toba villages, many Toba see their Criollo neighbors as even poorer than themselves.

3   Angel referred to this when he told me: "As the old man says, there's other people who were born with more knowledge. They can produce money. Then, they don't have necessities because they have [things]. And we were born with nothing, just like this, poor."

16. *Journeys to Strange Lands*

1   In the early 1980s small groups of men were still cutting posts and selling them to merchants or the ICA. But a few years later the production of quebracho posts came to a halt.

2   Producing a quebracho post involved different tasks: cutting the tree down (*voltear*), cutting off the trunk edges (*despuntar*), cutting off branches and bark (*devastar*), smoothing the post's surface (*labrar*), and carrying it to the camp (*rodear*).

3   However, YPF did not find oil in or near Toba lands. The only significant oil well in northwest Formosa is at Palmar Largo, Departamento Ramón Lista.

4   Before heading to the estancias, the Toba usually register themselves at the local quarters of the Paraguayan gendarmería.

5   Some of these migrations began sporadically years earlier. Horticultural farms in Colonia Santa Rosa (Salta), were among the first to hire Toba men and women after Tabacal's mechanization. Migrations to these farms were conducted on an irregular basis, involved few people, and eventually ended in the early 1980s.

6   In the 1990s, in spite of annual variations, the Toba were paid an average of one peso (then one U.S. dollar) per ten kilos of cotton. Experienced harvesters can gather up to 150 kilos a day but many do not get more than 80. In the 1996 bean harvest, the Toba were paid 22 pesos per hectare; an average person completes one hectare per day (experienced workers can

complete up to one and a half). As a result, people usually earn more than in the cotton farms. The amount people get paid in cash (every Saturday in tayíñi and at the end of the harvest in tadéwo) depends heavily on the deductions for food and goods obtained at the provedurías. On occasions, these deductions leave people with very little money (on the bean farms, see also Trinchero and Leguizamón 1995).

7 The group members often include their work in a single account and later split the gains. Forms of labor control in both types of farms are also similar, involving local foremen in the east and the contractor and his assistants in the west, who regularly supervise the pace and quality of work.

17. *Locations of Contention and Hegemony*

1 At the end of 1995, for instance, a Toba extended family that set up a camp near the marshes engaged in tense standoffs with Criollos living nearby, with both sides trying to intimidate each other by displaying firearms and shooting in the air.

2 Most adults obtained their ID papers for the first time through the intervention of David Leake (Alfred Leake's son) in June 1968 (see D. Leake 1968).

3 As Luis María de la Cruz and Marcela Mendoza have noted (1988), this gave them legal visibility as a group but also forced them to adapt to procedures alien to them: establishing an *estatuto* (the association rules), choosing representatives, and electing a land commission on a regular basis.

4 The government granted the settlers living outside Toba lands the right to use some tracts of land (*permiso de ocupación*). Their lands have been measured but they are obliged to invest in basic infrastructure (*mejoras*) in order to eventually receive their title, something that has not taken place yet (De la Cruz, personal communication, 1999).

5 Yet well-off Toba continue attempting to create more individual forms of land use. Some leaders have recently fenced off some areas for their cattle. These *piquetes* (wire fences) cover only a few dozen hectares and do not imply property rights; but they have partially restricted collective access to those tracts of land.

18. *The Other Side*

1 For instance, the Toba call the Pilagá *tainhikpí*, "people from down the river," and the latter refer to the Toba as *ñachilamolekpí*, "people from up the river." Most groups in the area also made a distinction between bands of the hinterland and bands that occupied lands on the river.

2 Additionally, land titling has fixed Toba legal ownership of land south of

the marshes. This factor alone would have certainly constrained any massive plan to move to the other side. My goal here, nonetheless, is not to evaluate the feasibility of such a displacement but to analyze why some people, even if briefly, considered it an option.

Conclusions

1 Kay Warren (1998:71–72), for instance, articulates this concern.
2 In fact, despite her tacit criticism of notions of negativity, this is one of the main points Massey makes about places in her *Space, Place and Gender* (1994).

References

Archives

AGN *Archivo General de la Nación*, Buenos Aires
AHF *Archivo Histórico de Formosa*, Formosa

Newspapers

El Mundo, Buenos Aires (1951)
La Nación, Buenos Aires (1946)
Página/12, Buenos Aires (1996)

Books and Articles

Abercrombie, Thomas. 1998. *Pathways of Memory and Power: Ethnography and History among an Andean People.* Madison: University of Wisconsin Press.

Adorno, Theodor. 1973 [1966]. *Negative Dialectics.* Trans. E. Ashton. New York: Continuum.

Amariglio, Jack, and Antonio Caliari. 1993. "Marxian Value Theory and the Problem of the Subject: The Role of Commodity Fetishism." In Emily Apter and William Pietz, eds., *Fetishism as Cultural Discourse*, 186–216. Ithaca: Cornell University Press.

Anderson, Benedict. 1991. *Imagined Communities: Reflections on the Origin and Spread of Nationalism.* London: Verso.

Appadurai, Arjun. 1996. *Modernity at Large: Cultural Dimensions of Globalization.* Minneapolis: University of Minnesota Press.

Aráoz, Ernesto. 1966. *Vida y obra del Doctor Patrón Costas.* Buenos Aires.

Aráoz de Lamadrid, Mariano. 1914. "Fundamentos del contrato que antecede." *Boletín del Departamento Nacional de Trabajo* 28: 37–44.

Arenales, José. 1833. *Noticias históricas y descriptivas sobre el país del Chaco y el río Bermejo, con observaciones relativas a un plan de navegación y colonización que se propone.* Buenos Aires: Imprenta Hallet.

Arengo, Elena. 1996. "Civilization and its Discontents: History and Ab-original Identity in the Argentine Chaco." Ph.D. diss., Department of Anthropology, New School for Social Research.

Arnott, John. 1933. "Progress in the Toba Mission." *South American Missionary Society Magazine* 67: 5–6.

———. 1934. "Los Toba-Pilagá del Chaco y sus guerras." *Revista Geográfica Americana* 1(7): 491–501.

———. 1936. "Misión Pilagá: The Society Youngest Mission." *South American Missionary Society Magazine* 70: 68–70.

———. 1937. "Misión Pilagá, April–June 1937." *South American Missionary Society Magazine* 71: 112–14.

Astrada, Domingo. 1906. *Expedición al Pilcomayo*. Buenos Aires: Estudio Gráfico Robles.

Balzac, Honoré de. 2002 [1845]. *A Prince of Bohemia and other Stories*. New York: Fredonia.

Bargalló, María Lía. 1992. "Shamanes, iglesias y atención primaria entre los tobas del oeste de Formosa: Etnicidad y hegemonización en el campo de la salud." Tesis de Licenciatura en Ciencias Antropológicas, Universidad de Buenos Aires.

Basso, Keith. 1996. *Wisdom Sits in Places: Landscape and Language among the Western Apache*. Albuquerque: University of New Mexico Press.

Beck, Hugo Humberto. 1994. *Relaciones entre blancos e indios en los territorios nacionales de Chaco y Formosa, 1885–1950*. Cuadernos de Historia Regional, Resistencia, Instituto de Investigaciones Geohistóricas, No. 29.

Bialet Massé, Juan. 1973 [1904]. *Las clases obreras argentinas a principios de siglo*. Buenos Aires: Nueva. Visión.

Bisio, Raúl, and Floreal Forni. 1976. "Economía de enclave y satelización del mercado de trabajo rural: El caso de los trabajadores con empleo precario en un ingenio azucarero del noroeste argentino." *Desarrollo Económico* 16(61): 3–56.

Bourdieu, Pierre. 1977 [1972]. *Outline of a Theory of Practice*. Trans. Richard Nice. Cambridge: Cambridge University Press.

Bourgois, Philippe. 1988. "Conjugated Oppression: Class and Ethnicity among Guaymi and Kuna Banana Workers." *American Ethnologist* 15(2): 328–48.

Bradberry, J. 1958. "Indian Preachers' Influence." *South American Missionary Society Magazine* 92: 58.

Briones, Claudia. 1996. "(Lo esencial es invisible a los ojos): Crímenes y pecados de (in)visibilidad asimétrica en el concepto de cultura." *Publicar en Antropología y Ciencias Sociales* 6: 7–56.

Cardiel, José. 1920 [1780]. "Recuerdos del Gran Chaco." *Estudios* 107: 372–83.

Carrasco, Morita, and Claudia Briones. 1996. *La tierra que nos quitaron: Reclamos indígenas en Argentina*. Buenos Aires: IGWIA-Asociación Lhaka Honhat.

Casey, Edward. 1987. *Remembering: A Phenomenological Study.* Bloomington: Indiana University Press.

Castañeda Vega, Rafael. 1920. *Colonia Buenaventura y Oeste de Formosa: Aspecto físico, habitantes y flora, oportunidades para el pequeño capital.* Buenos Aires: Compañía Gráfica Argentina.

Castro Boedo, Emilio. 1873. *Estudios sobre la navegación del Bermejo y colonización del Chaco en 1872.* Buenos Aires.

Chevalier, Jacques. 1982. *Civilization and the Stolen Gift: Capital, Kin and Cult in Eastern Peru.* Toronto: University of Toronto Press.

Coluccio, Félix, and Marta Isabel Coluccio. 1987. *Presencia del diablo en la tradición oral de Iberoamérica.* Buenos Aires: Ediciones Culturales Argentinas-Ministerio de Educación y Justicia.

Comaroff, Jean. 1985. *Body of Power, Spirit of Resistance: The Culture and History of a South African People.* Chicago: University of Chicago Press.

Comaroff, Jean, and John Comaroff. 1991. *Of Revelation and Revolution, Vol. 1: Christianity, Colonialism and Consciousness in Southern Africa.* Chicago: University of Chicago Press.

———. 1999. "Occult Economies and the Violence of Abstraction: Notes from the South African Postcolony." *American Ethnologist* 26(2): 279–303.

Comaroff, John, and Jean Comaroff. 1992. *Ethnography and the Historical Imagination.* Boulder: Westview Press.

———. 1997. *Of Revelation and Revolution, Vol. 2: The Dialectics of Modernity on a South African Frontier.* Chicago: University of Chicago Press.

Cole, Jennifer. 2001. *Forget Colonialism? Sacrifice and the Art of Memory in Madagascar.* Berkeley: University of California Press.

Connerton, Paul. 1989. *How Societies Remember.* Cambridge: Cambridge University Press.

Conti, Viviana, Ana de Lagos, and Marcelo Lagos. 1988. *Mano de obra indígena en los ingenios de Jujuy a principios de siglo.* Buenos Aires: Centro Editor de América Latina.

Coole, Diana. 2000. *Negativity and Politics: Dionysus and Dialectics from Kant to Poststructuralism.* London: Routledge.

Cordeu, Edgardo, and Alejandra Siffredi. 1971. *De la algarroba al algodón: Movimientos milenaristas del Chaco Argentino.* Buenos Aires: Juárez Editor.

Crain, Mary. 1991. "Poetics and Politics in the Ecuadorian Andes: Women's Narratives of Death and Devil Possession." *American Ethnologist* 18(1): 67–89.

de la Cruz, Luis María. 1989. "La situación de ocupación territorial de las comunidades aborígenes del Chaco salteño y su tratamiento legal." *Suplemento Antropológico* 24(2): 87–144.

———. 1993. "Apuntes para la topología del espacio toba." *Suplemento Antropológico* 28(1–2): 427–82.

———. 1997. *Y no cumplieron: Reflexiones acerca de la apasioanda relación entre los organismos de promoción de desarrollo y los grupos wichí.* La Plata:

Fundación para el Desarrollo Agroforestal de las Comunidades del Noroeste Argentino.

de la Cruz, Luis María, and Marcela Mendoza. 1988. "Les Tobas de l'ouest de Formosa, et le processus de reconnaisance légale de la propriété communautaire des terres." *Recherches Amérindiennes au Québec* 29 (4): 43–51.

Departamento de Guerra. 1889. *Memoria del Ministerio de Guerra y Marina. Departamento de Guerra: 1888–1889*. Buenos Aires: Editorial de Sud-América.

Dobrizhoffer, Martin. 1970 [1784]. *An Account of the Abipones, an Equestrian People of Paraguay*. New York: Johnson Reprint.

Dunk, Thomas. 1991. *It's a Working Man's Town: Male Working-Class Culture in Northwestern Ontario*. Montreal: McGill-Queen's University Press.

Edelman, Marc. 1994. "Landlords and the Devil: Class, Ethnic and Gender Dimensions of Central American Peasant Narratives." *Cultural Anthropology* 9(1): 58–93.

Estigarribia, José Félix. 1969 [1950]. *The Epic of the Chaco: Marshal Estigarribia's Memoirs of the Chaco War: 1932–1925*. New York: Greenwood Press.

Every, E. F. 1933. *South American Memories of Thirty Years*. London: Society for Promoting Christian Knowledge.

———. 1934. "Bishop Every at the Toba Mission." *South American Missionary Society Magazine* 68: 101.

———. 1936. "Bishop Every's 19th Visit to the Argentine Chaco Mission." *South American Missionary Society Magazine* 70: 110–12.

Fabian, Johannes. 1983. *Time and the Other: How Anthropology Makes Its Object*. New York: Columbia University Press.

———. 2001. *Anthropology with an Attitude*. Stanford: Stanford University Press.

Feld, Stephen. 1996. "Waterfalls of Song: An Acoustemology of Place Resounding in Bosavi, Papua New Guinea. In Stephen Feld and Keith Basso, eds., *Senses of Place*, 91–135. Santa Fe: School of American Research Press.

Feld, Stephen, and Keith Basso. 1996. "Introduction." In Stephen Feld and Keith Basso, eds. *Senses of Place*, 3–11. Santa Fe: School of American Research Press.

Feldman, Allen. 1991. *Formations of Violence: The Narrative of the Body and Political Terror in Northern Ireland*. Chicago: University of Chicago Press.

Fentress, James, and Chris Wickham. 1992. *Social Memory*. London: Blackwell.

Ferguson, James, and Akhil Gupta. 2002. "Spatializing States: Towards an Ethnography of Neoliberal Governmentality." *American Ethnologist* 29(4): 981–1002.

Fotheringham, Ignacio. 1910. *La vida de un soldado: O reminisencias de la frontera*. Buenos Aires: Kraft.

Foucault, Michel. 1990 [1976]. *The History of Sexuality, Vol. 1: An Introduction*. Trans. Robert Hurley. New York: Vintage.

Fox, Harold. 1958. "The Curse of the Cane-fields." *South American Missionary Society Magazine* 92: 24–25.

Geertz, Clifford. 1983. *Local Knowledge*. New York: Basic Books.

Gobelli, Rafael. 1916. *Mis memorias y apuntes varios*. Salta: Imprenta Rafael Tula.

Godbeer, Richard. 1992. *The Devil's Dominion: Magic and Religion in New England*. New York: Cambridge University Press.

González, Melitón. 1890. *El Gran Chaco argentino*. Buenos Aires: Compañía Sudamericana de Billetes de Banco.

González Trilla, Casimiro. 1921. *El Chaqueño: Apuntes sobre el Chaco santiagueño*. Santiago del Estero.

Gordillo, Gastón. 1992. "Cazadores-recolectores y cosecheros: Subordinación al capital y reproducción social entre los tobas del oeste de Formosa." In Hugo Trinchero, Daniel Piccinini, and Gastón Gordillo, *Capitalismo y grupos indígenas en el Chaco Centro-Occidental* (2 vols.), 13–191. Buenos Aires: Centro Editor de América Latina.

———. 1993. "La actual dinámica económica de los cazadores-recolectores del Gran Chaco y los deseos imaginarios del esencialismo." *Publicar en Antropología y Ciencias Sociales* 3: 73–96.

———. 1994. "La presión de los más pobres: Reciprocidad, diferenciación social y conflicto entre los tobas del oeste de Formosa." *Cuadernos del Instituto Nacional de Antropología y Pensamiento Latinoamericano* 15: 53–82.

———. 1995a. "Después de los ingenios: La mecanización de la zafra saltojujeña y sus efectos sobre los indígenas del Chaco Centro-Occidental." *Desarrollo Económico* 35 (137): 105–26.

———. 1995b. "La subordinación y sus mediaciones: Dinámica cazadora-recolectora, relaciones de producción, capital comercial y Estado entre los Tobas del oeste e Formosa." In Hugo Trinchero, ed., *Producción doméstica y capital: Estudios desde la antropología económica*, 105–38. Buenos Aires: Biblos.

———. 1996a. "Entre el monte y las cosechas: Migraciones estacionales y retención de fuerza de trabajo entre los tobas del oeste de Formosa (Argentina)." *Estudios Migratorios Latinoamericanos* 11(32): 135–67.

———. 1996b. "Hermenéutica de la ilusión: La etnología fenomenológica de Marcelo Bórmida y su construcción de los indígenas del Gran Chaco." *Cuadernos de Antropología Social* 9: 135–71.

———. 1996c. "La cultura como praxis material: Respuesta a Claudia Briones." *Publicar en Antropología y Ciencias Sociales* 6: 37–46.

———. 1999. "The Toba of the Argentine Chaco." In Richard Lee and Richard Daly, eds., *The Cambridge Encyclopedia of Hunters and Gatherers*, 110–13. Cambridge: Cambridge University Press.

———. 2001. " 'Un río tan salvaje e indómito como el indio toba': Una historia antropológica de la frontera del Pilcomayo." *Desarrollo Económico* 41(162): 261–80.

————. 2002a. "The Breath of the Devils: Memories and Places of an Experience of Terror." *American Ethnologist* 29(1): 33–57.

————. 2002b. "The Dialectic of Estrangement: Memory and the Production of Places of Wealth and Poverty in the Argentinean Chaco." *Cultural Anthropology* 17(1): 3–31.

————. 2002c. "Locations of Hegemony: The Making of Places in the Toba's Struggle for La Comuna, 1989–1999." *American Anthropologist* 104(1): 262–77.

————. 2002d. "Remembering 'the Ancient Ones': Memory, Hegemony, and the Shadows of State Terror in the Argentinean Chaco." In Belinda Leach and Winnie Lem, eds., *Culture, Economy, Power: Anthropology as Critique, Anthropology as Praxis*, 177–90. Albany: SUNY Press.

————. 2003. "Shamanic Forms of Resistance in the Argentinean Chaco: A Political Economy." *Journal of Latin American Anthropology* 8(3): 103–25.

Gordillo, Gastón, and Juan Martín Leguizamón. 2002. *El río y la frontera: Movilizaciones aborígenes, obras públicas y Mercosur en el Pilcomayo*. Buenos Aires: Biblos.

Gordillo, Gastón, and Gustavo Porini. 2001. "La declinación de la caza comercial entre aborígenes del Chaco argentino: Un análisis histórico-antropológico." *Suplemento Antropológico* 36(1): 325–54.

Gott, Richard. 1993. *Land without Evil: Utopian Journeys across the South American Watershed*. London: Verso.

Gould, Jeffrey. 1990. *To Lead as Equals: Rural Protest and Political Consciousness in Chinandenga Nicaragua, 1912–1979*. Chapel Hill: University of North Carolina Press.

Gramsci, Antonio. 1971 [1929–35]. *Selections from the Prison Notebooks*. Ed. and trans. Quintin Hoare and Geoffrey Nowell Smith. New York: International Publishers.

————. 1995 [1929–35]. *Further Selections from the Prison Notebooks*. Ed. and trans. Derek Boothman. Minneapolis: University of Minnesota Press.

Green, Linda. 1999. *Fear as a Way of Life*. New York: Columbia University Press.

Grubb, Barbrooke. 1911. "First Impressions of San Pedro de Jujuy." *South American Missionary Society Annual Report, 1910–1911*: 84–92.

————. 1915. "The New Station on the Rio Bermejo." *South American Missionary Society Magazine* 49: 42–43.

Grubb, Henry. 1931. "Early Days at the Toba Mission." *South American Missionary Society Magazine* 65: 87–89.

————. 1933. "Busy Days among the Tobas." *South American Missionary Society Magazine* 67: 41–43.

————. 1936. "A Scheme for a New Mission among the Southern Tobas." *South American Missionary Society Magazine* 70: 8.

————. 1948. "The Argentine Chaco Harvest Fields." *South American Missionary Society Annual Report, 1948*: 13–16.

————. 1965. *The Land between Rivers*. London: Lutterworth Press.

Grubb, Henry, and Alfred Leake. 1929. "An Account of a Visit to the Tobas of the Sombrero Negro District." *South American Missionary Society Magazine* 63: 94–95.

Gullón Abao, Alberto. 1993. *La frontera del Chaco en la gobernación del Tucumán, 1750–1810*. Cádiz: Universidad de Cádiz.

Gupta, Akhil, and James Ferguson. 1997. "Behind 'Culture': Space, Identity and the Politics of Difference." In Akhil Gupta and James Ferguson, eds., *Culture, Power, Place: Explorations in Critical Anthropology*, 33–51. Durham: Duke University Press.

Harvey, David. 1989. *The Condition of Postmodernity*. Oxford: Blackwell.

————. 1996. *Justice, Nature, and the Geography of Difference*. Oxford: Blackwell.

————. 2000. *Spaces of Hope*. Berkeley: University of California Press.

————. 2001. *Spaces of Capital: Towards a Critical Geography*. London: Routledge.

Hirsch, Silvia. 2000. "Misión, región y nación entre los guaraníes de Argentina: Procesos de integración y de re-etnización en zonas de frontera." In Alejandro Grimson, ed., *Fronteras, naciones e identidades: La periferia como centro*, 278–98. Buenos Aires: Ciccus-La Crujía.

Hunt, Richard. 1912a. "How the Argentine Chaco Mission Began." *South American Missionary Society Annual Report, 1911–1912*: 20–25.

————. 1912b. "San Pedro de Jujuy: The Base of Missionary Operations." *South American Missionary Society Magazine* 46: 71–73.

————. 1913. "Links in the Chain: Aims and Plans of the Argentine Chaco Mission." *South American Missionary Society Annual Report, 1912–1913*: 60–65.

————. 1928. "A Visit to Selva San Andrés' Mission." *South American Missionary Magazine* 62: 117–20.

————. 1933. *The Livingstone of South America*. London: Seely Service.

Ibazeta, Rudecindo. 1883–34. "Expedición argentina al Pilcomayo." *Boletín del Instituto Geográfico Argentino* 4: 227–31.

Iñigo Carrera, Nicolás. 1983. *La colonización del Chaco*. Buenos Aires: Centro Editor de América Latina.

————. 1984. *Campañas militares y clase obrera: Chaco, 1870–1930*. Buenos Aires: Centro Editor de América Latina.

Isla, Alejandro, and Julie Taylor. 1995. "Terror e identidad en los Andes: El caso del noroeste argentino." *Revista Andina* (13)2: 311–57.

Karsten, Rafael. 1970 [1923]. *The Toba Indians of the Bolivian Gran Chaco*. Oosterhout, Netherlands: Anthropological Publications.

Keenan, Thomas. 1993. "The Point is to (Ex) Change It: Reading Capital, Rhetorically." In Emily Apter and William Pietz, eds., *Fetishism as Cultural Discourse*, 152–85. Ithaca: Cornell University Press.

Kitchin, Barbara. 1958. "The Need at the Canefields." *South American Missionary Society Magazine* 92: 25–27.

Laclau, Ernesto, and Chantal Mouffe. 1985. *Hegemony and Socialist Strategy: Towards a Radical Democratic Politics.* London: Verso.

Lagos, Marcelo. 1995. "De la toldería al ingenio: Apuntes de investigación sobre el trabajo de las aborígenes chaqueñas." In Ana Teruel, ed., *Población y trabajo en el noroeste argentino: Siglos XVIII y XIX*, 125–42. Jujuy: Universidad Nacional de Jujuy.

Lambek, Michael. 1996. "The Past Imperfect: Remembering as Moral Practice." In Paul Antze and Michael Lambek, eds., *Tense Past: Cultural Essays on Trauma and Memory*, 235–54. London: Routledge.

Lange, Gunardo. 1906. *Río Pilcomayo: Desde la desembocadura en el río Pilcomayo hasta el paralelo 22 sud.* Buenos Aires: Oficina Meteorológica Argentina.

Leake, Alfred. 1933. "The Story of the Toba Mission." *South American Missionary Society Magazine* 67: 66–69.

———. 1934. "In the Toba Country." *South American Missionary Society Magazine* 68: 115–16.

———. 1937. "Misión El Toba." *South American Missionary Society Magazine* 71: 127–28.

———. 1940. "Notes from Misión El Toba." *South American Missionary Society Magazine* 74: 7–10.

———. 1944. "Lenguas Visit 'Toba' Land." *South American Missionary Society Magazine* 78: 11.

Leake, David. 1968. "David Leake." *Sent* March/April: 10–12.

Leake, Olive. 1932. "Toba Mission Staff Notes." *South American Missionary Society Magazine* 66: 93–94.

———. 1934. "News from Toba Land." *South American Missionary Society Magazine* 68: 9–10.

———. 1936. "Misión 'El Toba.' Argentine Chaco." *South American Missionary Society Magazine* 70: 126–28.

———. 1937. "Misión El Toba." *South American Missionary Society Magazine* 71: 37–39.

Lee, Richard B. 1979. *The Kung San: Men, Women and Work in a Foraging Society.* Cambridge: Cambridge University Press.

———. 1988. "Reflections on Primitive Communism." In Tim Ingold, David Riches, and James Woodburn, eds., *Hunters and Gatherers, Vol. 2: Property, Power and Ideology*, 252–68. Oxford: Berg.

———. 2003. *The Dobe Ju/'Hoansi.* 3rd ed. Orlando: Harcourt Brace College Publishers.

Lee, Richard B., and Richard Daly. 1999. "Introduction: Foragers and Others." In Richard Lee and Richard Daly, eds., *The Cambridge Encyclopedia of Hunters and Gatherers*, 1–19. Cambridge: Cambridge University Press.

Lee, Richard B., and Mathias Guenther. 1991. "Oxen or Onions? The Search for Trade (and Truth) in the Kalahari." *Current Anthropology* 32(5): 592–601.

Lefebvre, Henri. 1991 [1974]. *The Production of Space.* Trans. Donald Nicholson-Smith. Oxford: Blackwell.

Lehmann-Nitsche, Robert. 1925. "Vocabulario Toba (Río Pilcomayo y Chaco Oriental)." *Boletín de la Academia Nacional de Ciencias de la República Argentina* 28: 179–96.

Lewis, Laura. 2001. "Of Ships and Saints: History, Memory, and Place in the Making of Moreno Mexican Identity." *Cultural Anthropology* 16(1): 62–82.

Lozano, Pedro. 1989 [1733]. *Descripción corográfica del Gran Chaco Gualamba.* San Miguel de Tucumán: Universidad Nacional de Tucumán.

Luca de Tena, Torcuato, Luis Calvo, and Esteban Peicovich. 1976. *Yo, Juan Domingo Perón: Relato autobiográfico.* Buenos Aires: Planeta.

Lukács, Georg. 1971 [1923]. *History and Class Consciousness.* Trans. Rodney Livingstone. Cambridge, Mass.: MIT Press.

Luna Olmos, Lucas. 1905. *Expedición al Pilcomayo.* Buenos Aires: Imprenta Guillermo Krieger.

Luque Colombres, Carlos. 1991. *Patrón Costas en la historia.* Córdoba: Editorial Sepa.

Makower, Katharine. 1989. *Don't Cry For Me: Poor Yet Rich, the Inspiring Story of Indian Christians in Argentina.* London: Hodder Christian Paperbacks.

Malkki, Liisa. 1995. *Purity and Exile: Violence, Memory, and National Cosmology among Hutu Refugees in Tanzania.* Chicago: University of Chicago Press.

Marx, Karl. 1964 [1844]. *Economic and Philosophic Manuscripts.* New York: International Publishers.

———. 1966 [1846]. "Theses on Feuerbach." In Karl Marx and Friedrich Engels, *The German Ideology,* 197–99. New York: International Publishers.

———. 1970 [1859]. *A Contribution to the Critique of Political Economy.* New York: International Publishers.

———. 1977 [1867]. *Capital: A Critique of Political Economy, Vol. 1.* New York: Vintage.

———. 1981 [1894]. *Capital: A Critique of Political Economy, Vol. 3.* New York: Penguin.

Marx, Karl, and Friedrich Engels. 1966 [1846]. *The German Ideology.* New York: International Publishers.

Massey, Doreen. 1994. *Space, Place, and Gender.* Minneapolis: University of Minnesota Press.

Mendoza, Marcela. 1994. "Técnicas de observación directa para estudiar interacciones sociales infantiles entre los Toba." *Runa* 21: 241–62.

———. 1999. "The Western Toba: Family Life and Subsistence of a Former Hunter-Gatherer Society." In Elmer Miller, ed., *Peoples of the Gran Chaco,* 81–108. Westport, Conn.: Greenwood.

———. 2002. *Band Mobility and Leadership among the Western Toba Hunter-Gatherers of the Gran Chaco in Argentina.* New York: Edwin Mellin Press.

Mendoza, Marcela, and Michael Browne. 1995. "Términos de parentesco y términos de duelo de los tobas del oeste de Formosa." *Hacia una nueva carta étnica del Chaco* 6: 117–22.

Mendoza, Marcela, and Gastón Gordillo. 1988. "Las migraciones estacionales de los tobas ñachilamo'lek a la zafra salto-jujeña (1890–1930)." *Cuadernos de Antropología* 3: 70–89.

Métraux, Alfred. 1933a. "Nouvelles de la Mission A. Métraux." *Journal de la Societé des Americanistes* 25: 203–05.

———. 1933b. "La obra de las misiones inglesas en el Chaco." *Journal de la Societé des Americanistes* 25: 205–09.

———. 1933c. "A Remarkable Testimony and Appeal from an Argentine Scientist." *South American Missionary Society Magazine* 67: 79–80.

———. 1937. "Études d'ethnographie Toba-Pilagá (Gran Chaco)." *Anthropos* 32: 171–94, 378–402.

———. 1946a. *Myths of the Toba and Pilagá Indians of the Gran Chaco.* Philadelphia: American Folklore Society.

———. 1946b. "Ethnography of the Chaco." In Julian Steward, ed., *Handbook of South American Indians, Vol. 1: The Marginal Tribes*, 197–370. Washington: Smithsonian Institution Press.

———. 1967. *Religions et magies indiennes d'Amerique du Sud.* Paris: Gallimard.

———. 1978. *Itinéraires 1 (1935–1953): Carnets de notes et journaux de voyage.* Paris: Payot.

Miller, Elmer. 1975. "Shamans, Power Symbols, and Change in Argentine Toba Culture." *American Ethnologist* 2(3): 477–96.

———. 1979. *Los Tobas argentinos: Armonía y disonancia en una sociedad.* México: Siglo XXI.

———. 1995. *Nurturing Doubt: From Mennonite Missionary to Anthropologist in the Argentine Chaco.* Urbana: University of Illinois Press.

———. 1999. "Argentina's Eastern Toba: Vitalizing Ethnic Consciousness and Determination." In Elmer Miller, ed., *Peoples of the Gran Chaco*, 109–34. Westport, Conn.: Greenwood.

Ministerio de Guerra y Marina. 1889. *Memoria del Ministerio de Guerra y Marina, 1889. Departamento de Guerra.* Buenos Aires: Editorial de Sud-América.

Mitchell, Don. 1996. *The Lie of the Land: Migrant Workers and the California Landscape.* Minneapolis: University of Minnesota Press.

Molinari, Juan Luis. 1949. *Mangrullo entre tobas y pilagás.* Formosa: Talleres la Voz Popular.

Moore, Donald. 1998. "Subaltern Struggles and the Politics of Place: Remapping Resistance in Zimbabwe's Eastern Frontier." *Cultural Anthropology* 13(3): 344–81.

Morello, Jorge. 1970. "Modelo de relaciones entre pastizales y leñosas colonizadoras en el Chaco argentino." *IDIA* 276: 31–52.

Morello, Jorge, and Carlos Saravia Toledo. 1959. "El bosque chaqueño (I y II): Paisaje primitivo, paisaje natural y paisaje cultural del Oriente de Salta." *Revista Agrícola del Noroeste Argentino* 3(1–2): 5–82, 209–58.

Muir, Henry James. 1947. *Hoo Hooey: An Argentine Arcady, and How I Came There.* London: Country Life.

Myers, Fred. 1986. *Pintupi Country, Pintupi Self: Sentiment, Place, and Politics among Western Desert Aborigines.* Washington: Smithsonian Institution Press.

Nash, June. 1993 [1979]. *We Eat the Mines and the Mines Eat Us: Dependency and Exploitation in Bolivian Tin Mines.* New York: Columbia University Press.

Nelli, Ricardo. 1988. *La injusticia cojuda: Testimonios de los trabajadores del azúcar del ingenio Ledesma.* Buenos Aires: Punto Sur.

Niklison, José Elías. 1989 [1917]. *Investigación sobre los indios matacos trabajadores.* Jujuy: Universidad Nacional de Jujuy.

———. 1990 [1916]. *Los Tobas: Informe del Ministerio Nacional de Trabajo.* Jujuy: Universidad Nacional de Jujuy.

Nora, Pierre. 1989. "Between Memory and History: Les Lieux de Mémoire." *Representations* 26: 7–25.

Nordenskiöld, Erland. 1912. "La vie des Indiens dans le Chaco (Amerique du Sud)." *Revue de Geographie* Tome VI, Fasc. III.

Orta, Andrew. 2002. "Burying the Past: Locality, Lived History, and Death in an Aymara Ritual of Remembrance." *Cultural Anthropology* 17(4): 471–511.

Pagés Larraya, Fernando. 1982. *Lo irracional en la cultura.* Vols. 2 and 3. Buenos Aires: Fecic.

Palermo, Miguel Angel. 1986. "Reflexiones sobre el llamado 'complejo ecuestre' en la Argentina." *Runa* 16: 157–77.

Parry, Jonathan, and Maurice Bloch. 1991. "Introduction: Money and the Morality of Exchange." In Jonathan Parry and Maurice Bloch, eds., *Money and the Morality of Exchange,* 1–32. Cambridge: Cambridge University Press.

Pavón Pereyra, Enrique. 1974. *Perón: El hombre del destino.* Vol. 2. Buenos Aires: Abril.

Platt, Tristan. 1983. "Conciencia andina y conciencia proletaria: Qhuyaruna y ayllu en el norte de Potosí," HISLA: *Revista Latinoamericana de Historia Económica y Social* 2: 47–73.

Povinelli, Elizabeth. 1993. *Labor's Lot: The Power, History, and Culture of Aboriginal Action.* Chicago: University of Chicago Press.

Pryce, Paula. 1999. *"Keeping the Lakes' Way": Reburial and the Recreation of a Moral World among an Invisible People.* Toronto: University of Toronto Press.

Raffles, Hugh. 1999. " 'Local Theory': Nature and the Making of an Amazonian Place." *Cultural Anthropology* 14(3): 323–60.

———. 2002. *In Amazonia: A Natural History.* Princeton: Princeton University Press.

Rappaport, Joanne. 1990. *The Politics of Memory: Native Historical Interpretation in the Colombian Andes.* Cambridge: Cambridge University Press.

Regis, Helen. 2001. "Blackness and the Politics of Memory in the New Orleans Second Line." *American Ethnologist* 28(4): 752–77.

Revill, Winifred. 1949. "A Visit to the Cane-Fields." *South American Missionary Society Magazine* 83: 56–57.

Riaño-Alcalá, Pilar. 2002. "Remembering Place: Memory and Violence in Medellín, Colombia." *Journal of Latin American Anthropology* 7(1): 276–309.

Ricoeur, Paul. 1974. *The Conflict of Interpretations: Essays in Hermeneutics.* Evanston: Northwestern University Press.

———. 1976. *Interpretation Theory: Discourse and the Surplus of Meaning.* Fort Worth: Texas Christian University Press.

Rodas, Federico. 1991. *El pueblo de Ingeniero Juárez (Formosa): Sus antecedentes, su historia y la de sus instituciones y pioneros.* Córdoba: ABC Publishing.

Rodman, Margaret. 1992. "Empowering Place: Multilocality and Multi-vocality." *American Anthropologist* 94(3): 640–56.

Roseberry, William. 1989. *Anthropologies and Histories: Essays in Culture, History and Political Economy.* New Brunswick: Rutgers University Press.

———. 1994. "Hegemony and the Language of Contention." In Gilbert Joseph and Daniel Nugent, eds., *Everyday Forms of State Formation: Revolution and the Negotiation of Rule in Modern Mexico,* 355–66. Durham: Duke University Press.

Rosenberg, Tobías. 1936. *Palo'i Chalchal: Supersticiones, leyendas y costumbres del Tucumán.* San Miguel de Tucumán: Ediciones de la Sociedad Sarmiento.

Rosenzvaig, Eduardo. 1986. *Historia social de Tucumán y del azúcar.* 2 vols. Tucumán: Universidad Nacional de Tucumán.

———. 1995. *La cepa: Arqueología de una cultura azucarera.* vol 1. Buenos Aires: Universidad Nacional de Tucumán-Ediciones Letra Buena.

Rostagno, Enrique. 1969 [1911]. *Informe de Fuerzas de Operaciones en el Chaco — 1911.* Buenos Aires: Círculo Militar.

Rutledge, Ian. 1987. *Cambio agrario e integración: El desarrollo del capitalismo en Jujuy (1550–1960).* San Miguel de Tucumán: UBA, ECIRA-CICSO.

Sahlins, Marshall. 1981. *Historical Metaphors and Mythical Realities: Structure in the Early History of the Sandwich Islands Kingdom.* Ann Arbor: University of Michigan Press.

———. 1985. *Islands of History.* Chicago: University of Chicago Press.

———. 1993. "Goodbye to Tristes Tropes: Ethnography in the Context of Modern World History." *Journal of Modern History* 65: 1–25.

Saint, Enrique. 1936. "El norte argentino en automóvil." *Revista Geográfica Americana* 3(30–31): 153–80, 239–58.

Schama, Simon. 1995. *Landscape and Memory.* New York: Vintage.

Schleh, Emilio. 1945. *Noticias históricas sobre el azúcar en la Argentina.* Buenos Aires: Centro Azucarero Argentino.

Scott, James. 1990. *Domination and the Arts of Resistance: Hidden Transcripts.* New Haven: Yale University Press.

Scunio, Alberto. 1972. *La conquista del Chaco.* Buenos Aires: Círculo Militar.

Segovia, Laureano. 1998. *Nuestra Memoria-Olhamel Otichunhayaj.* Buenos Aires: Editorial Universitaria de Buenos Aires.

Shapiro, Samuel. 1962. "The Toba Indians of Bolivia." *América Indígena* 22(3): 241–45.

Sider, Gerald. 1986. *Culture and Class in Anthropology and History: A Newfoundland Illustration.* Cambridge: Cambridge University Press.

Sider, Gerald, and Gavin Smith. 1997. "Introduction." In Gerald Sider and Gavin Smith, eds., *Between History and Histories: The Making of Silences and Commemorations,* 3–28. Toronto: University of Toronto Press.

Sierra e Iglesias, Jacobino. 1998. *Un tiempo que se fue: Vida y obra de los hermanos Leach.* San Pedro de Jujuy: Editorial de la Universidad Nacional de Jujuy.

Smith, Gavin. 1989. *Livelihood and Resistance: Peasants and the Politics of Land in Peru.* Berkeley: University of California Press.

———. 1991. "The Production of Culture in Local Rebellion." In Jay O'Brien and William Roseberry, eds., *Golden Ages, Dark Ages: Imagining the Past in Anthropology and History,* 180–207. Berkeley: University of California Press.

———. 1999. *Confronting the Present: Towards a Politically Engaged Anthropology.* Oxford: Berg.

Smith, Neil. 1984. *Uneven Development: Nature, Capital, and the Production of Space.* Oxford: Blackwell.

Solway, Jacqueline, and Richard Lee. 1990. "Foragers, Genuine or Spurious? Situating the Kalahari San in History." *Current Anthropology* 31(2): 109–45.

South American Missionary Society. 1928. "A Toba Chief Comes In." *South American Missionary Society Magazine* 62: 100.

———. 1933. "The Argentine Chaco Mission." *South American Missionary Society Annual Report, 1933:* 32–44.

———. 1935. "The Toba Mission." *South American Missionary Society Magazine* 69: 128–29.

———. 1937. "On the Banks of the Pilcomayo River." *South American Missionary Society Magazine* 71: 54–59.

———. 1938. "Argentine Chaco Notes." *South American Missionary Society Magazine* 72: 39.

Stewart, Kathleen. 1996. *A Space on the Side of the Road: Cultural Poetics in an "Other" America.* Princeton: Princeton University Press.

Stoler, Ann. 1985. *Capitalism and Confrontation in Sumatra's Plantation Belt, 1879–1979.* New Haven: Yale University Press.

Susnik, Branislava. 1971. *El indio colonial del Paraguay: El chaqueño, Vol. 3.* Asunción: Museo Etnográfico Andrés Barbero.

Swedenburg, Ted. 1991. "Popular Memory and the Palestinian National Past." In Jay O'Brien and William Roseberry, eds., *Golden Ages, Dark Ages: Imagining the Past in Anthropology and History,* 152–79. Berkeley: University of California Press.

Sweeney, Ernest, and Alejandro Domínguez Benavides. 1998. *Robustiano Patrón Costas: Una leyenda argentina.* Buenos Aires: Emecé.

Taussig, Michael. 1980. *The Devil and Commodity Fetishism in South America.* Chapel Hill: University of North Carolina Press.

————. 1987. *Shamanism, Colonialism and the Wild Man: A Study in Terror and Healing.* Chicago: University of Chicago Press.

————. 1993. *Mimesis and Alterity: A Particular History of the Senses.* New York: Routledge.

————. 1995. "The Sun Gives without Receiving: An Old Story." *Comparative Studies in Society and History* 37(2): 368–98.

————. 1997. *The Magic of the State.* New York: Routledge.

Tebboth, Dora. 1989 [1938–46]. *With Teb, among the Tobas: Letters Written Home from the Mission Field.* Sussex, UK: Lantern Press.

Tebboth, Thomas. 1938a. "Misión El Toba." *South American Missionary Society Magazine* 72: 112–14.

————. 1938b. "Misión El Toba." *South American Missionary Society Magazine* 72: 146–47.

————. 1939. "Misión El Toba." *South American Missionary Society Magazine* 73: 95–96.

————. 1943. "Misión El Toba." *South American Missionary Society Magazine* 77: 36–37.

Teruel, Ana. 1994. "Zenta y San Ignacio de Tobas: El trabajo en dos misiones del Chaco occidental a fines de la colonia." *Anuario del IEHS* 9: 227–52.

————. 1995. "Introducción." In Ana Teruel, ed., *Misioneros del Chaco occidental: Escritos de franciscanos del Chaco salteño (1861–1914).* Jujuy: Universidad Nacional de Jujuy.

Thompson, Edward P. 1966 [1963]. *The Making of the English Working Class.* New York: Vintage.

————. 1978a. "Eighteenth-Century English Society: Class Struggle without Class?" *Social History* 3(2): 133–65.

————. 1978b. *The Poverty of Theory and Other Essays.* London: Merlin Press.

————. 1993. *Customs in Common: Studies in Traditional Popular Culture.* New York: New Press.

Thouar, Arthur. 1991 [1891]. *A travers le Gran Chaco: Chez les indiennes coupers de tétes.* Paris: Phebus.

Torres, María Irma. 1975. *Ingeniero Guillermo Nicasio Juárez y los parajes del oeste de Formosa.* Buenos Aires: Ediciones Tiempo de Hoy.

Trinchero, Héctor Hugo, and Juan Martín Leguizamón. 1995. "Fronteras de la modernización: Reproducción del capital y fuerza de trabajo en el umbral al Chaco argentino." In Hugo Trinchero, ed., *Producción doméstica y capital: Estudios desde la antropología económica,* 15–44. Buenos Aires: Biblos.

Trinchero, Héctor Hugo, and Aristóbulo Maranta. 1987. "Las crisis reveladoras: Historias y estrategias de identidad entre los mataco-wichí del Chaco centro-occidental." *Cuadernos de Historia Regional* 4(10): 74–92.

Trouillot, Michel-Rolph. 1986. "The Price of Indulgence." *Social Analysis* 19: 85–90.

————. 1995. *Silencing the Past: Power and the Production of History.* Boston: Beacon Press.

Tsing, Anna. 1993. *In the Realm of the Diamond Queen: Marginality in an Out-of-the-way Place*. Princeton: Princeton University Press.

Turner, Terence. 1986. "Production, Exploitation, and Social Consciousness in the 'Peripheral Situation.'" *Social Analysis* 19: 91–115.

Turner, Victor. 1974. *Dramas, Fields, and Metaphors: Symbolic Action in Human Society*. Ithaca: Cornell University Press.

Unsain, Alejandro. 1914. "Informe del Jefe de la División Inspección, presentado a raíz de su viaje de inspección al ingenio de la Compañía Azucarera de Ledesma." *Boletín del Departamento Nacional de Trabajo* 28: 45–89.

Uriburu, Napoleón. 1873. "Memoria elevada por el jefe de la frontera de Norte de Salta al Ministerio de Guerra." In Luis Jorge Fontana, *El Gran Chaco*, 105–10. Buenos Aires: Hachette Solar.

Vessuri, Hebe. 1971. "Aspectos del catolicismo popular de Santiago del Estero: Ensayo en categorías sociales y morales." *América Latina* 14(1–2): 40–69.

Vidal, I. 1914. "Informe sobre las condiciones en que los indígenas son contratados: Cargos formulados por los indígenas." *Boletín del Departamento Nacional de Trabajo* 32: 5–25.

Volosinov, Valentin. 1973 [1929]. *Marxism and the Philosophy of Language*. Trans. Ladislav Matejka and I. R. Titunik. Cambridge, Mass.: Harvard University Press.

von Rosen, Eric. 1904. *The Chorote Indians of the Bolivian Chaco*. Stockholm: Ivar Haeggströms Boktryckeri.

Warren, Kay. 1998. *Indigenous Movements and their Critics: Pan-Mayan Activism in Guatemala*. Princeton: Princeton University Press.

Weiss, Brad. 1997. "Northwestern Tanzania on a Single Shilling: Sociality, Embodiment, Valuation." *Cultural Anthropology* 12(3): 335–61.

Whiteford, Scott. 1981. *Workers from the North: Plantations, Bolivian Labor, and the City in Northwestern Argentina*. Austin: University of Texas Press.

Williams, Raymond. 1961. *The Long Revolution*. London: Hogarth Press.

———. 1973. *The Country and the City*. London: Hogarth Press.

———. 1977. *Marxism and Literature*. Oxford: Oxford University Press.

Wilmsen, Edwin. 1989. *Land Filled with Flies: A Political Economy of the Kalahari*. Chicago: University of Chicago Press.

Wilmsen, Edwin, and James Denbow. 1991. "Paradigmatic History of San-Speaking Peoples and Current Attempts at Revision." *Current Anthropology* 31(5): 489–523.

Wolf, Eric. 1982. *Europe and the People without History*. Berkeley: University of California Press.

Wright, Pablo. 1992. "Toba Pentecostalism Revisited." *Social Compass* 39(3): 355–75.

———. 1997. "Being-in-the-Dream: Postcolonial Explorations in Toba Ontology." Ph.D. Diss., Department of Anthropology, Temple University.

———. 1998. "El desierto del Chaco: Geografías de la alteridad y el estado."

In Ana Teruel and Omar Jerez, eds., *Pasado y presente de un mundo postergado*, 35–56. Jujuy: Universidad Nacional de Jujuy.

Young, Robert. 1905. *From Cape Horn to Panama: A Narrative of Missionary Enterprise among the Neglected Races of South America, by the South American Missionary Society*. London: Simpkin, Marshall, Hamilton, Kent.

Zapata Gollán, Agustín. 1966. *El Chaco Gualamba y la ciudad de Concepción del Bermejo*. Santa Fe: Departamento de Estudios Coloniales-Editorial Castellví.

Zavalía, Rafael de. 1915. "Trabajo de Indios en los ingenios azucareros." *Boletín del Departamento Nacional de Trabajo* 31. Buenos Aires.

Index

Abercrombie, Thomas, 265 n.2

Aboriginality: the body and, 60, 129, 133, 151, 153; the bush and, 24, 113, 174–75, 186–87, 206, 234–35; class and, 60, 66–67, 77, 111–14, 129, 161, 163, 174–75, 186–87, 196, 201, 229; dancing and, 150–53; ethnic hierarchies and, 112–14, 129, 133, 150–51, 156, 159–61, 184–85; local knowledge and, 184–85; party politics and, 234–38; poverty and, 19, 24, 160, 174–75, 184, 187, 201–5, 229. *See also* Ethnicity

Adorno, Theodor, 255–56

Agency: concept of, 256

Agriculture, 30, 268 n.14, 268 n.15

Alienation: concept of, 137, 256–57. *See also* Estrangement

Amariglio, Jack, 138

Ancient ones, 10, 21, 267 n.2; cattle and, 62, 224; clashes with the army, 62–65, 66, 196–97; their "ignorance," 57, 62, 65, 70–71; missionaries and, 69, 73–77; physical strength of, 58, 65, 71, 173, 185; in the plantations, 56–59, 60, 66–68; warfare and, 54–56, 68, 71, 78, 99, 224, 228; wealth and, 206

Anderson, Benedict, 169

Anglican missionization, 5, 11, 17; agriculture and, 82, 225; the army and, 85–87, 196–97; arrival in the Argentinean Chaco, 72–73, 270 n.1 (ch.4); the bush and, 84, 87, 96–99, 225; devil imageries and, 8, 88–92, 95–96, 97, 124, 138, 194–95; discipline and, 79–80, 88–99, 116, 153–55, 225; education and, 17, 80–

81; foraging and, 82, 96–99, 272 n.3 (ch.6); handicrafts and, 81–82, 225, 278 n.1 (ch.15); healing and, 179–80; plantations and, 73–74, 154–55; protection provided by, 73–77, 83–87, 197, 271 n.1, 271 n.4; shamanism and, 79, 89–91, 94–96, 99; tensions with government, 85–86, 271 n.6; Toba leaders and, 79; wealth and, 270–71 n.2 (ch.5); work and, 81–82. *See also* Misión El Toba

Appadurai, Arjun, 184

Arengo, Elena, 51

Army, 2; campaign in 1884, 48–49; campaign in 1911, 62; clashes with the Toba, 62–63, 66, 196–97; fear of, 65–68; massacres by, 46, 61, 84, 86; in Misión El Toba, 85–86; plantations and, 52, 66–67

Arnott, John, 266 n.9, 271 n.8

Arreglo grande, 59, 121–22, 141–42, 145, 198

Astrada Domingo, 56, 270 n.2 (ch.3)

Autonomy: from the army, 46, 48, 60–61, 65–66, 196; the bush and, 2, 5, 43–44, 60–61, 96–99, 174–75, 235, 251; from exploitation, 2, 5, 43–44, 59–61, 165–66, 174–75, 222, 224; gender relations and, 187, 192, 235–36; from missionaries, 96–99, 149–51, 153–55; from party politics, 234–38

Balzac, Honoré de, 248

Bean farms, 10, 34–36, 269 n.19; devils in, 210–11, 217–19; riches near, 211, 219–20; sex in, 218, 219, 221; souls in, 209–10, 217; work on, 214–20, 278 n.6, 279 n.7

GASTÓN R. GORDILLO
is an assistant professor in the Department
of Anthropology and Sociology at the University
of British Columbia.

Library of Congress Cataloging-in-Publication Data

Gordillo, Gastón.
Landscapes of devils : tensions of place and memory in
the Argentinean Chaco / Gastón R. Gordillo.
p. cm.
Includes bibliographical references and index.
ISBN 0-8223-3380-5 (cloth : alk. paper)
ISBN 0-8223-3391-0 (pbk. : alk. paper)
1. Toba Indians—Social life and customs. 2. Toba Indians—
Psychology. 3. Human geography—Argentina—Chaco.
4. Geographical perception—Argentina—Chaco. 5. Memory—
Social aspects—Argentina—Chaco. 6. Chaco (Argentina)—History.
7. Chaco (Argentina)—Social life and customs. I. Title.
F2823.T7G67 2004
304.2'089'987—dc22   2004015806